Annual Review of Golf Coaching 2009

Simon Jenkins
Editor

A Multi-Science Publication
ISBN 978 1907132 124

CW01496545

Annual Review of
Golf Coaching 2009

Contents

Editorial

This issue of the *Annual Review of Golf Coaching* features a leading article about John Jacobs, OBE, who on 17 December 2008, at The Dorchester, Park Lane, London, received the Lifetime Achievement Award from the UK Coaching Hall of Fame. In nominating Jacobs, Dr. Kyle Phillpots, who is Director of Training and Education for the PGA of Great Britain and Ireland, wrote the following:

> John Jacobs began coaching golf in the years after WWII. At first he combined this with playing tournaments (Ryder Cup player in 1955; Dutch Open and South African Match Play champion 1957). But he found his services as a coach were in such demand his playing suffered. He studied the golf swing as a player and was determined to learn as much as possible about it. He realized that he taught golf better than he plays it and set out to be the best he could. He quickly became the most sought after golf coach in the world and at some time worked with all the best players, including Jack Nicklaus, Seve Ballesteros, Nick Faldo, Sandy Lyle, Ian Woosnam, Gary Player, Jose-Maria Olazabal. He also brought golf coaching to the masses through his golf schools in the USA and the thousands of clinics he conducted throughout the world. John has also been heavily involved in developing golf in Europe and even at the age of 83 still goes to Spain each year to coach young golfers. He was also instrumental in establishing driving ranges in the UK and became the first Director of the European Tour in 1972. John received the OBE in 1997 and was inducted into the World Golf Hall of Fame in the USA in 2000. It is undoubtedly golf coaching that he has imparted upon more than any other person. He set the standard and style that others have followed.

Phillpots received a number of endorsements in support of nominating John Jacobs, including the following:

> I believe John Jacobs is the most important golf coach in Europe. His influence has been over-riding, not only as a coach, but also a teacher to many other trainers. John introduced the concept of a coach in European Golf. Before him, there was no tradition of receiving advice and training for top players.
> (Severiano Ballesteros)

> He has played a huge role in my development as a coach. Over the past twenty five years he has allowed himself to be obsessively questioned by

myself and at times even challenged. Yet at all time he showed both patience and benevolence to me, being prepared to pass on all his hard won secrets on teaching and coaching golfers of all abilities.
(Denis Pugh, PGA Master Professional)

John has a great passion for golf and is tireless when it comes to teaching the game, its traditions and sportsmanship.
(Jack Nicklaus)

Simon Jenkins
(Leeds Metropolitan University, UK)

The Impact of John Jacobs on Golf Coaching

Simon Jenkins
Carnegie Faculty of Sport and Education,
Leeds Metropolitan University, Leeds, LS6 3QS, UK
E-mail: S.P.Jenkins@Leedsmet.ac.uk

INTRODUCTION

I learned much about golf coaching as a caddie on the PGA European Tour during the years 1985 to 1992, observing the likes of Bob Torrance and David Leadbetter on a regular basis. However, it was through working with Peter Green that I learned most about golf coaching. I assisted him in the coaching of the Oxford University Golf Team, which I previously played on, from 1993-2001. Green, a former tour player, learned from John Jacobs:

> I was having a drink with John Jacobs after my second golf school with him and he asked me how I got on that day.
> "I felt that I needed to express myself better. I felt that I needed to do a bit more talking to the pupils," I replied.
> "You want to keep it as simple as possible, give them as little as possible, keep it as basic and simple as possible," John said in his strong and assuring manner.
> That was the best tip I ever learned as a golf teacher.
> As time went by, working with Jacobs and watching him, I was amazed at how quickly he could get someone to hit the ball better. He would quickly put them into the correct address position and get the backswing in a certain correct position.
> It was an apprenticeship, really, which started in 1966 and I've worked with him on and off ever since. (Peter Green, personal communication, 1992)

The purpose of this article is to stimulate commentaries from leading figures in the contemporary world of golf coaching who have been influenced by, and/or can provide insights into the development of, John Jacobs' golf instruction and coaching.

JOHN JACOBS: THE GOLFER

John Jacobs started playing on the professional tournament circuit in 1952. The highlights of his career were beating Cary Middlecoff in a singles match in the 1955

Reviewer: John Jacobs, OBE

Ryder Cup and beating Gary Player in the final of the 1957 South African match-play. He played in the British Open on 12 occasions, finishing 12th at St. Andrews in 1955.

Jacobs was always experimenting with his clubs – altering the grip thickness or lies of his short irons, for example – and the shape of shots he hit. With regard to the latter, his friend and successful tour player, Bernard Hunt has revealed:

> "John was a natural hooker, but whenever he got onto a golf course, he'd see a shot in terms of a fade or a draw, a cut-up ball or one floated in high, and so on; he would always see the "difficult" shot, the one which appealed to his fancy. He wouldn't stop mixing it up. In a way, he knows too much about the golf swing. He was for ever putting into practice what he had learnt about flighting the ball, moving it about and what he was teaching his pupils. I felt that he could have been a better player if he had been prepared to play more naturally and stuck to his natural shape.
> "But…it was the knowledge he had built up of flighting the ball, moving it about and what was necessary in a swing to produce these results that made him such a good teacher. [1, p. 55]

In light of the above, it is interesting to consider that Jacobs himself has stated that "great players were successful because they realized their limitations" in that they not only "knew that some shots were all but impossible for anyone to play successfully", but also they "knew that other shots were beyond their own particular abilities" [1, p. 211]. He has also remarked that Sam Snead "knew how to stay within the outer parameters of his tendencies":

> "When I asked Sam how he accounted for his long career, he told me that when he was hooking the ball in a tournament, he would allow for it by aiming right, put a check in his pocket, and then go home and practice aiming left". [2]

Jacobs has admitted his weakness on the mental side of the game, which he rates as "the most important element in golf", and has stated that if he was playing today he would "enlist the help of a sport psychologist" [3, p. 220]:

> "If I'd had half the confidence as a player I had as a teacher, I'd have been a very good player, but I wasn't confident. If I bogeyed before I birdied, I was always under pressure." [2]

HEROES

Jacobs' boyhood hero was Henry Cotton, who he first saw at the 1938 British Open. Later Byron Nelson became his hero:

> "I played with him three straight days in Palm Springs in 1955, and even then he was the best hitter I've ever seen. The way he flattened his swing at the bottom with his legs was genius. You could never teach that move. It was better than orthodox, almost beyond technique." [2]

Jacobs has recalled early memories of his "father talking about the remarkable exploits of Bobby Jones" [3, p. 196].

JOHN JACOBS: THE COACH

In the context of getting Jacobs on board in 1962 for a new golf magazine in the UK, *Golf World*, editor Ken Bowden had been impressed with Jacobs' instructional articles for *Golfing* magazine, which was edited by John Stobbs:

> "It caught my eye particularly because, apart from Bobby Jones' books, all instruction seemed to deal with the mechanics of the swing and positions, and what these were supposed to achieve. John, on the other hand, started from the other end. He stated what had to be achieved by the player and worked back from there." [1, p. 94]

Later, as editor of *Golf Digest* in the USA, Bowden gave Jacobs the opportunity to argue the case for his concepts with the magazine's instruction panel of Jim Flick, Eddie Merrins, Cary Middlecoff, Paul Runyan, Sam Snead, Bob Toski, and Gary Wiren:

> "John ran into a lot of opposition…because he was teaching a different concept. He was starting from the point where the ball reacts to the clubface, and how the flight of the ball tells you all you want to know about the swing path, the angle of attack and the set of the clubface." [1, p. 97]

Jacobs was able to change the thinking of the *Golf Digest* instruction panel. Bowden again refers to Bobby Jones:

> "What John was telling them in 1970 was really little different from what Bob Jones had been saying years before. It's all there in his books. If you read them you will see the extent of the common ground there is between the two men. Jones talked as freely as John does about the way the ball reacts to the clubface and the lessons to be learned from the flight of the ball.
> "But then Nelson, Hogan, the cult of the square-to-square method and Nicklaus intervened to obscure the Jones concept. The Americans are a practical, mechanical, statistical society. In golf, they were thinking in terms of methods and set-piece positions. They had lost sight of the end-product. In a word, they had forgotten Jones. What John did was to remind them of that heritage. He took the stiltedness – the mechanicalness, if you like – out of their game." [1, p. 98]

To make Bowden's point for him, Laddie Lucas uses extracts from Jones' book *Golf Is My Game* [4] including:

> Golf is played by striking the ball with the clubhead. The object of the player is not to swing the club in a specific manner, nor execute a series of complicated movements…nor look pretty…but primarily and essentially to strike the ball with the head of the club so that the ball will perform according

to his wishes. No one can play golf until he knows the many ways in which a golf ball can be expected to respond when it is struck in different ways. [1, p. 98]

'Ken Bowden read Bobby Jones. Bobby Jones didn't influence me,' said Jacobs (personal communication, June 2009). The impact of Jacobs' instructional material (magazine articles, books and videos) was due in no small way to the knowledge-elicitation role played by his collaborating authors, especially Ken Bowden. The discourse about Jones is an example of how the collaborator's beliefs are brought to bear.

Shelby Futch, one of Jacobs' associates in the USA, recalled what Jacobs once said soon after starting golf schools in the USA: "If golf was about the golf swing and 'positions', then someone on the tour has to be wrong" [1, p. 190]. Jacobs has offered the following explanation with regard to the issue of "swing, or move from position to position":

> Most of the great golfers to the early 1960s learned the game as caddies. They watched the people they carried for and tried to copy those who played well. They were copying an action, a fluid movement. It would never have occurred to them, even if they had known how, to break the swing down into parts and study it segment by segment in static form. Golf was an action and learned as such.
> … Instead of watching good players in the flesh, and trying to emulate the *action* of a good golf swing, they study static pictures and try to copy the positions in which the camera has frozen the players. They are learning positions which, in themselves, without the essential motivating force of swinging, are almost useless. [3, p. 15-16]

According to Jacobs, the most sought after positions seem to be the top-of-backswing and halfway-down positions; but: "I venture to say that the finest players never feel this position; they feel a much more complete thing, that of swinging the clubhead through the ball to the target" [3, p. 45]. Furthermore, "the 'secret' of golf lies in coordinating the turns with the actual swinging of the club – not in a series of geometrically exact, deliberate placement of the club in certain 'positions'" [3, p. 64].

JOHN JACOBS' TEACHING SYSTEM

Jamie Diaz has stated that Jacobs' greatest contribution was "diagnosing the golf swing through the flight of the ball" [2]. Jim Hardy, who served an apprenticeship under Jacobs at his Practical Golf school, has been quoted as saying that Jacobs "boiled all his knowledge into a system, and it just made teaching so much more efficient" [2]. Sir Michael Bonallack, five-times British Amateur champion and former secretary of the Royal and Ancient Golf Club of St. Andrews, has stated:

> "John has almost taught the game backwards. Instead of starting with the address and the swing, he begins by seeing where the ball has gone. And when he has found out what the ball is doing and what is happening to the

shots, then everything is worked backwards from there. He was the first person who taught you to think about golf that way." [1, p. 99]

The following extract from the PGA of Great Britain and Ireland's *2003 PGA Golf Coaching – Swing Manual* appears in *50 Years of Golfing Wisdom* [3] and sums up Jacobs' system in his own words:

> The shape of a golf lesson would normally take the form of: diagnosis, explanation, accompanied by demonstration and finally, correction. The pupil is best viewed down the line to facilitate this approach. The set-up to the target can be observed and the subsequent swing path through the ball can be clearly seen. The flight of the ball relative to the swing path will give a valid indication of the clubface at impact. ...
> It is vital that the correct diagnosis is made and that the explanation and accompanying demonstration be fully understood by the pupil in order to encourage the necessary perseverance since any correction is likely to be, initially, uncomfortable. [3, p. 10]

With regard to the correction being, "initially, uncomfortable", Jacobs has stated that this is "because in all likelihood it's an exaggerated contrary of what they've been doing" but that "if they can grasp the why, they will stay with it". [2] An example from Jacobs of an "exaggerated contrary" for the student who has difficulty 'clearing the left side' in the throughswing might be:

> 'Now, with this one, I want you to hit left – hit this ball left of the target – hit it at the left-hand side of the fairway – a Yorkshireman's left'. (Pause) 'I'll take the blame.' [1, p. 154]

Hardy's point about Jacobs' "system" not withstanding, it should be noted that Jacobs has stated:

> "I don't teach a method, I teach people. Once a golfer is presented with the fix to his fault, the trick is to impart it in a way that connects with that particular person. It's a human problem." [2]

In a similar vein, Bert Buehler has stated that: "[Jacobs] went from one student to another, never changing his basic philosophy, starting with impact and its effect on ball flight, but always, it seemed, picking out a different point with each person" [1, p. 185].

COACHING STYLE

Jacobs is enthusiastic and gives others enjoyment [1, p. 236]. His direct, logical and simple approach is nevertheless combined with patience, making the pupil feel comfortable. [1, p. 137; 153] His 'photographic memory' is legendary:

> With his built-in ability to 'photograph' a player, keep the picture fresh in his mind and, in a sentence or two, describe it sharply years afterwards, he can

> still recall vividly the swing actions of the 'names' of the 1950s and 1960s. [1, p. 27]

His ability to communicate includes the use of humour and entertainment:

> Especially in younger days, he could mimic a student's swing to illustrate a fault, and then demonstrate the fix in a way equally palpable. Jacobs also liked to show off by turning his back to a subject so that he could see the ball flight but not the actual swing, and then offer a spot-on diagnosis of the golfer's flaws. [2]

Most notable perhaps is his use of empathy: "When I'm teaching people, I genuinely feel, by what they do, that I know what is going on in their mind. I can feel what a pupil is sensing" [1, p. 194].

CRITICAL INCIDENTS

A critical incident has been defined as "an interpretation of the significance of an event" [5, p. 8]. Reflection is considered as essential to the development of professional judgement, requiring "some from of challenge to and critique of ourselves and our professional values" [5, p. 12] in order to be effective. Critical incidents are "not simply observed, they are literally created" [5, p. 27]; i.e., rendered 'critical' through analysis [5, p. 24]. An example of a critical incident for John Jacobs was his coaching of Bruce Critchley, which he can still recall and reflect further on at the age of 84 [personal communication, May 2009]. Below, the account from Lucas [1] is drawn from.

In growing up, Bruce Critchley had been taught by Tom Haliburton at Wentworth and Arthur Lees at Sunningdale:

> "Tom never taught me in the true sense," Critchley recalls. "He talked to me about the game, discussed it and its philosophy, told me how to think my way round a golf course and put a round together. But he did not teach me in the way that pros usually do. He left such talent as there was to develop. Arthur, afterwards, went rather deeper. He would point out what he thought was wrong. ..." [1, p. 43]

In 1962, Critchley, aged 19, was selected for England. A month before the home internationals, the English Golf Union sent its squad to Jacobs at Sandy Lodge. Critchley hit three shots with a 3-iron – "super shots, as it happened" before Jacobs said, in a direct manner: "You'll never hit the ball consistently with that swing." [1, p. 43]:

> "I had a long, sloppy, fairly attractive swing. John just told me to swing like Bernard Hunt, to try to get the idea of a rather short, compact, three-quarter swing..." [1, p. 44],

After another visit to Sandy Lodge, Critchley was not in a good state:

"My rhythm went and, with it, my swing. The base of it was taken away. I had never thought about it before; I had just played with what I had been given. For two years or so my game was a disaster. I hardly ever broke 80." [1, p. 44]

After this, Critchley returned to Haliburton and explained his situation, which included less time for golf as he had now developed a career outside of golf. Critchley expected Haliburton to take him out onto the practice ground right away, but:

'Instead, Tom said that he would finish his cup of tea and be out to see me in about twenty minutes. Meanwhile he told me to go out, forget everything – "empty the mind" – and just swing at the ball: "You used to have a swing once and I'll be surprised if it's not still there." When ultimately, he did come out I said to him: "Tom, that's all I want, I don't need any more. That's it for me."' [1, p. 44]

A few years later, Critchley was back in the England team and he also made it into the Walker Cup team. Laddie Lucas states:

Two decades on, he sees his experience in rational perspective. ... He recognizes that, had he been, in 1962, totally dedicated to the game or even about to embark upon it as a career, able to go frequently to Jacobs and to practise assiduously over a period, there is little doubt that he could have developed a commercial, repeating swing... [1, p. 45]

Furthermore, "Jacobs is adamant about only seeing a player who has his own familiar guru if that team member specifically asks him to do so; and then he much prefers it if the usual teacher can be present during the session" [1, p. 45].

Finally, Lucas presents Critchley's current (i.e., c. 1987) assessment of Jacobs's standing:

'John is clearly the outstanding teacher of the last twenty years. His approach is quite different from Tom Haliburton's in his time. Tom, as I knew him, was more concerned with the playing of the game and its philosophy, whereas John studied the mechanics, thought it all through, and is completely confident of his findings. He is a pro's pro.' [1, p. 46]

TEAM COACHING

There is reason to doubt Critchley's assessment, however, with regard to Jacobs' work with teams. Donald Steel recalled to Laddie Lucas his experience of the winter of 1957-58 when Jacobs was invited to spend a week at Rye with the Cambridge University golf team:

"We used to spend fascinating evenings in the pub at Rye just listening to John talking about golf and golfers. Naturally, he helped us on the course and the practice ground with our games, but what struck me as the most beneficial aspect of having him as a coach was the chance to hear him talk – not so much about the technical side of the game but about how to play a match, how to get it round – and to listen to his stories of his Ryder Cup conquest in 1955 and of the Middlecoffs, the Sneads, the Nelsons and the Hogans and what made them great..." [1, p. 60]

CONCLUSION

There are many golf coaches who have paid homage to the influence of John Jacobs in development of their teaching. Of the most well known of today's coaches, Butch Harmon points to his father and John Jacobs as his "two biggest influences" [3, p. 3] and he requires his assistants to read Jacobs' classic instruction book *Practical Golf* [6]: "John's way cut through everything because it gets down to the essentials; clubface and path" [2]. For Hank Haney, Jacobs is "the greatest golf instructor the game of golf has ever known" [7]:

> "The essence of what I teach I learned from John. Some people call him a band-aid teacher, the quick-fix guy. In a way they're right, because he needs only about 10 minutes to help anybody. What makes him special is, his band-aid is always the right one." [2]

While Haney's use of the term "golf instructor" in connection with John Jacobs, one can also use the term 'golf coach' as shown, for example, by his work with teams at university and international levels. It could be argued that 'instruction' is just one facet of golf coaching. His position of Captain of the European team for the Ryder Cups of 1979 and 1981 would be regarded by many followers of American sport as essentially a role of 'head coach'.

According to Jamie Diaz of *Golf Digest*, Tiger Woods, who has worked with Hank Haney since 2004, "calls the improved ability to learn from the ball flight his most important breakthrough in 2005" [2] While this points to Jacobs' impact in golf instruction, the bottom line is that the demand for his services as a coach owe much to his enthusiasm and ability to communicate in an empathic, effective and efficient manner. In the words of Bernard Gallacher, who Jacobs coached as a teenager and was three times Captain of the European team in the Ryder Cup:

> 'The thing about John is his enthusiasm for the game – he really likes to play golf. … It spills over into his teaching. Watch him when he is having a look at one of the tour players. John is working with him, carrying his load with him, understanding what is going on in his mind. You can feel his enthusiasm. It transmits to those whom he is helping. [1, p. 157]

REFERENCES

1.   Lucas, L., *John Jacobs' Impact on Golf: The Man and His Methods*, Stanley Paul, London, 1987.

2.   Diaz, J., Golf's Wise Man: The Genius of John Jacobs is Back in Style, *Golf Digest*, February, 2006, http://findarticles.com/p/articles/mi_m0HFI/is_2_57/ai_n26734513/

3.   Jacobs, J. and Newell, S., *50 Years of Golfing Wisdom*, CollinsWillow, London, 2005.

4.   Jones, R.T., *Bobby Jones on Golf*, Doubleday, New York, 1966.

5.   Tripp, D., *Critical Incidents in Teaching: Developing Professional Judgement*, Routledge, London, 1993.

6.   Jacobs, J. and Bowden, K., *Practical Golf*, Stanley Paul, London, 1972.

7.   Golf Link, Hank Haney: Philosophy (Video Transcript), http://www.golflink.com/tipsvideos/video.aspx?v=62134

The Impact of John Jacobs on Golf Coaching:

A Commentary

Gary Wiren
Trump International Golf Club,
3505 Summit Blvd, West Palm Beach, FL 33406, USA
E-mail: garywiren@aol.com

INTRODUCTION

In Simon Jenkins' article, he makes it clear that Jacobs is the "full package"...teacher, player, coach, writer, commentator, psychologist, motivator and, when the time is right, entertainer. I was privileged to personally experience some of John's wit as well as his eloquence while serving on the *Golf Digest* Teaching Panel along with Paul Runyan, Cary Middlecoff, Bob Toski, Jim Flick, Davis Love, and Sam Snead.

SIMPLICITY

One of the panel's many questions answered by passing it around the table for comment was, "Is golf primarily a left-sided, or right-sided game?" There were certainly some differences of opinion, but when it got to John he nailed it. In his classic British accent he opined, "Frankly, I don't think the ball gives a damn." You were spot on, John, while doing it in just a few words.

This is one of his characteristics when working the lesson tee, that of being "a man of few words." He keeps it simple, direct and understandable, which makes for rapid positive results. Although he can expound by the hour on golf theory over a pint while in a pub, he knows that theory is best left there rather than taken to the tee. In that respect he meets the master teaching criterion laid down by Tommy Armour who said, "You need to understand the golf swing in its total complexity so that you can teach it in its utter simplicity."

LAWS, PRINCIPLES AND PREFERENCES

While reading Jenkins' article, I became further aware of the genius of Jacobs. It is only human for one to place another in high regard when their beliefs so often coincide. So many aspects of Jacobs' teaching I support, such as the importance of impact; teaching people not methods; using a variety of ways to teach the same thing; and the importance of "through" not "to" in making a swing. My creation of the teaching model, "Laws, Principles, and Preferences" was borrowed directly from John and could be cited as another example of his influence on instruction.

PERSONAL CHARACTERISTICS

In addition to thoroughly researching his subject, Jenkins' use of quotations from others who knew Jacobs well adds to the authenticity of his remarks. Jenkins also brought to light several of Jacobs' special personal characteristics, such as:

Having an inquisitive mind. John is constantly looking for better ways to do things in his teaching as he did in his own game.

Being his own man. No amount of opposition or argument that favored focusing on positions in the swing or adopting some "magic method or move" can sway John. He maintains a resolute stand for simply "co-coordinating the body turns with the swinging of the clubhead."

Sticking to principles. Jacobs seems to care little for style or form, but rather has stuck to ball flight. This, I would concur, is particularly useful in teaching the less skilled player. He will support a player who may not "look good," but is able to produce a competent shot by correctly managing the principles that deliver it.

Employing logic to coaching. When John sees an errant shot, he instantly identifies the possible reason from a mental catalog of cause and effect. By rapid deduction, he can sort the many possibilities and come to an answer that is both logical and effective.

CONCLUSION

The most impressive item to me that Jenkins' writing revealed is quite rare. That is, whenever possible, Jacobs' habit of including a player's regular teacher in a training session so they can all work together. This demonstrates that John cares more about the player and that player's teacher than his own ego. If the golf world were filled with more coaches and teachers who adhered to this practice, we would all be the better.

The Impact of John Jacobs on Golf Coaching:

A Commentary

Jim Hardy

Jim Hardy Golf, 2918 E Lake Fall Circle, Spring, Texas 77386, USA

E-mail: tina@planetruthforgolfers.com

INTRODUCTION

I firmly believe John Jacobs is the father of modern golf instruction worldwide. His revelation on how to always correctly diagnose a student's problem was revolutionary. It was ground breaking when he introduced it and it still is today. Prior to John's method of diagnosis and still too often today, the method used by instructors was to start with an examination of the swing relative to the fundamentals that the particular instructor thought was important. The focus was to make the swing conform to a certain preconceived fundamental shape. John's approach started from an entirely different perspective. He started his diagnosis from the flight of the ball rather than swing shape. His idea claimed the golfer's mistake was the errant ball flight and you traced the cause of the mistake through a series of logical steps to find its origination.

JACOBS' METHOD

To understand his method, you first have to accept one of John's rules of golf as true; i.e., "the sole purpose of the golf swing is to produce a correct impact – the method employed is of no significance as long as it is repetitive." That statement is at the root of John's teaching and of his fault diagnosis. The swing might appear unorthodox – look at Jim Furyk, Lee Trevino, John Daly, etc. – but if we are to understand golf, we must first judge the ball flight as to its correctness and repetitive nature. All the game's great players with unorthodox swings seem to defy swing fundamentals but produce correct, repetitive impacts. If we can assume that a correct, repetitive impact is our goal rather than a correct appearing swing, then we have made the first step in correctly diagnosing all swings. To correct a swing, we must first understand what is wrong with it. The nature of the ball flight, either it's lack of correctness or repetition, is the student's problem. Once we start at this point, then we can trace the swing problem to its origination. In this manner, all swing mechanics the instructor applies to the student swing will have a positive effect on the flight of the ball. Through method, all students will see immediate improvement rather than suffer continue golf, or in many cases even worse golf.

IDENTIFYING AND FIXING SWING MISTAKES

The logical steps to correctly identify the swing's originating mistake is to first trace the ball flight mistake to impact; what the club was doing at impact to cause the ball flight mistake. Once the club's mistake at impact is understood, then trace what the club was doing in the swing to cause the impact mistake. Next trace what the golfer was doing to cause the club to be swinging incorrectly. Then understand why the golfer was swinging incorrectly. You are now at the root cause of the golfer's mistake. You have correctly identified the swing mistake because it is now directly related to the golfer's mistake; his ball flight. The method employed to fix the swing mistake might vary from one instructor to another, but if both instructors are working to solve the same problem, just using different techniques, they are both correct.

This diagnosis method is fool proof. It allows personal freedom for swing shape to fit the individual's body shape and athleticism. It allows the golfer to make some unorthodox moves within the swing as long as they arrive at impact correctly and repetitively. It explains all golf swings, why they work and why they do not. It eliminates guess work and absolute conformity to a model. It reinforces what we see in golf; that all great golfers do not swing alike. What they all do alike is produce correct and repetitive impacts.

CONCLUSION

It is through this diagnosis method that we can see John's greatest contribution to golf. That contribution is the impact he has had upon the game's instructors. Yes, John has helped thousands of golfers through his instruction, either personally or through books, articles and appearances; but it is the instructors he has influenced that represents his legacy. John's generous sharing of his life's work with other professionals is unparalleled. The hundreds, if not thousands of instructors that he has mentored in turn each teach thousands of golfers. These hundreds of thousands of golfers now have the chance to play the game better more quickly, easily, naturally and to understand why they do so. It is through these instructors, world wide, that he has lifted golf instruction out of personal preference and guess work into the light of logical understanding. It is because of this that John has earned the mantel of the true father of modern golf instruction.'

The Impact of John Jacobs on Golf Coaching:

A Commentary

Donald Crawley
GolfSimplified, The Boulders Golf Academy,
Boulders Golf Club, Carefree, Arizona 85377, USA
E-mail: donald.crawley@theboulders.com

INTRODUCTION

John Jacobs has been my golf mentor since I met him in 1976. I taught golf at John Jacobs Golf Centre, Delapre Golf Complex, England. As a keen minded, enthusiastic teenage golf apprentice, I was fortunate to learn from the 'master'.

In 1980 I moved to the United States to teach golf, initially at elegant country clubs employed by Jacobs 'disciples'. In 1983, I became the first full-time employee of the John Jacobs Practical Golf Schools headed by the marketer Shelby Futch. My title was Director of Instruction for twenty years, until I headed out to run my own golf teaching business GolfSimplified in 2003.

As mentioned by Jacobs to Peter Green: "keep it simple". John keeps it simple, direct, practical and effective. I have observed him give golf lessons to major tournament winners, prominent business leaders, brand new golfers and children alike. The message is the same. His delivery is right on cue. He gets results.

INSTRUCTOR VERSUS COACH

John Jacobs' resumé is second to none in the golf world. As mentioned in Jenkins' article, John was a world-class player, Ryder Cup 1955, Europe's most famous golf instructor post war, first European Tour commissioner, entrepreneur and business man (with partner Laddie Lucas), Walker Cup coach, Ryder Cup captain, World Golf Hall of Fame, O.B.E, and many accolades that far exceed any other golf instructor.

It is worth noting that the tem golf 'instructor' and golf 'coach' have a different meaning across the pond. Americans refer to a golf instructor as someone giving golf lessons, a 'swing coach'. A coach is referred to as a leader of a team, but the job description often covers more than just instructing. A golf coach could be no more than a bus driver and organizer, but not a golf instructor. However, a golf coach could be in charge of a junior, high school, college or professional team with duties ranging from fixing swing flaws to life coaching and fundraising.

In John's career, he has done everything under the sun related to golf. His impact golf coaching is huge on both sides of the Atlantic. Interest

better in Europe as an individual, a personality, a true leader and strong influence on the way golf is taught.

In America, his golf schools have been the most successful 'group coaching' business in the last 30 years. Part of that is more marketing than golf skills, but I will take a little credit in using John's teaching philosophy and turning it into a teaching system. This system, taught by multiple instructors at 42 different locations to as many as 20,000 students each year, has helped make John Jacobs a known figure in the amateur golf world in the USA.

John is highly regarded by the modern golf-instructor gurus in America. David Leadbetter, Butch Harmon, Hank Haney, Jim Hardy come to mind as they have had personal experience with John, and they all respect his strong teaching abilities. It is true that John's *Practical Golf* book is the golf instructor's bible at many facilities.

INFLUENCE ON EVOLUTION OF THE GOLF SWING

In my opinion, John strongly influenced the way the golf swing has evolved. In his lifetime, consider that in the 1950's golf was played an individual way – Hogan's swing was on one plane looking flat, yet Nelson was upright. In the 1960's, Nicklaus overpowered a golf course and Palmer was swashbuckling and wild. This was followed by the 'unorthodox' Trevino and inconsistent Watson in the 1970's, at a time when the square-to-square swing method was prevalent and influencing many. John's defiance of it explained the resistance Ken Bowden mentioned. John's simplistic yet fundamentally sound teaching philosophy finally won over, and his influence trickled down to Faldo, Ballesteros, Lyle and Langer in the 1980's. I would go as far to say that John's impact has strongly shaped Butch Harmon and Hank Haney's teaching style that has had a strong effect on Tiger Woods. Tiger's swing is envied and copied by many and I believe that John Jacobs has had an indirect influence on that major-championship winning swing.

CONCLUSION

About 18 months ago, I visited John and we were sitting for lunch in his garden. During our conversation, I mentioned how I had recently bumped into a new feel in my backswing and was going through a great ball striking spell. At 82 years age, he literally jumped up from the table inviting me to show him this feel, as we proceeded to a golf net behind his garage. In our enthusiasm to share information and swing 'feels', I ended up giving John a lesson, and vice versa. Furthermore, he gave my nine year-old son his first ever golf instruction. I wish I had had a video camera to record a classic and timeless experience. Whenever I reminisce on that day, my son Nigel says, "Oh, Mr Jacobs, he is funny; he told me to "hit England and turn through". Allow me to interpret John's humorous verbage. 'Hit England and turn through' means to strike the bottom of the ball and the turf at the same time as your hips unwind through impact. The 9 year-old boy understood the instruction, was able to do it, remembered it for the future, and had a good time taking the lesson. Delivered by a true master.

John remains sharp minded, curious, and a fun guy to be around regardless of your age or station in life. Without doubt, John has made a huge impact on golf teaching/coaching and I am honored to call him my friend.

The Impact of John Jacobs on Golf Coaching:

A Commentary

Peter Green

Peter Green Golf, 30 Minster Way, Bathwick, Bath, BA2 6RH, UK
E-mail: green786@btinternet.com

INTRODUCTION

My first meeting with John Jacobs happened in the early sixties, when I was lucky enough to be selected for English Golf Union (EGU) coaching at John's home club, Sandy Lodge. I remember in those days thinking to myself that here is a man who has tremendous presence and a deep knowledge of the game of golf. The main thing I got out of that weekend was John's advice not to change much, but to brush up on my course management. Little did I know then that John was to play such a big part in my future coaching career.

APPRENTICESHIP

When I turned professional and got on to the European Tour, our paths crossed again as we often played practice rounds together. During the winter, I worked for John at the driving ranges he had opened. My thoughts had always been about playing, so my big interest in coaching the game was still a way off. That happened when I finished the Tour and was the professional at Bristol and Clifton Golf Club. I rang John and asked him if I could follow him on some of his teaching weeks. My enthusiasm for coaching the game full time began with those weeks. It took me time to cotton on to John's way of doing things, but he made it so simple with his way of getting to the fault through the club face, clubhead path, and angle of attack, before providing the player with one move to get back on track.

THE SECRET TO CORRECTING FAULTS

Some coaches in the USA, who did not understand John's way, called it "Band Aid teaching," curing a mistake with a mistake, but it was actually exaggerating the other way to get the balance correct. As Sam Snead said: if you are hooking, then practice slicing; and if you are slicing, then practice hooking!

GOLF SCHOOLS

I started to work with John on his European golf schools and then in the early 1980s John set up a company in the USA called Practical Golf Schools. I had the great pleasure of working on those schools from 1981 until 1991. One of my proudest moments occurred when John was doing a Red Carpet School in Phoenix, for around a dozen pupils, the day I arrived to start working in the USA. Shelby Futch, who ran the Practical Golf Schools in the USA, asked me to walk behind John's pupils and tell him what I would do. He was amazed that I said almost word for word what John had said. As a result I was accepted straight away as somebody who could do the job, which was good news for me.

CONCLUSION

Working with and for John was always great fun. He was tough, but always fair. I have the greatest respect for him as a person, a business man, the best golf coach ever, and a friend.

The Impact of John Jacobs on Golf Coaching:

A Commentary

Stephen Rolley
Worthing Golf Club, Links Road, Worthing,
West Sussex, BN14 9QZ, UK
E-mail: stephenrolley@yahoo.co.uk

INTRODUCTION

I first met John Jacobs in the late 1970's at one of the early European Tour young players' schools in Jersey. At the time I was professional at Royal Guernsey Golf Club and still playing in a limited number of tour events. My friend Tommy Horton invited me to Jersey for the day to spend some time with John. I was excited yet slightly apprehensive on the flight over, because I was hitting the ball so well and really enjoying my golf and I was concerned that this great guru would change my swing and spoil my game. When it was my turn to see John, he watched for a few minutes and then asked me to hit some draw shots to a target, then a fade, a knockdown shot and a high floater. "No sense in spending any more time with you Steve, you know exactly what you are doing. Keep up the good work, practice your short game a lot and you can't fail," John said. That was such a powerful lesson and a great confidence boost. What impressed me most was that this internationally renowned instructor was only interested in results and not at all concerned with trying to impress the pupil with his knowledge of the fine detail and intricacies of swing technique.

BECOMING AN EFFECTIVE COACH

Some time later, I decided to concentrate on improving my own coaching skills and called John to ask for his advice. He couldn't have been warmer or more helpful and invited me to attend a clinic he was soon to give at Fulford Golf Club in York. Seeing John work that day with golfers of all standards was a priceless and career-changing experience. With one or two simple instructions, delivered in an easy and humorous style, John was able to almost instantly improve the pupil's ball striking and accuracy. Not only that, but his energy and enthusiasm for the game was infectious and everyone left the range to go to the course with a spring in their step and a smile on their face. It was clear to me that I was watching a genius at work. My own coaching improved overnight, because for the first time I truly understood that the basis of all golf instruction is simply to improve how the player controls the ball and any corrections in technique are most effective if they are delivered in the simplest and most uncomplicated language possible.

Prior to seeing John teach and getting the 'message,' I would have had great difficulty in dealing with a Jim Furyk, a John Daly or a Lee Trevino. My answer would have been to try to make them 'look' better and swing in a more orthodox fashion. I would have made Bernhard Langer weaken his grip and Jose-Maria Olazabal strengthen his grip, purely to get them to conform to my own preconceived ideas of the way you had to hold the golf club. In a way, I would just put everyone in a box. I was already becoming effective as a coach, so I obviously had some knowledge. However, I also had some knowledge I didn't realize I had and of course there was a lot I didn't know. When I saw John work, it put everything in order; it put all the pieces in place. I now realised that I had the opportunity to become a much more effective coach, capable of dealing with players at any level, so I went to watch John coach as often as my schedule would allow. I can't tell you how delighted I was when one spring John called and asked me to join his European coaching team. For more than 25 years, I was privileged to work alongside him on the range, listen to his wisdom and experiences, and to witness at first hand his enthusiasm and love for our game and his generosity in passing on his knowledge. Over time, he gave me more and more coaching tools and ideas, and more especially the confidence to deal with people.

DIAGNOSIS, EXPLANATION AND CORRECTION

Video is not enough to teach effectively. We need the whole package – movement, ball, and the sound – to get the complete picture. We diagnose and this gives us the ammunition to explain. A lot of the explanation is by demonstration. If I couldn't demonstrate, I'd find it difficult to teach. Because I was a player initially, I understand and can feel of a lot of what the pupil is feeling when hitting particular shots, be they good or bad. As all John's coaches come from a playing background, they are interested in their own golf and have a good sense of feel for the game. As a golfer, I learned how to play from my uncle, Len Boyd, a local pro, who was a good hitter and a good player. Standing behind the player we can get the posture, the swing path, etc. The ball gives us the clubface, but there is also the sound. There is an 'underneath' sound, an 'over-the-top' sound, and a 'dead-right' sound. Walk along the line on the range at a tournament and you can tell who is playing well from the sound. There is the noise the club makes either side of the ball and there is the sound of the impact. Video doesn't give sound. Some players don't look totally correct, but have a natural confidence and authority of strike that far outweighs any potential weakness in technique. You can tell from the sound that they can hit it. Lee Trevino and Lee Westwood are good examples. As part of their research, Ping wanted to take the sting out of clubs, so they put two plugs in the shaft; one at the head end, the other under the grip. This gave a 'dead feel,' so they then tried it with one plug and it improved the feel. Testing golfers with ear plugs, they found that more than half of the players couldn't feel their shots if they could not get the noise.

I like watching other coaches, especially the English Golf Union regional and national coaches, more so on the correction than the diagnosis. After my first two years of doing eight weeks of golf schools each year around Europe, John and I would bounce ideas off each other. It got to the stage where, with a line of 20 players, John would start at one end and I would start at the other, and we would meet in the middle. He might say, "What you have said to that woman, I don't want to change because she's hitting it great" or "I've done such and such with this man [explaining why] and I don't want you to interfere with that".

CONCLUSION

John was an absolute joy to work with, a great friend and a wonderful mentor. He will help anyone who asks and has never charged golf professionals (and many amateurs) for a lesson in his life. I have seen him instruct winners of major tournaments, countless tour players, leading amateurs, club players and complete beginners and I am convinced that no other coach has the ability to instantly connect with golfers of any level and with a few simple, easy to follow instructions get results as quickly, as simply and as effectively as John Jacobs. We are truly fortunate to have had such an exceptional and generous man at the forefront of our game for so many years.

The Impact of John Jacobs on Golf Coaching:

A Commentary

Paul Hoad

Director of Instruction, St. Paul Golf Academy,
86 Yanquing Road, Qingdao, China 266216
E-mail: pgjhoad@hotmail.com

INTRODUCTION

It would not be too great a statement to call John Jacobs the grandfather of modern day professional golf coaching. Since the mid-fifties, his presence as a player and teacher has been felt throughout the whole golfing world. Since 1972, his pioneering work in uniting European golf has had an amazing effect on the development of the game at both professional and amateur levels. I count myself lucky to have spent time with John Jacobs.

I first met John Jacobs in 1980 at an Apollo-sponsored golf training camp at Meon Valley Golf Club in Hampshire, UK. This camp was aimed mainly at the young talent on the European Tour. I remember John Jacobs as confident and positive in what he was saying. For my own swing changes, I remember I had a fairly upright swing at this time and he was trying to get me swinging on a slightly flatter plane. I remember the emphasis he placed on turning the left side out of the way or as he termed it "not getting in my own way". This was probably referring to my habit of trying to keep the club online for as long as possible through the impact area, which made my knees slide toward the target and reduced my ability to rotate my hips left out of the way.

It is indeed an honour for me, as one of John Jacobs's students, to be asked to write a commentary on this article by Dr. Simon Jenkins. It is also very interesting for me to offer another view as a player turned teacher/instructor/coach.

FROM PLAYER TO INSTRUCTOR TO COACH

John Jacobs' boyhood hero was Henry Cotton whom he first saw in 1938 at the Open Golf Championship. Indeed Henry Cotton's first Open Championship win at Sandwich in 1934, which my own father watched as a young man, was remarkable by the amazing 67, 65 start and, equally amazing, the very nervous, unconfident 79 final round. Jacobs admits he himself was "not confident as a player", which is an interesting opinion as he was a tournament winner and Ryder Cup player.

John Jacobs realised the importance of mental strength, as some players did in his era. In today's game at the highest levels, mental coaching is very much more prevalent. In fact, most of the top tour players have a variety of coaches, trainers and advisers so that they can find support quickly in their less strong areas of performance. Padraig Harrington would be a good example of this.

It is this area that I myself can have some degree of empathy as playing, instructing and coaching seem to require very different sets of skills. These skills are instinctive and I don't think they can be developed to the highest level by any amount of skilful training and practice. There is now a much higher level of training to PGA members and trainees than ever before, but true levels of greatness success will not come just through academic qualifications and large numbers of training seminar points.

I think John Jacobs possessed a rare skill in that he could not only play to a high level, but also instruct his students to an even higher level after his tournament playing days were over. The author reflects that John Jacobs' success as coach for the EGU, R&A and many other amateur and professional teams' was I feel sure, in no small measure due to his extensive experience as a player and his rare communication gifts.

JACOBS' TEACHING SYSTEM.

Teaching from ball flight and impact geometry is what has characterised Jacobs' teaching system. With a little help, people can understand why the ball reacts to clubface angle, club head path and angle of attack.

It is fair to say that John Jacobs' book *Golf*, written in 1963, with John Stobbs was at the time an interesting insight into the Jacobs's ideas on the golf swing, players and the development of the game to that point. Regarding his teaching technique, much of what he writes is being used today. The only difference is in his language use, which is much friendlier and not technical. An example would be on hand action, which "should be natural, the hands will be kept swinging as they are both working in the backswing and the downswing. This will groove the club head swing and will be found to stand up to the pressure of the really big occasion." [1, p. 68]. In this quotation, Jacobs refers to the hands being "kept swinging"; this could well refer to his concept that the hands should work as one unit, together. Also they keep moving or flowing without hesitation in the backswing and downswing, thus giving the player the best link and connection, sense and feeling for the clubhead and clubface position.[1]

John Jacobs's very sharp eye, use of humour and natural sense of showmanship also made him a very attractive communicator, with a soft, Yorkshire brogue delivery. I can clearly remember some of his now famous adages such as "the swing is simply two turns with a swish of the arms in the middle"; "clear the left side", clicking his long fingers either side of his body demonstrating these two areas of interest.

During the time prior to the mid-seventies, there was little video technology available for use for swing analysis and golf instruction. This is probably one reason why John Jacobs did not care to use video cameras during his lessons. I remember asking John in the early 1980's why he didn't use video and he simply replied that "until you can see the clubface as it hits the ball there isn't much point in using it".

Golf instruction has moved into a new era where technology tries to back up the words and explanation of the instructor. But the question still hangs; does having lots of technical information help the student really understand better what he needs to do

---

[1]Editor's Note: Jacobs stated, 'That's the same thing as saying "swing the arms". Every time Henry Cotton said "hands", I would say "arms". (Personal Communication, June 2009)

to improve or does it simply give him more reasons to doubt his own ability to repeat his unique, signature swing?

CRITICAL INCIDENT

The author defines the term "critical incident" very clearly and draws attention to the case of the promising amateur golfer Bruce Critchley, who was placed before the master Jacobs in 1962. It was not the first time nor, I am sure, the last, that a young talent may seemingly fall away after hearing a comment from a gifted coach in a one-off lesson. It seems that making a distinction between instructor and coach is very necessary, particularly in top amateurs. Players who are searching for that little extra help to get them into a lucrative tournament playing career can still be susceptible to a negative change by seeking another opinion. A more recent, well-reported case could be American player Michelle Wie, who was undoubtedly the World's best 15 year-old player. She was encouraged to change her coach and, despite all kinds of professional assistance, went into a prolonged slump which she only now, aged 19, happily seems to be recovering from.

GOLF COACHING IN CHINA

In the world's fastest growing golf market, it is easy to forget some of the traditions from the home of golf! However, as much as the local marketers try to state that golf started in China some 500 years ago, the game is still in its infancy and without any real level of sophistication. If it is possible to "catch up" fast, then maybe China with some positive government influence will do the best job around – with Chinese characteristics of course!

Golf is governed by the China Golf Association (CGA) and is included currently as one of the seven small-ball sports. It controls all professional and amateur play. There is currently a strong desire by the Government for the China National Men's and Women's teams to win the Asia games in November 2010. There is an Olympic training style approach to this. The team leaders are gathering from the resources of the elite training locations in Beijing and around the country. Some of the video motion and biomechanical technology being used is currently the best in the world and it helped create record numbers of gold medallists in the 2008 Olympics. It will be interesting to see the results of this approach. It seems, however, that creating a group of high-level golfers in one place is not quite that easy. I am fortunate to have been involved in this coaching program, but the lack of raw talent to draw from is still a major limiting factor.

As there is still an official moratorium on any new golf course developments, golf is a game for the elite rich. The new talent is still coming mainly from the wealthier or well connected families of China and so despite all the best training practices and facilities allied to some foreign instructors, there are still not enough good players.

It is interesting to note that some of the positive effects of rapid economic growth and business involvement in golf still cannot create a sustainable environment to create more young talent. The spirit of the game is rarely mentioned out here and still only Tiger Woods and the elite image are being promoted. Amateurs and professionals are difficult to distinguish between and as such are all under the governing body of the CGA, which itself is under the control of the Government.

John Jacobs' Golf Schools are the longest running and best known schools in the world of golf. They introduce many thousands of new golfers into the game and have built a strong brand name in the game. I suppose that I have been very fortunate to have been exposed to both John Jacobs and later David Leadbetter, as a player first and then as an instructor/coach. In my own golf academy now, in the north east of China in the beautiful city of Qingdao in Shandong province, I find a great sense of security in what I am trying to offer to my students and instructors in terms of technical knowledge as well as a broader understanding in many other areas of this very diverse game. The influence of John Jacobs in my early days on the PGA European Tour was very helpful. I found many interesting subjects in those meetings and discussions on technique, mental and physical training, as well as the stories that go along with any gathering of golfers!

CONCLUSION

Dr. Jenkins rounds off his article with reference to Hank Haney and Tiger Woods' work on learning from better ball flight. This clearly references back to John Jacobs as an instructor. John Jacobs's strong Yorkshire character, golfing background, enthusiasm and ability to communicate in an emphatic, effective and efficient manner put him at the top of any list, and in any golfing era.

REFERENCES

1.   Jacobs, J. and Stobbs, J., *Golf*, Stanley Paul, London, 1963.

The Impact of John Jacobs on Golf Coaching:

A Commentary

Keith Williams

Keith Williams Golf, 11 Hunston Road, Woodhall Spa,
Lincolnshire, LN10 6PE, UK
E-mail: keithwcoach@aol.com

INTRODUCTION

My earliest memory of John is a 1960/70's ITV series "Learn to Play Golf", which was televised on Sundays around lunchtime. It was basically presented by the producer and there were no high-tech aids to help illustrate the teachings, but John was wonderful at describing and demonstrating how to learn the game. His students on the show hit the ball better and better and inspired the viewer to 'give it a go'.

John Jacobs' playing career was at its height when I was born, so I don't feel qualified to comment on his playing proficiency or successes. What I will say, however, is that he has always maintained his love and enthusiasm for playing the game. Whenever I have had the pleasure of being in his company and, despite his keenness to talk about the golf swing, he still has great enthusiasm for playing the game as often as possible.

I have always sensed that playing was his first love, but perhaps at times his self expectations were just too high for him to feel satisfied with his own performances. Perhaps, for a man of such high ideals, his move from player to teacher gave him the luxury and satisfaction of helping others achieve the heights without the personal frustration!

JOHN JACOBS: THE COACH

John's ability to communicate via words, demonstration and physical manipulation are in my opinion the best in the world and account for so much of his successes in getting players to achieve improvements in the simplest and most effective manner possible.

Simon Jenkins highlights John's ability to focus on the impact position and what that is telling the golfer and the coach needs to be achieved with the swing action. It reflects a parallel of thinking with reference to the comments made by Bobby Jones in *Golf Is My Game* – both understood the science of ballistics extremely well both as players and educators of the swing.

John took the simple factors of clubface, swing path, angle of attack and clubhead speed and delivered a philosophy that was simple and logical. While acknowledging that grip, aim, alignment, ball position and posture are all essentials (fundamentals) for the golfer, he was the first coach to explain that because the ball was positioned to the side of the player and on the ground, the swing was an inside-to-square-to-inside movement. He then described the swing as a turn of the body with the hands and arms swinging up, down and up again in unison with the body action.

He regularly stated that the flight of the ball tells all and that "the correct 'geometry' of impact" is the "single most important step in becoming a good golfer" [1, p. 27].

John's 'method' is not one based on exact physiological movements, angles or positions for the golf swing. Rather it is one founded on what the clubface is doing at impact and what factors have controlled or influenced this. He does not ignore how much influence the body has in accomplishing a consistent and repeatable action and his coaching epitomizes the need to stand correctly at address and to make the appropriate body movements and hand/arm actions during the swing itself. Above all, he gets the player to focus on what the ball is doing or what that player would like the ball to do during its flight and from there how impact has caused the result. Thereafter, most aspects fall into place because it's what the player does with the club to achieve success rather than getting too way laid with perfecting technical positions first and then waiting for results further down the line.

TOUR SCHOOL

John was probably the first teacher to be regarded as a Tour coach. Without his contribution, I doubt the PGA European Tour's annual coaching school initiation for Tour School graduates would have generated such enthusiasm and reward. The first ever school was sponsored by John Brown Engineering Ltd. and took place at Meon Valley, Hants. In addition to John Jacobs, coaches were Bernard Gallagher, Tommy Horton, John Stirling, and John Gracey. Attendees included Sam Torrance, John O'Leary, Billy Longmuir and several other more established players who wanted some guidance along with a larger number of 'rookie' Tour players. John took the lead in all technical areas while using Bernard and Tommy to do the demonstrations. This was valuable in showing the younger players how his method of teaching could be simple, effective and quick to achieve. More importantly it was the first time that I, as a player and coach, had ever been shown that this method of understanding and influencing ball flight through impact positions did not require a 'one style' of swing method to achieve results which was the influence coming from the USA. While Tommy and Bernard demonstrated great skills around the greens, John was able to best describe and explain how the club head was working at impact making the learning more effective for the younger players. John Gracey was the first medical expert to deliver a psychology lecture to European Tour players. Sports science is now widely acknowledged in golf, but John Jacobs was very clear even in those days that the mental side was a key aspect in competing successfully at top level and not to be taken for granted.

CONCLUSION

Seminars, conferences and coaching summits around the world have all prospered by John speaking and talking openly about his thoughts. He's as much 'at home' talking to 1000 coaches as he is one-to-one. John's presence as a speaker almost guaranteed a successful attendance at events. For me, it wasn't just John's knowledge of the swing and how to play the game that provided my best learning experiences from him. It was also the way he delivered his presentations – generally a couple of clubs, a few lightweight balls and thereafter an ability to hold his audience with the odd demonstration to show how simple it actually all ought to be! He never struggled to give a logical and practical answer to any question simply because he knew exactly how it all worked within his philosophy for the swing. On one occasion at a large coaching summit, I was also presenting and one leading coach asked me a slightly 'curved ball' question. I fumbled a little and rued my answer somewhat, but John came up to me immediately afterwards and said: "Keith, the answer was simply, 'I'd watch the player's ball flight and teach him from there'".

REFERENCES

1.   Jacobs, J. and Newell, S., *50 Years of Golfing Wisdom*, Collins Willow, London, 2005.

The Impact of John Jacobs on Golf Coaching:

A Commentary

David Colclough
PGA National Training Academy,
Ping House, The Belfry, Sutton Coldfield, B76 9PW
E-mail: david.colclough@pga.org.uk

INTRODUCTION

Simon Jenkins' article is yet further recognition, if it was needed, of the position that John Jacobs holds in the world of golf coaching. As well as his contribution to our understanding of what makes an effective swing, Jenkins rightly draws attention to the delivery style of Jacobs's teaching. Specifically, the effective way in which he puts his students at ease with phrases such as "I'll take the blame" when they try to execute a new grip, or exaggerated feeling in the swing.

Jenkins also touches on Jacobs's career as a player and very briefly on the golf schools that Jacobs set up with Shelby Futch in the 1970's. Alongside the development of John Jacobs' Golf Schools and becoming one of the world's most prominent golf teachers, it must not be forgotten that Jacobs is also credited as the man who led the emergence of the PGA European Tour in the early 1970's; a result of an internal power struggle within the PGA between the club professionals and tournament-playing professionals of the day [1].

My own personal awareness of John Jacobs was raised by his television series that brought golf instruction to the nation, as well as his books. Jacobs also influenced golf professionals all around the world with his lectures on how to teach golf at Teaching and Coaching conferences and seminars. For those teachers not as fortunate as someone like Hank Haney to get the same chances to work with Jacobs at close quarters, the release of videos showing him teaching at his golf schools in America [2] allowed them to observe the process he went through.

PGA GOLF COACHING EDUCATION

Jacobs influence on golf coaching today is quite clear for all to see, with his teaching ethos permeating through all the PGA's golf coaching education programmes. Understanding the factors (clubhead path, clubface direction, centredness of strike, angle of approach and clubhead velocity) which create the flight characteristics of the golf ball (initial direction, curvature, trajectory and distance) is fundamental to the approach taken when introducing aspiring PGA Professionals to techniques involved in coaching the game. From this standpoint, in a lesson scenario the golf coach is encouraged to anticipate how any technical advice offered to the player will alter the flight characteristics of the ball flight *before* they suggest a change; and this same approach is encouraged when analysing movements that appear to some to be 'quirky' or unconventional, and to understand how they are able to produce performance that holds up under the highest pressures that the game can offer (e.g., Jim Furyk, Colin Montgomerie)

LONG GAME VERSUS SHORT GAME

It has been noted by previous students of Jacobs, and other coaches, including Haney, that when used in isolation of the rest of the game (on the practice ground, looking only at the full swing) there can be pitfalls to this approach. In a lecture at a past European Teaching & Coaching conference, Haney described working as part of the instruction team at a golf school where Jacobs set about fixing a player's horrible slice, making changes to his set-up and swing shape that produced a number of shots hooking gently from right to left. However, when the same player came to him for the short-game part of the golf school, the player had little chance of executing a high pitch over a bunker with the same instructional advice that had been so successful in the long game. This observation is substantiated elsewhere by a professional reflecting on instruction taken with Jacobs on his own game whilst on the European Tour [2]. He related a similar experience, which resulted in the realisation with his own game, and subsequently his own coaching, that:

> If you change one area of the swing, whilst you have positive effects in some departments of the game, i.e. the long game, it had detrimental effect on my short game. [3, p. 63]

BEYOND BALL FLIGHT

While remembering the mantra of 'working to improve technique through observation of ball flight', Jenkins' presentation of the experiences of Bruce Critchley while he was under the tutelage of Jacobs as an England international requires further explanation. Billed as a 'critical incident', the lack of reflection offered from Jacobs's standpoint on this incident might be viewed as contradictory, if as Critchley suggests he was hitting 'super shots' with a 3-iron. It suggests a slightly differing approach to the 'typical' analysis process attributed to Jacobs; seeing beyond just the ball flight presently being executed and recognising that there was an inherent potential weakness in the technique. However, without comment from Jacobs himself the reader is left to surmise what was happening.

CONCLUSION

Today, where a PGA Professional's education and coaching practice is delivered with underpinning knowledge and research of the various sports sciences, the PGA would stand behind Butch Harmon's statement that the teachings of John Jacobs are required reading and essential for the rounded development of the serious golf coach.

REFERENCES

1. Holt, R., Lewis, P.N. and Vamplew, W., *The Professional Golfers' Association 1901-2001*, Grant Books, Droitwich, Worcestershire, 2002.

2. Jacobs, J., *John Jacobs: Doctor Golf's Advanced Surgery*, Quadrant Video, Carshalton, Surrey, 1995.

3. Colclough, D., *The Construction of Knowledge Amongst Expert Golf Coaches from Europe, Working at Elite Level*, Unpublished Masters Dissertation, University of Birmingham, 2008.

The Impact of John Jacobs on Golf Coaching:

A Commentary

Peter Mattsson
Director of Coaching, The English Golf Union Ltd,
The National Golf Centre, Woodhall Spa, Lincolnshire, LN10 6PU, UK
E-mail: pmattsson@englishgolfunion.org

INTRODUCTION

I first saw John Jacobs in person at a PGA Teaching Coaching Conference in Torremolinos, Spain, sometime in the mid 90's. At that time, I was very much a beginner coach trying to learn the ropes of coaching and still wanting to play my own golf in order to one day make a living from it.

GOLF IS WHAT THE BALL DOES

As a coach, I was taking in all sorts of influences from the coaches I met and I was a bit of a sponge in wanting to find out as much as possible and test it myself. This was the time when Leadbetter was the big name in coaching and I wanted to learn as much as I could from his methods. Therefore I was thrilled to pieces when I had the opportunity to cooperate with the Leadbetter Academy in Spain where I was working, playing and practicing at the time. The use of video and computer analysis had once and for all come into the art of coaching and I was quick to take that on in trying to develop both my own game and my coaching. The new technical developments and the highly motivated coaches that I came across greatly helped me in my search for "the perfect swing". The only problem was that it seemed to get me more and more confused. My golf swing and my playing abilities were going drastically downhill. Most of the speakers at the Torremolinos Conference kept giving me the same answers – all technical and down to the point about what the swing was supposed to be. I particularly remember Dr Ralph Mann's model golf swing (see [1]), which seemed like an excellent idea to me at the time.

When John Jacobs came on stage he was a complete breath of fresh air. There was this "old man", about 70 at the time, and in my eyes he completely contradicted and turned everything that had been said before on its head. How could this man make something so incredibly complicated sound so simple? His mantra of "Golf is what the ball does" kept echoing in my head and it still does some 15 years later. I was very confused now and the only thing I knew was that I had to find out a lot more about this thing.

FROM THE RANGE TO THE COURSE

Several years later, after years of studying motor learning and motor control along with a deep dive into Rod Thorpe's and David Bunker's model of Teaching Games For Understanding (see [2]), I am only just starting to get an understanding of why John Jacobs was right and most of the rest of us were desperately wrong. Of course the rest of us were doing all the best we could by trying to utilise the new technology that had become available to us. The problem was that we understood way too little about its impact and thereby also its pitfalls. I remember Dr Gary Wiren once saying something along the lines of, "We know enough about the golf swing and what it should look like. What we don't know is how to get that across to the player".

Only a short while ago, I had the opportunity to meet John again. A fellow coach and I went for a visit to his house where we spent about six hours talking. And believe me, John would not stop talking. One thing he said that particularly stuck with me was that everything he did and tried in coaching came from what he had learned from trying to become a better player himself. What a complete contrast again to what I had been doing in my early days! I was trying to become a better player, but in fact I was getting worse. Perhaps that is why John had already understood what it took to learn, re-learn and most important of all, to be able to put that into the context in which it is meant to be used. It is often said that the ranges are full of great swingers of the golf club who often are also very good ball strikers. On the range that is. Put them on the golf course and it is a completely different ball game. John Jacobs has known that for a long time and his way of not just simplifying instruction but also finding that magical key to unlock the whole door to improved performance is a skill that is and should be admired by anybody who wants to call him or herself a golf coach.

CONCLUSION

John is not a youngster anymore and we do not know for how much longer he will be here to share his wisdom with the rest of us. It is our collective responsibility to make sure that his legacy continues to live long after he is gone. This article is one excellent way of keeping the message alive and when I asked John if he would spend a day with our England Regional and National Coaches, you would not be surprised as to what his answer was: "I would be happy to do that!". In John's mind, of course, there is not that much that we can learn from him. To me, it is a chance to feed off somebody who is more modern in his coaching than any technical development can ever make any coach out there!

REFERENCES

1.   Mann, R. and Griffin, F., *Swing Like Pro*, Broadway Books, New York, 1998.

2.   Griffin, L.L. and Butler, J.I., *Teaching Games For Understanding: Theory, Research, and Practice*, Human Kinetics, Champaign, IL, 2005.

The Impact of John Jacobs on Golf Coaching:

A Commentary

David F. Wright
Wright Balance Research Institute,
31731 Via Coyote, Coto de Caza, CA92679, USA
E-mail: drwright@wrightbalance.com

INTRODUCTION

Simon Jenkins writes that the purpose of his article is to stimulate commentaries from leading figures in the contemporary world of golf coaching who have either been influenced by and/or may provide insights into the development of John Jacobs' golf instruction and coaching. John Jacobs' coaching has shaped both my approach to instruction as well as my research over the past 25 years.

MECHANICS AND POSITIONS

Former *Golf World* editor, Ken Bowden identified John Jacobs as different from other golf coaches during the 1960s and 70s. He said that apart from Bobby Jones' books, Jacobs was one of the only professionals who did not focus his coaching on the mechanics and positions of the golf swing and what these positions were supposed to achieve. Bowden went on to describe how "Americans are a practical, mechanical, statistical society. In Golf, they were thinking in terms of methods and set-piece positions" [1, p. 98]. Sadly, I believe US coaching has moved deeper into the analytical model and position teaching since the early 70's with the advent of video instruction.

Fundamentals are a gold standard for every sport. That is Jacobs' focus in his coaching. He watches ball flight and makes changes in a player's set-up to produce flight changes. US coaches advocate the importance of sound fundamentals in building a solid foundation from which to begin the swing motion. However, most of their coaching remains position instruction, not the correction of one or more fundamentals to produce a different motion and subsequently ball flight as Jacobs so adeptly does.

Jacobs says that how a player places his hands on the golf club is the primary determinant of the success or failure of every golf shot. He considers the grip 50 percent of the golf swing and the address position 40 percent, the fundamentals of golf. [2]

Wright et al. [3] determined that the orientation of a player's hips was the final path of the putter in 88 percent and the final path in 76 percent with irons in a biomechanics-laboratory golf study. They also found that a player's grip, stance width, grip size and foot flare were a few of the variables that modified the orientation of the hip line at address, a fundamental in the set-up to the golf ball. Correcting grip, stance width or foot flare at address to change club path is more enduring than placing the club in positions after swing motion has begun.

WHOLE LEARNING

During my graduate education years, I had a professor of "motor learning" direct the seminar participants through an exercise that I use in my golf coaching to this day. He had us sign our name at the top of a piece of paper. Then he instructed us to look carefully at our signature and copy it exactly as we had signed our name. We were told to look at the length of every vertical and horizontal line and to be certain it was exact, that every elliptical curve was precise and so on. Then we were asked to sign our name again and leave out the second letter of our first name and the third letter of our last name. Needless to say there was an immediate, predictable degradation in performance for each of us in both tasks. The lesson was that breaking a motor task into pieces diminishes quality when you introduce active volition. Motor tasks need to be learned either as a whole or in very large chunks that can be blended together until they are automatic. Removing a link in even a short chain of motor events creates havoc in the resulting performance and interferes with motor learning. Most important was the preparation to perform the motor skill or routine. The set-up prior to the performance of the motor skill, with practice, facilitates an automatic motion without thought.

CONCLUSION

John Jacobs was and is one of the greatest golf coaches of our era. He intuitively understands what fundamentals drive ball flight. He corrects those fundamentals before swing motion begins. He understands the relationship between grip and address positions that produce a foundation for optimum ball flight better than anyone in the last 50 years. I believe his contributions to golf coaching should be resurrected, taught and celebrated.

REFERENCES

1.   Lucus, L., *John Jacobs' Impact on Golf: The Man and His Methods*, Stanley Paul, London, 1987.

2.   Jacobs, J. and Bowden, K., *Practical Golf*, Stanley Paul, London, 1972.

3.   Wright, D.F., Mellman, M. and Watkins, R., Temporary Correction of Transverse Pelvic Plane Rotation Via a Three-Minute Exercise Program, *Annual Review of Golf Coaching* 2008, 2, 99-116.

The Impact of John Jacobs on Golf Coaching:

A Commentary

Fredrik Tuxen
TrackMan A/S, Stubbeled 2, DK-2950 Vedbæk, Denmark
E-mail: ft@isg.dk

INTRODUCTION

John Jacobs has had a lot of success watching ball flight to determine the appropriate corrective measures for a given swing in order to correct ball-flight issues. However, science has helped us to realize that the ball flight can be very misleading. In fact, we now know that using ball flight to determine club path and face angle can be very problematic. Consider a straight ball flight from a driver with a PGA Tour average ball speed of 166 mph, launch angle of 11 degrees, and 2700 rpm of spin rate. There is an indefinite number of club delivery combinations that can produce this ball flight: It could be a result of a perfectly optimal center impact shot for a player with 113 mph club head speed with perfect zero club path and face angle – these data would match a perfect tee shot from Jim Fyruk. However, the exact same ball flight could also be the result of a very inefficient shot from a player with 120 mph club head speed (like Phil Mickelson) who heavy toe's the shot while also having an outside-in club path with an open face angle – but the shot will be more than 20 m shorter than the perfect shot from a 120 mph club head player. This example tells us that only looking at the ball flight is not enough to understand the causes of the ball flight.

The effect of the bottom forward arc of the club head and ball impact position on the ball flight are described by some fundamental principles that must be understood to accomplish an effective game plan for improving ball flight. Detailed measurements of club delivery and ball flight parameters from TrackMan™ over the last couple of years have given us insights in understanding the cause and effect of club delivery on ball flight. I believe that, specifically, one thing has prevented an effective understanding of the club/ball collision and this is the confusion or missing sharp definition around the terms *swing plane* and *club path*.

SWING PLANE VS. CLUB PATH

TrackMan™ defines the *horizontal swing plane* as being the direction of the bottom arc of the club head both pre- and post-impact relative to the target line. The *club path* is the direction of the club head relative to the target line at time of impact. Only in two special cases will the club path equal the horizontal swing plane: i) if the attack angle is zero (ball impacted in the bottom of the swing); or ii) in the case of 90 degrees inclined swing plane (a putter stroke?).

To illustrate the difference between horizontal swing plane and club path, consider a situation with a 45° inclined swing plane (vertical swing plane equal to 45°) 'pointing' straight at the target – a horizontal swing plane of 0°. With this swing, if the ball is impacted at the bottom of the swing (attack angle 0°), then the club path will be 0°. However, if the attack angle instead is +5° (hitting up 5° on the ball) with the same horizontal swing plane of 0°, then the club path would be -5° (outside-in). Note that a swing with a horizontal swing plane of 0° from a video taken directly down the target line would show the club being on the perfect plane both before and after impact.

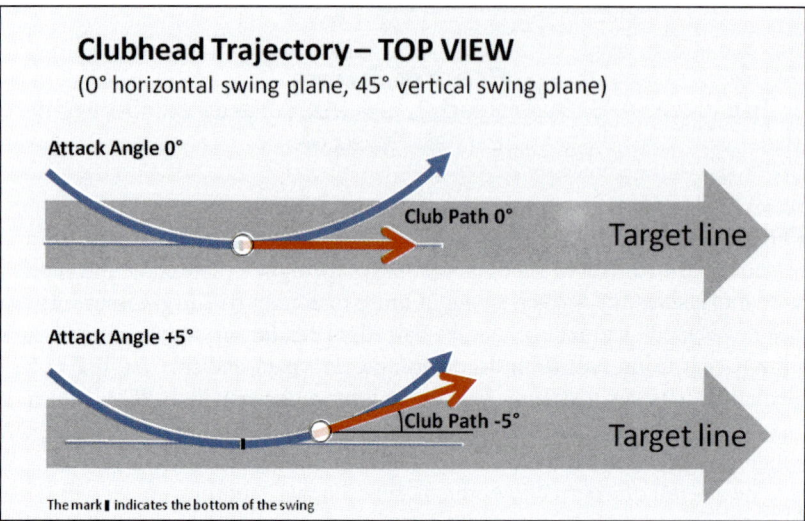

Figure 1. Difference between Horizontal Swing Plane and Club Path

BALL FLIGHT CHARACTERIZATION

The horizontal movement of the ball can easily be described by just two parameters: *horizontal launch angle,* which is the initial direction of the ball relative to the target line; and *spin axis*, which is the tilting of the ball's axis of rotation relative to the horizon. The spin axis will, in no wind conditions, fully describe the drawing/fading action of the ball flight.

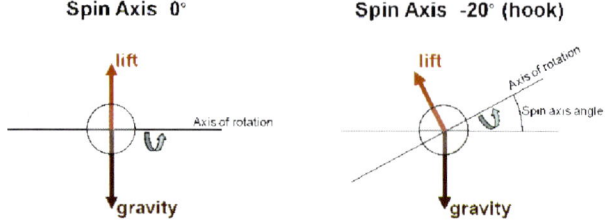

Rule of thumb:
A spin axis of 10° will take the ball 7% to the side – Meaning a 200 m carry shot with a +10° spin axis will curve 14 m to the right

Figure 2. Spin Axis Tilting Influence on Horizontal Ball Flight

The nine traditional shot shapes (pull/straight/push and draw/straight/fade) can then be characterized by the values of horizontal launch angle (HLA) and spin axis (SA) as shown in Figure 3.

Shot	Type	HLA	SA
1	Pull Hook	Negative	Negative
2	Pull	Negative	0
3	Pull Slice	Negative	Positive
4	Hook	0	Negative
5	Straight	0	0
6	Slice	0	Positive
7	Push Hook	Positive	Negative
8	Push	Positive	0
9	Push Slice	Positive	Positive

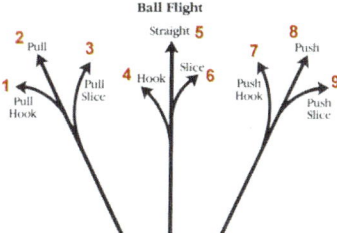

Figure 3. Traditional Shape Shots

HORIZONTAL LAUNCH ANGLE

The horizontal launch angle is determined by only two parameters, the *club path* and the *face angle*. As a rule of thumb, the horizontal launch angle is 15% determined by the club path and 85% determined by the face angle for normal dry club/ball impact.

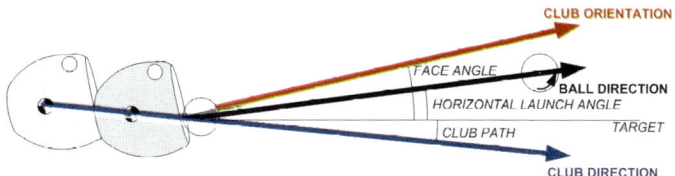

Figure 4. Club and Ball Collision in the Horizontal Plane

For example, assume a club path of +6.7 degrees (6.7 degrees inside-out for a right-handed player) and a face angle of -1 degrees (1 degree closed for right hand player). This would result in a horizontal launch angle of 0 degrees (ball starting at the target line). If the friction is less than normal between the club and the ball, such as a wet ball or grass between club face and ball, the face angle's impact on the horizontal launch angle will increase above 85%; in extreme cases, the face angle can dictate 95% of the ball's horizontal launch angle.

D-PLANE

For the spin axis, there are two contributions. The first is related to any difference between club path and face angle, where any difference between the two will tilt the spin axis. As a rule of thumb, for a 6-iron the ball's spin axis will be tilted 2 times the difference between the face angle and the club path, whereas for the driver, the ball's spin axis will be tilted 4 times the difference between the face angle and the club path. So if the face angle is 3° and the club path is 5°, then for a driver the spin axis will be around -8°; whereas for a 6-iron the spin axis would be around -4°. To understand why, we have to look at the so-called D-plane.

The D-plane is the wedge-shaped plane between two 3-dimensional directions: i) clubhead direction at impact which is described by attack angle and club path; and ii) clubface orientation at impact which is described by dynamic loft and face angle. In Figure 5, the yellow shaded wedge-shaped plane is the D-plane. Note that the angle of the D-plane is actually the spin loft. The laws of physics tell us:

- the initial direction of the ball will always happen in the D-plane and,
- assuming center impact on the clubface, the spin axis will be 90 degrees relative to the D-plane.

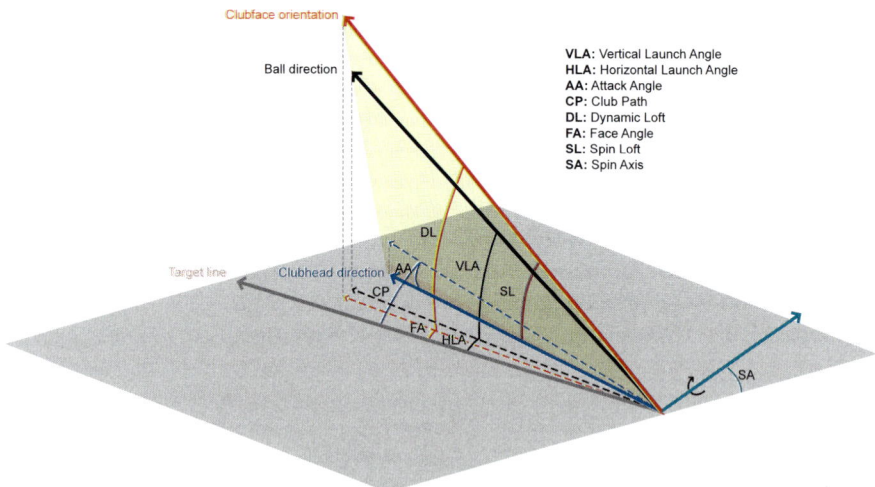

VLA: Vertical Launch Angle
HLA: Horizontal Launch Angle
AA: Attack Angle
CP: Club Path
DL: Dynamic Loft
FA: Face Angle
SL: Spin Loft
SA: Spin Axis

Figure 5. The D-Plane
The D-plane is the wedge-shaped plane between the two 3 dimensional directions: 1) the clubhead direction, and 2) the normal to the clubface, clubface orientation. The initial direction of the ball will always happen in the D-plane.

For a driver, the D-plane is a much narrower 'wedge' than for a 6-iron. This is because the club loft is much less with a driver. The consequence is that for a certain difference between face angle and club path, the D-plane will be tilted more the lower the loft of the club. Since the spin loft of a driver shot is around half the spin loft of a 6-iron shot, the result is that the spin axis of a 6-iron shot will only be half that of a driver shot having the same delta between club path and face angle.

TWO DIFFERENT SWINGS NEEDED

For years, we have heard the mantra 'swing all clubs the same way'. But I would not agree to that. Golfers need different swings to be most effective with their shots. In order to take a divot after impacting the ball with irons, you need to hit down on the ball – negative attack angle. Conversely, hitting up on the ball – positive attack angle – with the driver enables you to maximize your distance for your club head speed. So, let's assume that your vertical swing plane with a 6-iron is 60° and your attack angle is -5°. In order to create a straight shot, your goal is a club path of 0°. How can this be achieved? The answer is a horizontal swing plane of -2.5°, which means aim 2.5° left of the target line with your swing plane. In summary, for a swing having a 60° vertical swing plane, an attack angle of -5°, and a horizontal swing plane of -2.5°, the result will be a club path of 0°.

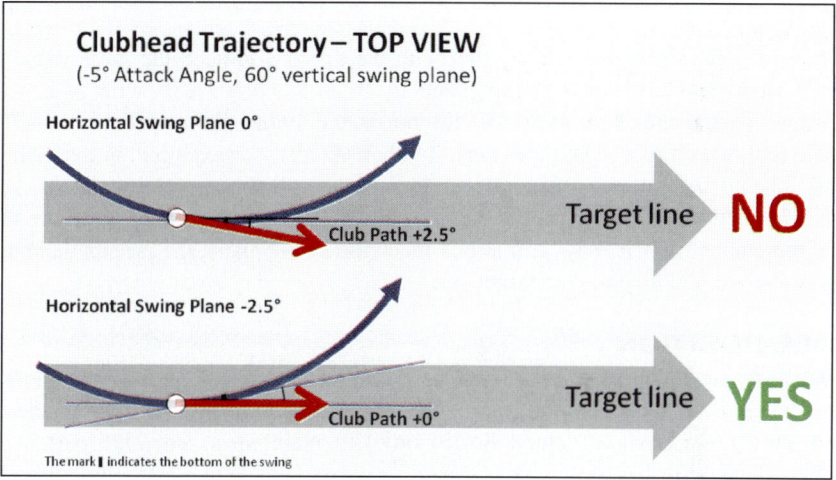

Figure 6. Adjustment of Horizontal Swing Plane Required to Achieve Zero Club Path

With the driver, the vertical swing plane is typically around 45°. Assuming a positive attack angle of 2° is desired, a horizontal swing plane of +2° is required to achieve the goal of club path 0°. With the driver, aim 2° right of the target with your swing plane. In summary, you need two different swings – or at least two different set-ups – to be most effective with the driver and irons.

If you are hitting down -5° with every iron, the shorter the iron you hit the steeper your vertical swing plane will be and the less you'll have to compensate your horizontal swing plane to achieve a club path of 0°. The shorter the iron with the same attack angle, the more direct at the target you should aim. In other words, it is more important to compensate – aim left – with the 3-iron than with the 8-iron.

	ATTACK ANGLE [deg]	VERT. SW.PLANE [deg]	HORZ. SW.PLANE [deg]		CLUB PATH [deg]
"DRIVER"	+2	45	0	=>	-2
"DRIVER"	+2	45	+2	=>	0
"6 IRON"	-5	60	0	=>	+2.5
"6 IRON"	-5	60	-2.5	=>	0
	doesn't matter	90 *	0	=>	0

*In the hypothetical scenario of vertical swing plane equals 90 degrees, club path would always equal horizontal swing plane.

Figure 7. Correlation between Horizontal Swing Plane and Club Path

In more simple terms, we can say that with the driver you need the same value for attack angle and horizontal swing plane in order to obtain a 0° club path – for example, if your attack angle is +3°, the horizontal swing plane needs to be +3° to obtain a club path of 0°. And for irons, it is half effect – for example, if attack angle is -4°, the horizontal swing plane needs to be -2° to obtain zero club path. In short, aim left when hitting down on the ball and aim right when hitting up upon the ball. And remember – when I say 'aim left', I mean the swing plane; the face angle should always be aligned towards the target line.

BALL POSITION

If you move the ball back towards your right foot for the same horizontal swing plane, the effect will be a steeper attack angle (more negative value) and a more inside-out club path (more positive value). So, in order to maintain a zero club path while moving the ball further back in your stance, you simply have to rotate your horizontal swing plane towards the left (more open stance).

Before we discussed that the shorter the club and the steeper the vertical swing plane, the less you had to compensate your horizontal swing plane away from the target line. However, if you add the effect of moving the ball backwards in your stance progressively with the shorter club, it is possible to counter balance this so you can end up with the same horizontal swing plane (aiming) for all your irons!

Beyond that, ball position is very much a teaching philosophy in which I will not take a strong position – but I can analyze the data! Some teachers want to maintain a consistent ball position throughout the set of clubs, while others speak for moving the ball progressively towards the right foot the shorter the club. Analyzing the data, I would tend towards the idea of moving the ball progressively, since this could enable your setup to be the same for all irons and hybrids.

OFF CENTER HIT – GEAR EFFECT

The second contribution to the tilting of the spin-axis is the result of the horizontal gear effect. The horizontal gear effect occurs when the ball is impacted anywhere but the center of gravity of the club head in the heel-toe direction. If the ball is hit towards the toe, the club head will twist clockwise, and the gear effect causes the ball spin-axis to tilt anti clockwise i.e., a draw spin. If the ball is hit towards the heel, we'll get the opposite effect, or a fade spin-axis tilt.

Impact location and gear effect have a surprisingly significant effect on the curvature of a golf shot. If we start with the ideal situation with a face angle of 0° and a club path of 0° and impacting the ball in the center of gravity of the club face, then the ball will go straight. However, with same face angle and club path if you impact the ball just 1 dimple (app. 3.6 mm) towards the heel of your driver, it creates a spin axis of +6° (fade spin), then the ball will start on the target line but end up 10 m right on a 250 m carry shot. You will probably be on the fairway, but in a major golf championship with very narrow landing areas and firm turf conditions, the shot may be in jeopardy of missing the fairway. If you impact as much as 10 mm towards the heel, the dispersion will be 28 m right of the target line on a 250 m carry!

CLUB PATH [deg]	FACE ANGLE [deg]	FACE IMPACT	HORZ. LAUNCH [deg]	SPIN AXIS [deg]	SIDE OFFLINE [m]
0	0	Center	0	0	On target
0	0	1 dimple (3.6mm) towards heel	0	+6	10 m R at 250 m
0	0	10 mm towards heel	0	+17	28 m R at 250 m

*Typical MOI and COG assumed

Figure 8. Driver: Effect of Off-Center Hits
MOI is moment of inertia; COG is centre of gravity

To counteract the horizontal gear effect, the club manufactures have added a curvature to the club face (the *bulge*) on woods and drivers. This means that when you impact the ball on the heel, your face angle at the impact point will normally be closed, hereby starting the ball more left and tilting the D-plane towards a draw spin. The net effect will be a much straighter shot compared to the zero face-angle situation.

The spin created by the gear effect is a spin around a vertical axis (sidespin) that is added to the spin from the D-plane. The vertical spin from the horizontal gear effect tilts the spin axis. The contribution to the vertical spin is roughly the same in rpm's throughout the set for the same off-center distance, but because you get much less spin with the driver the effect of the added vertical spin is much more pronounced than with a wedge, for example. If we have a spin rate of 2,500 rpm with the driver and 10,000 rpm with a wedge, the effect of 500 rpm of sidespin on the spin axis will be 11° for the driver and only a quarter of that, or 2.8°, for a wedge.

If we take an example of hitting a 6-iron with zero club path and face angle, and impacting the ball 1 dimple towards the toe of the club face, this will cause a spin axis of -2°, resulting in a shot starting on the target but being 2.5 m offline at 170 m carry. A spin-axis of -2° is not a serious problem and often is what we refer to as a 'baby draw'. For comparison, a 2° spin axis could originate from a center-impact 6-iron shot where the club path is 0° and the face angle is +1°; so a 1 dimple off-center impact has the same effect as 1° difference between club path and face angle on the spin axis for a 6 iron shot! For a driver shot, 1 dimple off-center corresponds to 1½° difference between club path and face angle.

CLUB PATH [deg]	FACE ANGLE [deg]	FACE IMPACT	HORZ. LAUNCH [deg]	SPIN AXIS [deg]	SIDE OFFLINE [m]
0	0	Center	0	0	On target
0	0	1 dimple (3.6mm) towards toe	0	-2	2.5 m L at 170 m
0	0	10 mm towards toe	0	-5.5	7 m L at 170 m

*Typical MOI and COG assumed

Figure 9. 6-Iron: Effect of Off-Center Hits
MOI is moment of inertia; COG is centre of gravity

Another important consequence of impacting the ball off center on the club face is the loss of initial ball speed and thereby loss of distance.

JOHN JACOBS *PRACTICAL GOLF*
The new knowledge about the cause and effect on the ball flight makes it necessary to comment on some quotations from John Jacobs' classical instruction book *Practical Golf* [1].

IMPACT LOCATION ON THE CLUBFACE
In *Practical Golf*, it is stated:

> The only purpose of the golf swing is to move the club through the ball square to the target at maximum speed. How this is done is of no significance at all, so long as the method employed enables it to be done repetitively. [1, p. 15]

What should be added to the above statement is: 'impact the ball in the center of the clubhead'. Other than that, Jacobs' statement is in total agreement with what science tells us. The only thing to be aware of is what 'moving the club square through impact' means; i.e., that the club head at impact moves towards the target (zero club path) with a square club face (zero face angle). Furthermore, the following is stated in *Practical Golf*:

> There are four possible impact variations produced by the golf swing that, in concert, determine the behaviour of the ball. They are:
>
> 1.   The direction in which the clubface looks.
> 2.   The direction of the swing.
> 3.   The angle of the club's approach to the ball.
> 4.   The speed of the club.

Of these four, the alignment of the clubface at impact is the most vital. If it is not reasonably correct, it will cause errors in the other three areas. For example, the clubface being open – pointing right of target – invariably leads at impact to an out-to-in swing path through the ball. This in turn forces the club into too steep an angle of approach to the ball. The clubface cannot meet the ball either squarely or solidly. Conversely, a closed face at impact generally leads to an in-to-out swing path. That causes too shallow an angle of approach – the club reaches the bottom of its arc before it reaches the ball. Again, the clubface cannot meet the ball either solidly or square. [1, p. 15]

We know that there is more to it than the four variations listed by Jacobs. The importance of impact location on the club face cannot be neglected. Further it is important to differentiate between the 'direction of the swing' (horizontal swing plane) and the 'club head direction at impact' (club path). Only the latter matters for the ball flight, whereas the former is the means to achieve a certain club path. In total, there are five rather than four impact variations:
1. Direction of club face (face angle and dynamic loft)
2. Direction of club head at impact (club path)
3. Club head's approach angle to the ball (attack angle)
4. Club speed
5. Impact location on the club face

CLUB FACE ORIENTATION
In *Practical Golf*, it is stated:

The direction in which the clubface looks is the most important of the four impact elements that determine the behavior of every shot you hit. If your clubface aims left or right of target during impact, instinctively you will make "matching" errors in the path of future swings.

If your clubface consistently points right of the target at impact, you will swing the clubhead through the ball from outside to inside the target line…, in an instinctive effort to prevent the ball from going to the right. If your clubface consistently points left of target at impact, you will do the opposite – swing through the ball from inside to outside the target line in an instinctive effort to stop the ball from going left…. .

If your clubface consistently points right of the target at impact, you will swing the clubhead through the ball from outside to inside the target line…, in an instinctive effort to prevent the ball from going to the right. If your clubface consistently points left of target at impact, you will do the opposite – swing through the ball from inside to outside the target line in an instinctive effort to stop the ball from going left…. .[1, p. 16]

The behavior of every shot you hit is caused by a specific inter-relationship of the clubface angle and the swing direction at impact. [1, p. 19]

The orientation of the club head is by far the most important of all the five impact variations. And as Jacobs correctly says, any misalignment of the club face at impact will lead to compensations in the other four impact variations to achieve a less effective straight shot.

In general, it is equally important for the shot shape to impact the ball in the center of the club face as it is to square up your club orientation and direction at impact.

HORIZONTAL GEAR EFFECT
In *Practical Golf*, it is stated:

> First, take a driver to the practice ground and hit half a dozen shots. If they bend from left to right in the air, the clubface is open to your swing line at impact. If they curve the other way the clubface is closed. By using a club with very little loft, you will always get an honest picture of your clubface alignment at impact. Why? Because, since the club's loft is minimal, little backspin is created by a back-of-the-ball blow – too little, in fact, to override the sidespin imparted by the oblique contact of an open or shut clubface.

> Next, take a nine-iron and hit a few more shots. Because of its greater loft, this club contacts the bottom back of the ball, imparting heavy backspin. Consequently, the influence of sidespin is reduced to the point where the direction in which the ball flies accurately reflects the path of the swing. [1, p. 23]

Unfortunately this is not true at all. For a driver, the impact of the horizontal gear effect is so pronounced on the curve of the shot, that there is simply no way by looking only at the ball flight you can determine anything about club path or face angle. Determination of club path and face angle is almost impossible without a dedicated measuring device such as TrackMan™ . Severe inside-out or outside-in club path's can be observed by the naked eye, but with the desired accuracy being around 1 degree for these parameters to be truly actionable, there is no way around the need to accurately measure it.

CONCLUSION
The ball flight is primarily determined by four things only:
I: Clubhead direction at impact (attack angle and club path)
II: Clubhead orientation at impact (dynamic loft and face angle)
III: Impact location on the club face
IV: Club speed

There are other factors such as ball and club properties that play a role for the ball flight. Since various combinations of I-IV above can produce the same launch conditions for the ball and thereby the same ball flight, it is consequently not possible to derive from the ball flight alone what exactly caused the ball flight – some additional information is needed. In particular, ambiguity exists in whether the club face is closed, square or open relative to the club path versus whether the ball is impacted towards the heel, center or toe. The effect of the practical variations on ball impact and club path/face angle are more or less of the same magnitude, which means that aligning club path and face angle is only equally important to impacting the ball in the center of the club face.

While it only matters how the clubhead is presented to the ball and not how it 'got there', there are some important differences in the swings required for the different clubs in order to achieve the perfect straight shot. The key lesson is to realize that it is the clubhead's direction at impact; i.e., *club path* that matters and that this is different from the direction of the overall swing. ie., *horizontal swing plane*. As a direct consequence of this, it is a minimum requirement to have different horizontal swing planes for the driver, woods and irons.

REFERENCE
1.   Jacobs, J. and Bowden, K., *Practical Golf*, Stanley Paul, London, 1972.

The Impact of John Jacobs on Golf Coaching:

A Commentary

TJ Tomasi
PGA Center for Golf Learning and Performance,
PGA of America Golf Schools,
8565 Commerce Center Pkwy,
Port St. Lucie, FL 34986, USA
E-mail: pblion@aol.com

INTRODUCTION

There is no doubt that John Jacobs is a giant in the world of golf – a good player, a great teacher and a wonderful role model for us all. But the thing that stands out most in my mind is that Jacobs is such an innovator. When everyone else was sure that teaching body positions was the only way to go, Jacobs was "swimming against the flow chart" — and that can be exhausting. Fortunately for teachers of golf and their students, he persevered and today the tutorial nature of ball flight is [or should be] part of every teacher's pedagogy.

BALL FLIGHT IS NOT ALWAYS TUTORIAL

But in my opinion there is more to the story. Relying *solely* on ball flight as some of his devotees do (Jacobs not included), ignores how humans learn a motor movement. The efficacy of ball flight depends on the stage of the learning process. During the stages where you are teaching tasks such as the grip, stance or takeaway, the ball flight is not tutorial and often distracts from the student's learning focus. It is not until these tasks are completed that ball flight becomes the central issue.

I believe that when you're teaching a swing piece like the grip, your evaluation system is how well your student matches the model not the quality of ball flight. However, once the pieces are in place the ball flight becomes tutorial. In fact, at this point the teacher should: i) trouble-shoot the golf swing on the basis of ball flight both on course and in practice; and ii) help the student develop images that "pull up" the body movements necessary to create proper ball flight.

JACOBS' EYE

Jacobs' eye for ball flight has its modern extension in the newest teaching technologies such as TrackMan, FlightScope and the SAM system, devices that aid the teacher in adjusting body motion and equipment based on ball-flight and ballistics.

As might be expected since his original thesis on the ball-flight laws, additions and amplifications have been made. We know the face accounts for approximately 80% of the flight pattern while the clubhead path is around 20%. The newest research from the TrackMan people show that the angle of attack (AofA) is a key variable, far more than formally supposed.

This may explain why many golfers spend their entire careers bouncing back and forth between hitting their irons well but not their woods, and vice versa. Research shows that the most efficient angle of attack changes depending on the club. If the player wants the club path square at impact with a negative AofA, the horizontal swing plane of a three-wood through wedge needs to be out-to-in (right-handed swing) in order to accommodate the downward angle of attack. For the driver, it needs to be in-to-out.

In addition to AofA, TrackMan measurements show that where on the face you make contact influences not only the direction of spin or curve of the ball but also the *amount* of curve — something a keen eye needs to evaluate. If we make an assumption that the face is square, then the following obtain:

Impact on low heel = fade, slice; highest spin

Impact on high heel = fade, slice; lower spin

Impact on low toe = draw, hook; higher spin

Impact on high toe = draw, hook; lowest spin

YOU STILL NEED A HUMAN ON THE OTHER END

Today, on the ballistics-end of ball flight, there are a bunch of wires and sensors taking the place of the Jacobs eye, but nothing so far has come along to take the place of the brain on the analysis end. Even with all its power, modern science is but an enhancement of the Jacobs algorithm, proving that no matter how reductionist science becomes there must always be a human on the other end to tweak the template.

Jacobs has never made the mistake that some of his alumni have – he knows a lot about the human factor and how it's related to ballistics. One zealot I spoke with pointed to a ball boy picking the range and bragged that he could teach the young man to be a good teacher by simply memorizing the ball-flight laws. My response was "only if the boy also understands human nature."

Here is Jacobs recognizing the human factor: "The thing we all react to most is the face of the club. You must realize…that the clubface at impact on shot one, affects the entire swing on the next" [1, p. 18]. Contained in this simple sentence is the Rosetta stone of human behaviour – our outcomes are conditioned responses and by understanding the process we can intervene and change those outcomes if we're not happy with them.

Or how about this for understanding the role of the person swinging the clubface: "the technique of striking the ball…is no more than 50 per cent of the game. Temperament, intelligence, nerve, desire, and many other mental qualities make up the other 50 per cent" [1, p. 19].

PERFECT IS THE ENEMY OF THE GOOD

Jacobs realizes that lockstep reconstruction of every golf swing to fit a theoretical norm can have disastrous results for both the student and the teacher. It's like performing a lung transplant on everyone with a cough. It was Voltaire who said "Perfect is the enemy of the good," but it is John Jacobs who applied Voltaire to golf:

> We all suffer from some kind of built-in fault. ... [If the average golfer] wants the maximum fun for the minimum effort...[he must make] himself completely aware of his own natural swing errors; then, depending on their severity, either [compensate] for them or [play] within them. [1, p. 187]

CONCLUSION

But of all the things John Jacobs is, he is one of us – a teacher — albeit at the highest rank. He teaches us not as some stone-faced authority figure whose pronouncements carry the air of the snooty butler, but as a kind and helpful colleague: "The golfer who makes me mad", says Jacobs, "is the chap who wants to play like Tony Jacklin after one lesson and no practice, and blames me if he doesn't" [1, p. 190]. You've got to love a fellow teacher who says these kinds of things.

REFERENCE

1.   Jacobs, J. and Bowden, K., *Practical Golf*, Atheneum, New York City, 1972.

The Impact of John Jacobs on Golf Coaching:

A Response to Commentaries

Simon Jenkins
Carnegie Faculty of Sport and Education,
Leeds Metropolitan University, Leeds, LS6 3QS, UK
E-mail: S.P.Jenkins@Leedsmet.ac.uk

INTRODUCTION

I would like to thank all twelve colleagues for writing insightful commentaries on my target article and, in doing so, paying tribute to one of the most influential figures in the history of golf. I would also like to thank John Jacobs for meeting me at Weetwood Hall, Leeds on 30 June 2009 – the day after he was involved in a Ryder Cup reunion event at nearby Moortown Golf Club – for an interview and conversation about the commentaries; all of which he had read beforehand except for the one by Fredrik Luxen which I did not receive until some time later. In this response to commentaries, I draw on this interview/conversation, in addition to published sources (mainly *John Jacobs' Impact on Golf* by Laddie Lucas [1]) and unpublished material from knowledge I elicited from Peter Green, who has worked with Jacobs for many years. Along with Donald Crawley, Jim Hardy and Stephen Rolley, Green was a commentator on the target article. All these colleagues learned directly from Jacobs and they would agree that Jacobs can be regarded as a 'master' golf coach or instructor in terms of the definition of 'master' given below:

> Traditionally, a master is any journeyman or expert who is also qualified to teach those at a lower level. Traditionally, a master is one of an elite group of experts whose judgments set the regulations, standards, or ideals. Also, a master can be that expert who is regarded by the other experts as being "the" expert, or the "real" expert, especially with regard to subdomain knowledge. [2, p. 22]

With regard to the title of Lucas' book, it is important to recognise that Jacobs' impact went beyond golf coaching. As Director-General of the PGA of Great Britain and Ireland's Tournament Division for five years from 10th October 1971, Jacobs "masterminded and built up what has since come to be called the PGA European Tour" [1, p. 113]. Mark McCormack, who was once dubbed by *Sports Illustrated* magazine as "the most powerful man in sport", stated the following in *The World of*

Professional Golf: Mark McCormack's Golf Annual (1973) and was cited by Lucas:

> I for one, do not doubt that [1972] was a year of high significance. It might be no more than a slight exaggeration to say that these twelve months saw British golf progress by a quarter of a century. And that is quite a trick. [1, p. 134]

RELUCTANT TEACHER

Jacobs is a teacher, but was a reluctant one. 'I got this reputation, so any young amateur who got down to 1 [handicap] was sent to me, the R&A,' said Jacobs. 'I charged four times as much as anyone else to keep people away. I wanted to play. If I hadn't been a teacher, I would have had quite a good record as a player. In match play, when I stood on the first tee I knew I was going to win.'

The first time he didn't know he was going to win was when he stood on the tee with Christy O'Connor, Snr. I asked Jacobs about O'Connor golf swing: 'Just better than orthodox – greased, not loose,' said Jacobs. 'Neutral in the sense that with the ball to the side, the natural shot is a little draw – but he could play all the shots. And he had a wonderful temperament.'

Jacobs was competitive as a player, but probably over-experimented with shot-making and admits to weaknesses as a player in terms of temperament. He also did not possess the understanding of putting he later gained as a teacher. After he finished his playing career, Jacobs was on the putting green at Wentworth with Gary Player and Arnold Palmer: 'I watched them both and they were both in-to-straight and I'd tried to go straight-to-straight.' Compared to his old method, Jacobs found he could get a release rather than 'overcontrolling', which tended to take the feel away.

In his commentary, Donald Crawley noted that, "Americans refer to a golf instructor as someone giving golf lessons, a 'swing coach'" while the term 'coach' is used in connection with a team at, say, a college (p. 15). Jacobs regards himself as a teacher and he doesn't like the word 'coach'. In the target article, I suggest that "instruction is just one facet of golf coaching" (p. 8). A recent article by coaching scientists Jean Côté and Wade Gilbert suggests that "to be called a coach, an individual must be in contact with one or more athletes regularly for at least one sporting season with a goal of developing, not only athletes' competence, but also confidence, connection, and character" [3, p. 318]. Therefore, Côté and Gilbert contend: "sporadic interactions between an apprentice and an instructor, who teaches a specific skill (i.e., golf lessons), would fall outside the boundaries of this definition" [3, p. 318]. 'Chema Olazabal is one of the few that I've taught over an extended period,' says Jacobs. However, numerous great players have asked for and received 'lessons' from Jacobs; Jack Nicklaus, Tom Watson, Seve Ballesteros and Nick Faldo, to name but a few. Jacobs was Captain of the Great Britain and Europe Ryder Cup Team (1979 and 1981): 'I said to both teams, "I'm not going to start teaching you, but I'm here if anyone wants to ask me"', says Jacobs. 'But I broke my rule with Faldo, "I know you're not playing well. I'm not going to teach you, but I want to give you a lesson tomorrow morning."'

In their commentaries, both David Colclough and Paul Hoad discussed the 'critical incident' concerning Bruce Critchley. Jacobs is at pains to explain what happened with Critchley. 'I only recollect Critch coming once and then he was naïve,' said

Jacobs. 'I knew I was right. He was a slinger; he loved being the guy that hit it miles. He would get fliers. You have to consider face, path but also the angle'.

Jacobs admitted that it is difficult when it is a one-off lesson and a player's regular coach is not there. Regarding Tom Halliburton, Jacobs said: 'Tom was a nice lad but he was not a teacher, he was a coach.'

WORKING ON HIS OWN GAME

Jacobs' understanding of how top players work on their swing is grounded in his own playing experience and understanding (including empathy) of 'fear of hooking'. 'There are certain basic things that are true for everybody and then when you get to a certain stage most good players draw the ball…and they're frightened of the hook,' said Jacobs. In his commentary, Peter Green referred to Sam Snead's dictum that "if you are hooking, then practice slicing; and if you are slicing, then practice hooking!" (p. 17). Jacobs followed Snead's advice when he was hooking the ball: 'I went straight to the practice ground and aimed left, and eventually I started fading everything,' he said. Jacobs pointed out that Arnold Palmer had a stronger grip with his driver than he did with his wedges: 'The great players do those things automatically, without thinking; I don't think they work it out.'

BALL-FLIGHT LAWS

In his commentary, Fredrik Tuxen acknowledges the success that Jacobs has had from looking at the ball flight to determine what needs to be done with the swing, but he argues that "science tells us now that the ball flight can be very deceiving" (p. 39). He points out that Jacobs' classic instruction book *Practical Golf* needs to add "impact location on the club face" to the other four impact variations (p. 46) and to take into account horizontal gear effect when considering the ball flight from hitting the ball with a driver (p. 48). At the theoretical level, most of what Tuxen states in his commentary can be found in *The Search for the Perfect Swing* [4], which was published in 1968 (horizontal gear effect, for example, received several pages of coverage). Where Tuxen has made a significant contribution with his Trackman™ device is in providing empirical data.

Jacobs read *The Search for the Perfect Swing* before he wrote *Practical Golf* [5]. He said it was knowledge that he knew. It might seem surprising therefore that he didn't articulate that: "The direction the ball start off on…depends more on where the clubface is pointing than on the direction of swing" [4, p. 125, Figure 20:6].

'Where I knew I was wrong, but I didn't want to complicate it: When you swing out-to-in with the face open, the ball doesn't start left it starts a little bit right and goes more right', said Jacobs. Jacobs' model of the ball-flight is simplified, but perhaps by necessity – both in terms of the target audience for his book and the fact that the interrelationship between the factors that determine the ball flight is complex, as the authors of *The Search for the Perfect Swing* explain:

> The player can usually tell which error is responsible for a curving shot of this kind by observing the flight of the ball.
> If it is only the swing which is off line to the target, the ball will start off slightly to one side of the line up the middle of the fairway, but then curve

back and away towards the rough on the other side.

If the swing is straight, and it is the clubface which is out of true to it, then the ball will again start off to one side of the centre-line but this time curve further away into the rough on the same side.

Very often both the swing and the clubface are misaligned to the target. *Under these circumstances almost any result is possible…*

[4, p. 124, italics added]

In addition to observing the ball flight, Jacobs also paid attention to the divot with iron clubs. He certainly understood the horizontal gear effect, having served an apprenticeship under master clubmaker Willie Wallis at the Hallamshire Golf Club in 1947 and was able to experiment with clubs for his own game. He had a practical understanding of gear effect and bulge. He used his knowledge of golf club technology later to develop 'anti-slice' clubs which were marketed by Dunlop in 1983 [1, p. 203-205]. Furthermore, echoing what Stephen Rolley stated in his commentary about sound (p. 20), Jacobs said, 'I feel devoid of something if I can't hear the sound of impact'.

Not withstandingTuxen's Trackman™ device, it is worth heeding the words of TJ Tomasi, who stated the following in his commentary:

> Today, on the ballistics-end of ball fight, there are a bunch of wires and sensors taking the place of the Jacobs eye, but nothing so far has come along to take the place of *the brain* on the analysis end. Even with all its power, modern science is but an enhancement of the Jacobs *algorithm*, proving that no matter how reductionist science becomes there must always be a human on the other end to tweak the template. (p. 52; italics added)

It can be argued that Jacobs' work is based primarily on practical intelligence, which can be defined as "ability to acquire *tacit knowledge* from everyday experience and to apply this knowledge to handling everyday practical problems in which the information necessary to determine a solution strategy is often incomplete" [6, p. 616]. Tacit knowledge is procedural rather the factual; i.e., it is about knowing *how* rather than knowing *that*. It is knowledge that is *usually* learned without explicit instruction and is not openly articulated. That is *not* to say, however, that tacit knowledge cannot be made accessible to conscious awareness or be articulated [6, p. 615].

While Jacobs did not excel in the classroom at school, he did get a distinction in woodwork. When I asked Jacobs to make explicit his understanding of the gear effect and the bulge of wooden clubheads, he said: 'I had this explained to me in detail, I've forgotten, it wasn't a simple answer – something much more engineering.'

GRIP, AIM, STANCE AND POSTURE (GASP)

In his commentary, TJ Tomasi states:

> Relying *solely* on ball flight as some of his devotees do (Jacobs not included), ignores how humans learn a motor movement. The efficacy of

ball flight depends on the stage of the learning process. During the stages where you are teaching tasks such as the grip, stance or takeaway, the ball flight is not tutorial and often distracts from the student's learning focus. It is not until these tasks are completed that ball flight becomes the central issue. (p. 59)

In line with what Tomasi states, Jacobs does indeed start beginners with the fundamentals of grip, aim, stance and posture (GASP): 'The first time I tell them about GASP, I relate it to impact. I wouldn't start teaching group until I've explained what GASP does.'

'I would give them the concept in the beginning,' said Jacobs. 'When you've got a beginner, you've got to get them to hit the ball in the air otherwise they'll give it up. It's easy enough with children because they'll go and hack it and chip it up but any grown up starting golf will find it difficult to get the ball in the air and if they don't have a little success, they won't play.

'I would have children competing straight away on the putting green. Then I would have them chipping by putting with a 5-iron off the green. I want it to be a game very quickly, not just learning, not just teaching. I mean I hated school!'

SWING PLANE

'When did you first come across swing plane concept? I asked Jacobs. 'Hogan's book – that was probably the first time it had been spelt out in such simplicity,' he replied. 'That pane of glass of Hogan's, that's as good a description of the plane as you can have. It's very difficult to be specific – is it through the neck, is it through…? For me, it's neck down to the ball, straight line; it's the same thing as saying that the swing is in-to-in. It's one of my swing thoughts sometimes when I'm not playing well,' he said. For further discussion of Jacobs' notions of swing plane, see Jenkins [7, p. 12-13].

Jacobs also believes that swing plane can be used with beginners. Furthermore, it is central to his philosophy of teaching. Shelby Futch has been quoted as follows:

> '…We've tried so hard all the while to keep the integrity of our teaching so sound and simple in terms of John Jacobs' basic philosophy. From the outset of these schools our philosophy has run like this: "You stand to the side of a golf ball which is on the ground. This means that the body must make two turns to give the arms room to swing up and down. Let's no make our basic concept any more complicated than that."' [1, p. 184]

In Jacobs' words, many years later: 'Swing plane is an extension of: the ball is to the side of you so you have to swing in-to-in and it's on the ground so you have to swing up at the same time; they're all interrelated.'

STRAIGHT VS. UPRIGHT

It would appear that Jacobs played an influential role in the development of golf instruction and even the golf swing; the latter in terms of the move away from the 'square-to-square' swing and towards a swing in which the clubface is neutral to the path of the clubhead. In asking the question of why Jacobs' *Practical Golf* was so successful, Jenkins [8] contended:

> One reason was that he understood a fundamental difficulty about the golf swing: coordination of upward movement of the arms with rotation of the body. The difficulty in achieving this co-ordination lies in the fact that the ball is at ground level but the centre of body rotation is at chest level. Also, the hands start the swing at a height in-between chest and ground level, while the clubhead is at ground level. [8, p. 1]

Jacobs is well known for his dictum that 'the body turns while the arms swing up and down'. His understanding of the distinction between 'straight' and 'upright' is crucial yet often looked. 'When good players go wrong, the majority of them tend to swing too straight,' said Jacobs. Here is what Peter Green states about 'straight':

> It's very easy for the human mind to think in terms of straight lines and angles. People – I fell into this trap – think that if they can take the club straight back from the ball with the clubface square then it would return square and the ball would fly straight. Purely from where we're standing – the golf ball is in front of us – it is impossible to swing the club on a straight line; it has to go on an arc. That arc is inside the target line on the way back, back to straight and inside the target line on the way through. And the analogy there is that it is like a door opening and closing, but the other thing is you have an angle because the ball is on the ground, so you've got to have an up and down movement. The body is what gives you the inside of the arc by turning to the right and to the left, and the angle is given to you by the arms swinging up and down. And that gets rid of the thing of the body and the arms swinging on the same plane.
>
> Most handicap golfers swing on a straight line and they hit the ground behind the ball because the angle is too steep, so there is a huge change of direction to create a bit of space. The club is going too steeply and too much to the left. If they don't pull it, they'll slice it depending on the reaction of the clubface through the ball.
>
> Another reaction from the straight line is that the body tends to follow the golf club. You tend to get this curl under aspect where the clubface curls under and then the underneath thing where the body gets in the way and you bottom out the arc too far behind the golf ball. And that will result in a push to the right or a snap hook. I would say that although more handicap golfers slice from coming over the top, more and more people are push slicing it from coming underneath, because of thinking about the Jack Nicklaus straight line theory; trying to do what he's doing.

A subtle nuance of Jacobs' theory of 'getting too straight' is his heuristic concerning the top edge of the clubhead and how it can facilitate a correct backswing. (A heuristic is a 'rule of thumb' based on experience or practice [9, p. 208].) This is articulated in *John Jacobs' Impact on Golf* [1], but not *Practical Golf* [5]; it is not 'textbook knowledge'. Jacobs talks about the clubface being 'strong' or hooded versus it being 'weak' or 'laid off'; this is different from the distinction between 'closed' or 'shut' versus 'open'. The former distinction concerns "the difference in angle between the top and bottom of the blade of an iron club" [1, p. 140]:

> If the top edge of an iron club is set off – laid off – to a greater angle to the bottom angle of the blade, a more inside swing is encouraged. This helps those whose tendency is to swing too much 'underneath' – too much 'up and under' – and, therefore, to rock and block. Conversely, if the angle is narrowed and brought more into line with the bottom of the blade – a stronger clubface position – this helps to counteract too flat, too shallow a swing, and so assists the player whose tendency is to 'fan it too much open' going back. [1, p. 204]

The case below concerns Tom Watson, who asked for Jacobs' advice in 1983 at Gleneagles, Scotland:

> The Yorkshireman asked Watson what his problem was.
> The answer came back pat: 'I rock and block.' He went on to say that, in his opinion, the standard golf shot should be a slight draw – which tied in nicely with Jacobs' own thinking. ('The fact that the ball is to the side of the player leads to an arc which tends to close the club through the ball.') The Englishman wanted to see Watson's set-up. The American then threw a ball down on the turf and lined up with his 5-iron on a distant bush. As he addressed it, he hooded the club – strengthened it – so that the top rather than the bottom of the blade was square to the line. A very strong position, it turned the 5-iron into a 4.
> Jacobs gave his view: 'I believe that sometimes you have the clubface too strong. It has the effect of making you push the club back too straight from the ball for too long. This is what causes the shoulders to tilt rather than turn...'
> Running his finger over the bottom of the blade and then over the top of it to demonstrate, he went on: 'If you square the bottom of the blade to the line and retain the correct loft on the club, the top of the blade will give you a better indication of the correct swing path and so help to turn the shoulders rather than tilt them. You would at first get the feeling that the clubface was more open at the address than you've been accustomed to, but the effect would be to help the rest of the action and let you turn out of the way going through the ball, thus releasing the clubhead and allowing the blade to square up. The golf swing is upright – yes; but straight – no.' [1, p. 196-197]

CORRECTING FAULTS

Jacobs' teaching involves 'diagnosis, explanation and correction'. In his commentary, Peter Green drew attention to how Jacobs' way of correction has been misunderstood as "Band Aid Teaching"; it was regarded as "curing a mistake with a mistake" when it was in fact "exaggerating the other way to get the balance correct" (p. 17). Because there is a difference between what golfers try to do or feel that they do and what they actually do, there is a need for pedagogical devices such as drills and exaggerated movements [7, p. 18].

A good example of a Jacobs corrective comes from his work with Scottish amateur player Charlie Green:

> 'Charlie knew that if you're hooking the ball, there's no better exercise (I've spent hours doing it myself) than just dropping a lot of balls down on some good, firm turf and hitting them with a driver. It avoids a player being too much in-to-out because, if you get too much to the inside coming in to the ball, there's no way that you can make contact with a driver hitting the ball off the turf. ...' [1, p. 36-37]

He has also used it with Olazabal when the Spanish player was getting underneath it with a driver.

Extracts from my knowledge elicitation work with Peter Green provide further insight into the Jacobs way of correction (see Appendix).

COACHING STYLE

'I've come to love teaching and going down the line and meeting a lot of people, and getting a quick result, and making it fun," said Jacobs. 'I don't teach everybody with the same degree of forcefulness or gentleness.' In their commentaries, Paul Hoad and Stephen Rolley both referred to Jacobs's use of humour and ability to make it fun for his students:

> John Jacobs's very sharp eye, use of humour and natural sense of showmanship also made him a very attractive communicator, with a soft, Yorkshire brogue delivery. (p. 24)

> With one or two simple instructions, delivered in an easy and humorous style, John was able to almost instantly improve the pupil's ball striking and accuracy. Not only that, but his energy and enthusiasm for the game was infectious and everyone left the range to go to the course with a spring in their step and a smile on their face. (p. 19)

I reminded Jacobs of his work with Bernhard Langer, which was reported by Lucas:

> ...in the late seventies, when Bernhard Langer, then at the start of his climb, asked Jacobs if he would have a look at him. After the German had hit a few shots, the comment was brief and forthright. 'People will tell you your shoulder turn is too flat, but it is perfect. You need to swing your arms and the club a little higher. The easiest way to achieve this is to put your best girlfriend in the way of a flat arc – but don't change that shoulder action.' [1, p. 195]

'Not last year's girlfriend, the current one,' said Jacobs. 'It means something to them, it really makes the point and it can be funny as well.'

KEEPING UP TO DATE

Even at 84 years of age, Jacobs is astutely aware of what the world's leading players are doing, especially with their swing. 'Mark O'Meara has probably the best golf swing I've seen, said Jacobs. 'I don't think Tiger's swinging a patch on how good he was with Butch [Harmon].' When I asked Jacobs about the difference in Tiger's swing from working with Hank Haney, he replied: 'Much firmer at the top; but firmer flat, he's having to drive through to hold the thing straight, but he's a marvellous short-iron player. The best part of his game is his nut; and the second is his short game; the two things go together.'

When I brought up Peter Green's comments to me[1] about how Tiger's backswing was relatively short and laid off when he drove accurately in this year's Memorial tournament, Jacobs related that getting the club parallel at the top of the backswing does not work for a lot of good players. 'John O'Leary yesterday wanted me to see his boy, and he was spot on at the top of the backswing in a parallel sense, but he hit from the inside all the time from there,' Jacobs said. 'His lesson was 'point left, hit left'. But he was really grooved, I didn't have much success. He understood it, but he'd get one in three right. He hated that feeling, but you're not actually doing that…you're going to end up with the shaft over there. He hit enough good ones – ball, turf. He couldn't get any turf from where he was; he was right in here – too wide and too shallow; a lot of good players do tend to drop it backwards.'

Jacobs then referred to a pair of photographic illustrations of top-of-the swing positions in the copy of a recent PGA swing manual; the right-hand of which was Nick Faldo's swing: 'I'd say the right hand one is perfect; because it's upright left; that's a lovely position,' Jacobs said. 'You can hit like hell from there and clear the left side. That's where I'd like John's boy to get for a little while and it might suit him perfectly. That's the top of backswing position for most good players. It's become much more prevalent in the last ten years.'

CONCLUSION

In his commentary, Gary Wiren acknowledged the influence of Jacobs on the creation of his teaching model, "Laws, Principles, and Preferences" [10]. The following words from Wiren pay homage to Jacobs as a master teacher:

> He keeps it simple, direct and understandable, which makes for rapid positive results. Although he can expound by the hour on golf theory over a pint while in a pub, he knows that theory is best left there rather than taken to the tee. In that respect he meets the master teaching criterion laid down by Tommy Armour who said, "You need to understand the golf swing in its total complexity so that you can teach it in its utter simplicity." (p. 11)

---

[1]Personal Communication, June 2009

REFERENCES

1.   Lucas, L., *John Jacobs' Impact on Golf: The Man and His Methods*, Stanley Paul, London, 1987.

2.   Chi, M.T.H., Two Approaches to the Study of Experts' Characteristics, in: Ericsson, K.A., Charness, N., Feltovich, P.J. and Hoffman, R.R., eds., *The Cambridge Handbook of Expertise and Expert Performance*, Cambridge University Press, New York, 2006, 21-30.

3.   Côté, J. and Gilbert, W., An Integrative Definition of Coaching Effectiveness and Expertise, *International Journal of Sports Science and Coaching*, 2009, 4(3), 307-323.

4.   Cochran, A. and Stobbs, J., *The Search for the Perfect Swing*, Heinemann, London, 1968.

5.   Jacobs, J. and Bowden, K., *Practical Golf*, Stanley Paul, London, 1972.

6.   Cianciolo, A.T., Matthew, C., Sternberg, R.J. and Wagner, R.K., Tacit Knowledge, Practical Intelligence, and Expertise, in: Ericsson, K.A., Charness, N., Feltovich, P.J. and Hoffman, R.R., eds., *The Cambridge Handbook of Expertise and Expert Performance*, Cambridge University Press, New York, 2006, 613-632.

7.   Jenkins, S., Golf Coaching and Swing Plane Theories, *Annual Review of Golf Coaching*, 2007, 1, 1-19.

8.   Jenkins, S., *Golf Swing Revolutions*, Sunningdale Publications, Sunningdale, UK, 1995.

9.   Jenkins, S., The Use of Swing Keys by Elite Tournament Professional Golfers, *Annual Review of Golf Coaching*, 2007, 1, 199-217.

10.   Wiren, G., *The PGA Manual of Golf: The Professional's Way to Play Better Golf*, MacMillan, New York, 1991.

APPENDIX: THE JACOBS WAY OF CORRECTING SWING FAULTS, AS TOLD BY PETER GREEN

A simple way to get people to swing on the correct arc is to get them to feel that the left arm rolls to the right as you go back and rolls to the left as you go through; just a simple counting exercise – one to the right as you go back; two to the left as you go through. You don't want them to open the clubface as they go back in respect to the arc of the swing and you don't want them to close over too quickly, but the feeling they have is they're opening and closing. But what's actually happening is that the face of the golf club is staying square to the arc of the swing and they can then release the golf club. That then gives them the release through to where they want the golf ball to go. The clubface will take care of itself. Their immediate thought will be, "Gosh, he's asking me to open the face wide open and close it". That's how it feels to them, but in fact the clubface is staying square to the arc of the swing.

We put the low-handicap player square at address and then try to get him to 'hit left'. This means getting the feeling that he is swinging the clubhead through the ball to the left; i.e., inside-to-square-to-inside. In the golf swing, the clubhead travels from inside-to-square-to-inside. Inside what? Inside the ball-to-target line. This applies to putting as well as the long game. If you have a short putt, however, the arc of the clubhead will appear straight back and straight through.

The golf teacher may put an umbrella in the middle of the fairway twenty yards ahead and encourage the player to start the ball left of it, in order to get the body out of the way and let the club go through on the correct arc which is back to the inside. There are other ways of helping the player to get his body out of the way, such as getting him to address the ball and move it forward six inches or teeing it high with a three wood and addressing the club above the ball so that he can turn either side of the ball.

There was a low handicap player who would either snap hook it or push it to the right. After he'd lost an important match, he said that he was going to have an operation on his right shoulder because he couldn't stop coming across the ball.
"It's the complete opposite, you're too much underneath," I said,
"Tee it up and I want you to hit as far left as you can with your right shoulder."
He was soon hitting the ball straight down the middle.

An eleven handicapper was across the line at the top of the backswing and was underneath it coming through.
"Point to the left at the top of the swing and hit left," I said to him.
That's not what I wanted him to do, but that's what I wanted him to feel – just to get the club in the correct direction and plane and it worked like a charm. That was all I had to say.

The technique of playing off sloping lies can help tremendously with people's mistakes. For example, the ball above the feet is a very good exercise for someone who tends to tilt their shoulders and not turn their shoulders correctly because if you tilt your shoulders, you'll hit the ground behind the ball. It makes you turn on the angle of the ground and there are a lot of players, like Seve Ballesteros and Nick Faldo, who have done this.
Swinging with the ball below the feet is tremendous for people who tend to follow their body too much with their hands and arms, like Arnold Palmer. Palmer used to practice with the ball below his feet, so did Peter Thomson, to try to get the club to go up and down a bit more.
The best slope of all is the one that you put beginners on; the one that slopes up and away from you. This gets them to hit with the golf club because if they hit with the body, they just bury the club into the ground. I used to start all my beginners on an upslope for the simple reason to get them to hit with the golf club, rather than too much with their body.
The slope that goes down and away from you, you need to know the technique but it really isn't any use for people's practice. It doesn't do anything for the body turn. It's just like playing a bunker shot. You've got to aim left and because you're trying to get the club up and down the slope very quickly, the golf swing is very straight and you're going to cut it; you need to swing up and down the slope.

The Vicious Circle Involved in the Development of the Yips

Christian Marquardt

Science&Motion Sports GmbH,
Schaefergasse 4, 65428 Ruesselsheim, Germany
E-mail: christian.marquardt@scienceandmotion.de

ABSTRACT

Data was collected using the SAM PuttLab from 264 amateur golfers who were measured during an amateur tournament series in Germany. Each golfer had to hit seven straight putts on a regular putting green at a distance of four meters using their own putter. Findings include that Heavy-Yips golfers showed an impaired control of face rotation and face angle at impact. It is proposed that the Yips is a Contextual Movement Disorder and a number of specific factors seem to be involved in its development: anxiety, overcontrol, interference, and awareness of the problem. These factors operate in a vicious circle and any of the factors could trigger the start of the Yips. A behavioural treatment approach can be used to interrupt this vicious circle, based on the premise that the putting movements can normally be executed without breakdown in a different context.

Key words: Golf Putting, Kinematic Analysis, Motor Control

INTRODUCTION

The term "Yips" generally describes the inability to execute a regular putting stroke, in particular the occurrence of involuntary and uncontrollable jerking of the hand or the wrist. The problem has been described as being organic (focal dystonia) or psychological (choking), or as a continuum between both aetiologies. According to research of the Mayo Clinic more than 30% of golfers are affected by this problem which adds on average 4.7 strokes to a round of golf [1]. The Yips can affect professional golfers as well as amateurs and often leads to a high level of frustration and desperation about their golf game. Similar breakdowns of motor performance in highly skilled athletes are also known in other sports like darts, bowling or cricket [2].

Reviewers: Paul Glazier (Sheffield Hallam University, UK)
Paul Hurrion (Quintec Consultancy Ltd, UK)

It is typically not the difficult putts that are affected, but rather the simple ones. The Yips often only appears on short putts, which are limited in the complexity of movement demands. It becomes impossible for the affected golfer to access their normal movement pattern even if they try to force it consciously. On the contrary, the more the player tries to avoid the problem, the harder it tends to break out. Many prominent golfers have been affected by the Yips, including Bernhard Langer, Sam Snead, Ben Hogan and Tom Watson.

YIPS SYMPTOMS

According to various case reports, many players mention a sporadic beginning after a long personal history of golf. In particular, the resistant nature of the problem is significant. Once affected, many players suffer from the Yips for the rest of their career. Some players report that once in a while they are able to putt normal again after quitting golf for some time, but that the problem soon returns (especially in pressure situations).

Typically, the Yips is assigned to involuntary movement jerks during the putting stroke [1, 3]. The substantial cocking and twisting of the wrist or the forearms result in an unpredictable ball action. *Choking* is a general symptom of decreased motor performance in sports due to increased performance anxiety, resulting in a disconnection from the movement. *Freezing* describes increased grip pressure and stiffness of a player, the inability to initiate the movement, and cramping during movement execution. Some players also report tremors of wrists or arms throughout the stroke, inhibiting control of the putter at impact.

RESEARCH ON THE YIPS

The discussion of the Yips being either a psychological disorder or an organic disorder has a long history. Various articles and studies have been published, but with yet insufficient understanding of the aetiology of the problem. Consequently, there is not yet any accepted treatment approach available. Although anxiety seems to play an important role in the development of the Yips, the exact mechanisms underlying an increased level of anxiety and the fundamental breakdown of movement performance are still unclear. McDaniel et al. [4] defined the Yips as a focal dystonia, where anxiety is exacerbating the problem, but is not the cause of the problem. Although 77% of the affected golfers reported the severity of the Yips being proportional to their anxiety level, no differences were found between affected and normal golfers with regard to the general level of performance anxiety. Sachdev [5] confirmed these results and found that more severely affected golfers tended to rate themselves more anxious, but the severity of the Yips did indicate more severe ratings of psychopathology. Anxiety was seen as a modulating effect which has also been found in other movement disorders.

The diagnosis of the Yips as a focal dystonia is based on the motor impairment involved in Yips which seems similar to the problems of cramping, tremors and clumsiness reported in other focal dystonias [6, 7]. Adler et al. [7] found abnormal co-contractions in Yips-affected golfers and also assumed evidence of the Yips being a focal dystonia. Focal dystonia is generally described as focal cramping of a muscle or group of muscles and is mainly observed in persons who professionally need to execute a specific movement for a long period of time (hence 'writer's cramp', 'musician's cramp'). The pathology of focal dystonia is assigned to structural changes of the basal ganglia and its corresponding transmitters. However, the aetiology of focal dystonia is not yet completely understood. Focal dystonia could also comprise mechanical, psychological and other task-specific problems and can be modulated by anxiety. Recent studies show that the disturbed movements can be retrained in a very short amount of time, thus contradicting the pure neurological definition of focal dystonia being an overuse syndrome [8]. Additionally it has been shown that in writer's cramp it is not the basic movement competences that are disturbed, but rather the execution of a movement in a specific context [9]. It is conjectured that writer's cramp develops as a consequence of exaggerated movement control strategies where increased level of movement control interferes with the execution of automated, open-loop movements.

Comprehensive studies of the Yips conducted by the Mayo Clinic [1, 3] suggest that the Yips should be defined as a motor phenomenon with multiple possible aetiologies, ranging from focal dystonia to choking. For golfers with handicaps of less than 12, it was found that the prevalence of the Yips is between 32.5% and 47.7%. They suggest that a clear definition cannot be made due to the variety of symptoms and underlying mechanisms. Besides an evaluation of personal habits, and the nature and onset of symptoms, the researchers measured vital parameters and discovered an elevated level of blood pressure, heart rate and elevated grip pressure in Yips-affected golfers. They concluded that the increased sympathetic activation is a consequence of the increased level of anxiety. However, it seems questionable whether the definition of a continuum from an organic neurological disease (focal dystonia) to a common psychological phenomenon in sports (performance anxiety) truly describes one and the same putting problem.

Most previous studies on the Yips focused on either psychological abnormalities or neuro-structural deficits involved in Yips. Adler [7] used EMG to measure muscle activity in the arms during putting and found increased level of co-contraction in Yips-affected golfers. In this study, we used kinematic movement analysis to investigate the putting movements in Yips-affected and normal golfers. Part of the study has already been published in another article [10]. In this article, we want to more precisely describe the disturbed functional aspects of the putting movements in Yips-affected golfers. Based on the results, we will discuss the aetiology of the problem and propose a theoretical model for development of the Yips which could also be used to tailor systematic treatment of the problem.

METHOD
PARTICIPANTS
The data sample contains 264 amateur golfers who were measured during an amateur tournament series in Germany. Each golfer had to strike seven straight putts on a regular putting green at a distance of four meters and using their own putter. For each golfer, two practice putts were allowed before the measurement began. The players were not informed about the purpose of the study. All players were invited to participate in the study, but received no remuneration for evaluation of their data. Table 1 shows the biometrical data for the participants.

Table 1. Participants in the Study

	N	Age	Sex Ratio Males:Females	Handicap	Years Golfing
Mean	264	44.7	208:56	16.6	8.7
SD		14.0		6.5	5.3

APPARATUS

The putter movements were captured in high resolution using the SAM PuttLab technology. The system consists of a sender unit mounted to the shaft which contains three miniature ultrasound transmitters. The weight of the triplet amounts to about 50 grams. A receiver unit is standing in front of the golfer. The system is calibrated with a laser for ball position and target direction. The overall sampling frequency is 210 Hz. During measurement, the registered data is continuously transferred from the receiver unit to a PC via USB. The recording software scans the data stream and automatically detects valid putting strokes to be stored to file. The analysis software can calculate more than 30 characteristic parameters for each putting stroke. Only a set of parameters was analysed in this study. A graphic report was printed for each player to validate the reliability of the data before statistical analysis with the software package SPSS 15.0.

GROUP SELECTION

To identify Yips-affected golfers, the kinematic characteristics of six self-confessing Yips-affected golfers were used as a template. The kinematic data of the Yips golfers clearly showed a severe disturbance of the rotation signal corresponding to the twitches of the hand or the lower arms. Around the moment of impact, the Yips golfers showed irregular large oscillations of face rotation which additionally were inconsistent throughout the movement repetitions. An oscillation was defined as at least one excessive opening and closing action of the putter face during a putting stroke.

Strong oscillations with high inconsistencies were rated as "heavy Yips", mild oscillations but still with high inconsistencies were rated with "mild Yips". Irregular rotation (i.e., high amount of either closing or opening the face only) was not rated as a Yips problem irrespective of the level of consistency. The selection of the test groups is described in more detail in Marquardt and Fischer [10]. The data for the resulting Yips groups are shown in Table 2. Yips golfers tended to be slightly older, but no differences in handicap were found.

Table 2. Data of the Subdivided Yips Groups

Group	N	Percent	Age	Handicap	Sex Ratio
Unaffected	224	84.8%	44.0	16.9	177:47
Mild Yips	21	8.0%	48.7	14.1	16:5
Heavy Yips	19	7.2%	47.6	15.7	15:4

RESULTS

A set of variables was statistically analyzed to reveal differences in the putting movements of the test groups. The mean values describe the general putting technique. The standard deviations (SD) represent the variability of performance. The data was sorted according to functional groups for setup, direction control and distance control. Parameters representing Setup are only direction of face angle at address position. Parameters determining the direction of the ball are face angle and path direction at impact. Additionally, we looked at putter face rotation, putter path arc and face rotation relative to the arc which are critical for face angle and path direction at impact; these are consistent and smooth for a natural and unaffected putting stroke. Parameters representing distance control are impact speed, and duration of backswing and time back to impact. Consistent timing is a typical characteristic of skilled movement execution and is critical for good distance control in putting. The mean values and the corresponding standard deviations for the test groups for the seven putts are shown in Table 3.

Table 3. Mean Values and Standard Deviations (SD) for 7 putts for Unaffected Golfers, Mild Yips and Heavy Yips
ANOVA tests and post-hoc t-tests (Bonferroni) were calculated to reveal significance levels: * $p < 0.05$; ** $p < 0.01$; *** $p < 0.001$.

	Variable	Unaffected	Mild Yips	Heavy Yips	F	p
SETUP						
Face angle at aim	FaceAim [°]	0.26	-0.02	-0.73	1.96	n.s.
	SD	1.14	1.24	1.50	2.74	n.s.
DIRECTION						
Path direction at impact	Direct [°]	-0.47	-0.37	0.04	0.41	n.s.
	SD	1.41	1.54	1.68	1.95	n.s.
Face angle at impact	FaceImp [°]	-0.03	0.08	-0.25	1.18	n.s.
	SD	1.29	1.19	1.61 *	3.36	*
Rate of face rotation	RotRate [°/s]	42	38	31 *	3.4	*
at impact	SD	9.0	12.2	22.9 ***	46.9	***
Arc of path at impact	Path Arc [°]	7.3	4.4	2.7	2.4	n.s.
	SD	5.0	5.4	7.7 ***	8.5	***
Rotation relative to arc	RelRot [°]	-3.1	-3.1	-3.1	0.02	n.s.
inside of +-10 mm	SD	1.5	1.5	2.1	2.9	n.s.
DISTANCE						
Impact speed	ImpSpeed [mm/s]	1688	1741	1674	0.70	n.s.
	SD	100	114	105	0.75	n.s.
Duration of backswing	BSTime [ms]	715	795 *	710	3.36	*
	SD	40	49.1	38.2	3.33	*
Time to impact in	ImpTime [ms]	322	352	317	2.78	n.s.
Downswing	SD	17.7	24.5 ***	17.3	8.33	***

SETUP PARAMETERS
Heavy Yips golfers tend to aim more left and tend to aim more inconsistently, but the statistical analysis did not reveal significant effects for mean aim angle or for consistency of aim between unaffected golfers, mild Yips and heavy Yips golfers.

DIRECTION PARAMETERS
The ANOVA group comparison showed significant main effects for *RotRate*, *SD*

FaceImp, *SD RotRate* and *SD PathArc*. Values for *Direct*, *FaceImp*, *PathArc*, *RelRot*, *SD Direct* and *SD RelRot* did not show significant differences between groups. Post-hoc t-tests (Bonferroni) showed significant differences between heavy Yips and unaffected golfers for *RotRate* ($p < .05$), *SD FaceImp* ($p < .05$), *SD RotRate* ($p < .001$) and *SD PathArc* ($p < .001$). Heavy Yips golfers rotate less through impact and have a more inconsistent face angle at impact, inconsistent face rotation and inconsistent path arc compared to unaffected golfers. If the face rotation is calculated relative to the amount of path arc (*RelRot*), no differences were found. No significant differences at all were found between mild Yips golfers and unaffected golfers for direction control parameters.

DISTANCE PARAMETERS

The ANOVA group comparison showed significant main effects for *BSTime*, *SD BSTime* and *SD ImpTime*. Values for *ImpSpeed*, *ImpTime* and *SD ImpSpeed* did not show significant differences between groups. Post-hoc t-tests (Bonferroni corrected) showed significant differences between mild Yips and unaffected golfers for *BSTime* ($p < .05$) and *SD ImpSpeed* ($p < .001$). Mild Yips golfers show an increased duration of the backswing. The time from top-of-backswing through to impact is also more inconsistent. No significant differences at all were found between heavy Yips golfers and unaffected golfers for distance control parameters.

DISCUSSION

Kinematic analysis of a putting stroke proved to be an adequate method to systematically investigate the characteristics of Yips affected putting movements. Although the studies of the Mayo Clinic used analysis technology to measure heart rate, EEG or EMG in Yips-affected golfers [1, 7], they were not able to draw conclusions on the disturbed functional aspects of the movement. It seems unclear if the measured abnormal brain activity and the co-contraction of the forearms represent basic motor control problems (i.e., dystonia) or rather represent consequences of a more complex movement problem. Consequently, this research was not able to provide relevant information to develop a conclusive treatment approach for curing the Yips. In contrast, the kinematic analysis in the current study revealed that in the Yips it is not the complete movement that breaks down but rather specific, functional aspects. Heavy Yips golfers show an impaired control of face rotation and face angle at impact. Other functional aspects such as movement timing or length of the backswing could play an important role in the early development of the Yips.

DIRECTION CONTROL PROBLEM

Part of the data already published [10] revealed that in heavy Yips golfers the amount of face rotation through impact is reduced and the consistency of all rotation parameters is drastically impaired. In this article, we sorted the parameters into the different functional groups for Setup, Direction control and Distance control. Significant differences for heavy Yips golfers were found in the level of Direction control, but not in the level of Setup or Distance control. Consequently we interpret the manifestation of the Yips as a problem connected to direction control, but not directly connected to distance control. This result corresponds to the fact that the Yips mostly occurs in short putts, where control of ball direction is critical. Longer putts, which are generally more associated with distance control, are not normally affected by Yips.

In this study, we analysed the arc of the putter path and the face rotation relative to the putter path. The results show a tendency of Yips-affected golfers to reduce the arc of the putter path at impact. The variability of path arc is significantly increased in heavy Yips. We previously found that, in heavy Yips golfers, face rotation through impact is reduced and variability of rotation is increased. Yips-affected golfers seem to interrupt both natural face rotation closing the putter face and movement of the putter to the inside on a natural arc. Surprisingly, if face rotation is seen relative to the putter path arc, no more differences between the groups could be found. The simultaneous impairment of face rotation and putter path suggests that in the Yips face angle and putter path are still somehow coupled and that both the hands and the forearms are simultaneously involved. This could also be a consequence of a generalization of dystonic movement problems from distal joints to proximal joints which has also been described for other task-specific movement disturbances such as writer's cramp, where the problem starts in the hands and develops into the arms and shoulders [9].

YIPS IN THE EARLY STAGES

The kinematic analysis could also help to identify the Yips problems at an early stage. Most of the golfers who show mild Yips symptoms are not yet aware of a specific putting problem. They may only recognize some inconsistency in their putting. Golfers who showed mild but inconsistent oscillations of face rotation were classified as mild Yips golfers in this study. Surprisingly, for this group of golfers no direction parameter showed significant differences. In contrast, significant differences were found for distance control parameters. Mild Yips golfers showed a significantly longer backswing time and an increased variability of time to impact.

Consistent movement rhythm and timing are typical characteristics of automated movement execution [11]. Automated movements are always executed in an open-loop mode of motor control where no feedback information is processed during the execution of the movement [12]. The processing of feedback information is always associated with considerable time demands, thus slowing down the movement and increasing the variability of movement timing. Increased movement time is a general sign of an increased level of conscious or subconscious movement control. The tendency for increased movement control in mild yips golfers could be interpreted as one of the triggers to develop the Yips at early stages.

FOCAL DYSTONIA

The cramping and jerking involved in the Yips is often assigned to focal dystonia. Our data does not support the contention that the movement problems involved in the Yips are a consequence of a neurological disease. Only specific functional aspects of the putting movements are disturbed in the Yips, whereas other aspects are not affected. From this result, we conclude that in the Yips the original movement program is still active but is superimposed by a second and conflicting movement program which is connected to the functional aspect of direction control.

Although cramps or co-contraction are typically involved in the Yips, a convincing explanation is still lacking as to why the movements can still be executed perfectly well if the context of the task is only slightly changed. The Yips often disappears if the ball is hidden under a cover and the golfer does not know if there is always a ball to be hit or not. The Yips can also disappear if the ball is fixed to the ground, the hole is removed, or is replaced by a symbolic target like a tee. Other golfers appear to experience the Yips for a specific distance on short putts, but if the putt is slightly longer or shorter the movement is all of a sudden perfect. If the movement program is disorganized by overuse (repetitive strain injury), which is assumed as an origin of focal dystonia, or if any other neurological sensory-motor deficit is the cause of the problem, it would be impossible to switch back and forth between normal and disturbed execution if exactly the same movement is executed but in a different context.

It is also unclear how people who never played golf before could be affected by the Yips. These golfers are explicitly excluded from most Yips studies, because they do not conform to the definition of the Yips being a disorder acquired over a long period of time. We have seen many novices or high-handicap golfers being measured on the PuttLab who show severe Yips, but without being aware of any problem of their movement. These golfers might have brought in the problem from other sports such as tennis. Our future research will focus on these groups of golfers to better understand the development of the Yips.

These phenomena seem to contradict the clinical diagnosis of the Yips as being a focal dystonia. Furthermore, the prevalence of the Yips seems much too high for focal dystonia. The prevalence of focal dystonia in the population is 3 in 10,000 [13]. The Mayo Clinic suggests that up to 47.7% of golfers are affected by Yips [1]. Is it plausible that a very high percentage of golfers are affected by focal dystonia when it has such a low prevalence in population as a whole? Rather, the high percentage of golfers affected with the Yips suggests that it is a *normal* phenomenon in golfers.

THE VICIOUS CIRCLE

If the putting stroke is only disturbed in a specific context, but can be executed perfectly well in other contexts, then it is not the basic movement itself that is disturbed but rather the execution of the movement in a specific context. Therefore, we propose to describe the Yips as Contextual Movement Disorder (CMD). A number of specific factors seem to be involved in the development of contextual movement disorders. Typically, task-specific movement disturbances only occur under high-precision demands, which *per se* focus attention on a successful movement outcome. This would appear true for hitting short putts where a miss will be interpreted as failure. Our data analysis showed that critical factors for the development and manifestation of the Yips are impaired movement timing associated with increased level of movement control in early Yips and impaired face rotation and path arc associated with jerking of the hands and forearms in heavy Yips. The jerking could then be interpreted as an interference in the execution of an open-loop movement and the activation of a feedback-controlled, closed loop. Smith et al. [1] described the Yips as a problem with multiple possible aetiologies, but, in their model, initial performance anxiety results in a continuum of problems ranging from focal dystonia to choking. In our model, the different factors can occur and influence each other at the same time and are connected by a vicious circle which accelerates once it is closed (see Figure 1).

Anxiety. Several studies showed that anxiety is modulating the problem, but it is not the cause of the problem. The severity of the Yips symptoms also increases with the level of anxiety. Other critical factors modulating the problem are avoidance of failure or estimated consequences of missing an important putt.

Overcontrol. The Yips is connected to conscious or sub-conscious control of impact. Without a ball or without impact, there is no Yips. We found increased movement time representing increased level of movement control in mild Yips golfers. McDaniel et al. [4] found increased level of obsessional thinking in Yips golfers. Processing of visual feedback information also tends to interrupt ongoing, open-loop movements [14].

Interference. In the Yips, it is not the complete movement that breaks down. The existing open-loop movement is superimposed by a second conflicting movement connected to direction control which results in jerking on short putts. By interrupting face rotation and path arc, the conflicting movement is working against a ball direction to the left. The results from Smith et al. [1] confirm that the Yips more often occurs on short putts and on left-to-right breaks.

Perception. Jerking only without awareness of the problem is different from the Yips. Jerking only does not seem to directly result in a pathologic putting problem. But the perception of the problem will trigger anxiety, which again triggers interference and thus will accelerate the process. In Yips-affected golfers, increased self-perception and subsequent self-rating play an important role.

Due to a vicious circle, the starting point of developing Yips could be any of the factors involved. The assumed interdependency between the different factors throws a very different light on the continuum of problems. Some golfers experience their first Yips-affected putt under increased performance anxiety, while in other golfers the Yips may develop as a consequence of a generally increased level of movement control or increased focus of attention to details of the putting stroke. High-handicap golfers can show jerking where anticipation of impact seems to play an important

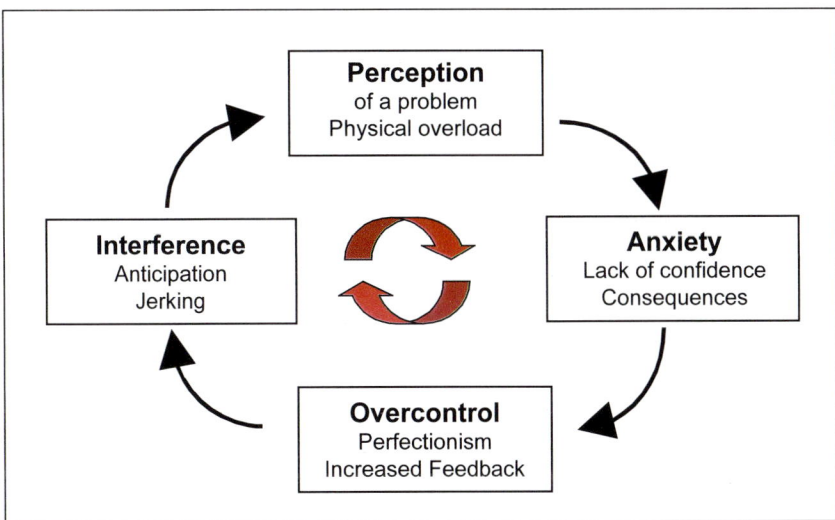

Figure 1. The Vicious Circle Involved in the Development of Yips.

role. Other golfers may first perceive a problem in their putting, then try to correct the problem, but the more they focus attention to their putting the worse it becomes. Once the vicious circle starts accelerating, the problems develop in a downwards spiral and the devastating movement strategies and compensations become established as an automated movement pattern.

THERAPY

The understanding of the Yips as a vicious circle could facilitate a better understanding of the inter-dependency of the factors involved in the development of the Yips. The variety of factors involved in development of the Yips seems to correspond to the variety of treatment approaches suggested to cure the Yips. Depending on the individual severity of the factors involved, different treatment approaches might in fact be adequate. In some golfers, the anxiety problems might dominate whereas others apply inadequate control strategies. In some golfers, the jerking itself is out of control whereas in others exaggerated self-perception is a problem. However, we use a treatment approach where we first search for preserved movement capabilities on a lower level of movement complexity that may be selected as reference movements and as a starting point for re-training of the intended movements [9]. The level of complexity of movement where undisturbed movements can be found can vary considerably between golfers. For some golfers, it is enough to put more focus on a consistent stroke rhythm, whereas others need to swing the putter freely without a ball. Once an undisturbed movement is found, the task complexity is reintroduced step by step. When a condition is reached where the movement is becoming impaired again, we work back and forth until we are able to shift the problem to the next level. The result of such a training session is shown in Figure 2.

The problem facing this golfer is indicated by large oscillations of the wrist and of the putter rotation around impact (Figure 2, Left). The speed and acceleration signals of the putter are less affected. A portion of movement beginning in the forward swing also seems unaffected. After 4 hours of training (Figure 2, Right), the problem almost disappeared. The wrist movements are now smooth and follow the movement of the putter. Rotation signals are now also in a normal range. It needs to be noted that the putter movements before and after the training look very similar apart from a slightly smoother finish of the forward stroke after training.

CONCLUSION

Kinematic analysis of putting is an adequate method to distinguish between the different putting problems summarized under the notion of the Yips. The vicious circle proposed in this article may promote a better understanding of the inter-dependency of the different factors involved in the Yips. Choking and freezing need to be clearly distinguished from the manifestation of the pathologic phenomena in the Yips. A more precise diagnosis for the Yips will be needed in the future to no longer summarize all uncontrollable putting problems under the same notion. A more precise definition of Yips will also enable more specific treatment approaches to be developed. Using kinematic analysis to identify the Yips at early stages or even before outbreak could be another emphasis of future research.

The Yips does not involve a complete breakdown of movement, but rather a

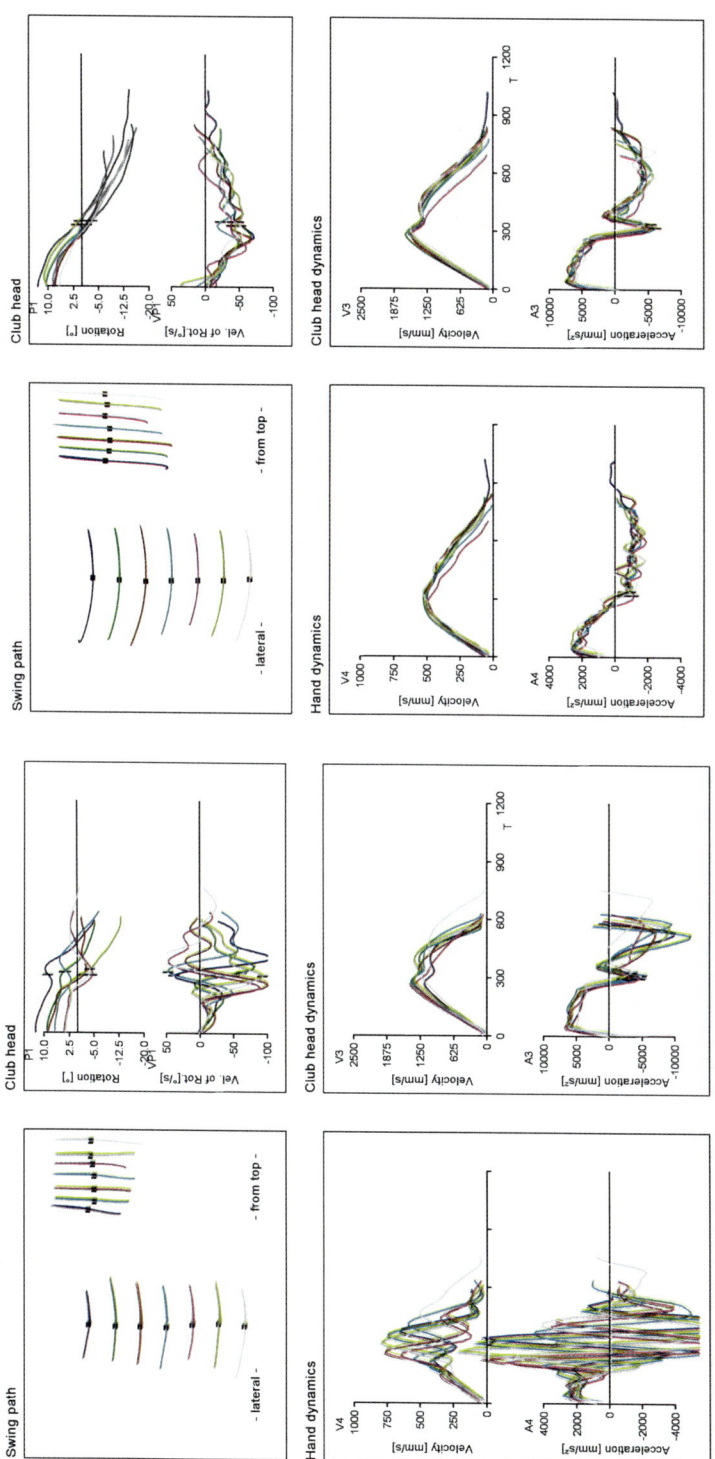

Figure 2. PuttLab Analysis of a Yips-Affected Golfer Before (Left) and After (Right) 4 Hours of Training
The data of 7 putts is superimposed. All graphs show only the forward swing. In each graph, the following is displayed: Upper left: Path in lateral and top view. Upper right: Club face rotation and velocity of rotation. Lower left: Velocity and acceleration of the right wrist. Lower right: Velocity and acceleration of the putter. Impact is the downpeak in the acceleration signals.

disturbance of direction control in a specific movement context. These findings contradict the clinical definition of focal dystonia. The Yips seems to be a "learned" disorder based on fatal movement strategies introducing an increased level of movement control in automated movements which results in jerking and is amplified by anxiety.

We propose a behavioural treatment approach to interrupt this vicious circle. As the movements can normally be executed perfectly well in a different context, it seems promising to exploit these preserved movement competences to tailor individual treatment and to retrain the originally intended movements. Yips-affected golfers trained with this method showed very promising results after short treatment time. A continuation study also needs to more precisely investigate the psychometric variables of the golfers.

REFERENCES

1.   Smith, A.M., Malo, S.A., Laskowski, E.R., Sabick, M., Cooney III, W.P., Finnie, S.B., Crews, D.J., Eischen, J.J., Hay, I.D., Detling, N.J. and Kaufman, K., A Multidisciplinary Study of the 'Yips' Phenomenon in Golf, *Sports Medicine*, 2000, 30 (6), 423-437.

2.   Bawden, M. and Maynard, I., Towards an Understanding of the Personal Experience of the 'Yips' in Cricketers, *Journal of Sports Science*, 2001, 12, 937-953.

3.   Smith, A.M., Adler, C.H., Crews, D., Wharen, R.E., Laskowski, E.R., Barnes, K., Bell, C.V., Pelz, D., Brennan, R.D., Sorenson, M.C. and Kaufman, K.R., The 'Yips' in Golf: A Continuum between a Focal Dystonia and Choking, *Sports Medicine*, 2003, 33 (1), 13-31.

4.   McDaniel, K.D., Cummings, J.L. and Shain, S., The "Yips": A Focal Dystonia of Golfers, *Neurology*, 1989, 39, 192-195.

5.   Sachdev, A., Golfers' Cramp: Clinical Characteristics and Evidence Against it Being an Anxiety Disorder, *Movement Disorders*, 1992, 4, 326-332.

6.   Sheehy, M.P. and Marsden, C.D., Writer's Cramp – A Focal Dystonia, *Brain*, 1982, 105, 461-480.

7.   Adler, C.H., Crews, D., Hentz, J.G., Smith, A.M. and Caviness, J.N., Abnormal Co-contraction in Yips-Affected but not Unaffected Golfers: Evidence for Focal Dystonia, *Neurology*, 2005, 64, 1813-1814.

8.   Candia, V., Schäfer, T., Taub, E., Rau, H., Altenmüller, E., Rockstroh, B. and Elbert, T., Sensory Motor Retuning: A Behavioural Treatment for Focal Hand Dystonia of Pianists and Guitarists, *Archives of Physical Medicine and Rehabilitation*, 2002, 83, 1342-1348.

9.   Mai, N. and Marquardt, C., Treatment of Writer's Cramp: Kinematic Measures as an Assessment Tool for Planning and Evaluating Training Procedures, in: Faure, C., Keuss, P., Lorette, G. and Vinter, A., eds., *Advances in Handwriting and Drawing: A Multidisciplinary Approach*, Europia, Paris, 1994, 445-461.

10.   Marquardt, C. and Fischer, M., Movement Kinematics of the Golfers' Yips, in: Crews, D. and Lutz, R., eds., *Science & Golf V. Proceedings of the World Scientific Congress of Golf*, 2008, Energy in Motion, Mesa, AZ, 2008, 216-223.

11.   Delay, D., Nougier, V. and Orliaguet, J.P., Movement Control in Putting, *Human Movement Science*, 1997, 16, 597-619.

12.   Schmidt, R.A., A Schema Theory of Discrete Motor Skill Learning, *Psychological Review*, 1975, 82, 225-260.

13.   Nutt, J.G., Muenter, M.D., Melton, N.J., Aronson, A. and Kurland, L.T., Epidemiology of Dystonia in Rochester, Minnesota, *Advances in Neurology*, 1988, 50, 361-365.

14.   Marquardt, C., Gentz, W. and Mai, N., On the Role of Vision in Skilled Handwriting, in: Simner, M.L., Leedham, G. and Thomassen, A.J.W.M., eds., *Handwriting and Drawing Research*, IOS Press, Amsterdam, 1996, 87-97.

The Vicious Circle Involved in the Development of Yips:

A Commentary

Paul Glazier

Centre for Sport and Exercise Science, Sheffield Hallam University,
Collegiate Campus, Sheffield, S10 2BP, UK
Email: paul@longdrivegolf.co.uk

INTRODUCTION

The term the 'yips' is a colloquialism that refers to the debilitating movement disorder characterised by the production of perceived involuntary movements (often described anecdotally as 'jerks', 'tremors', 'spasms' and 'twitches') that occur during the course of executing a motor behaviour requiring fine control. This affliction reportedly affects between 12% and 28% of golfers [1], of which most are experienced single-figure handicap amateurs or professionals, and costs, on average, 4.7 strokes per 18 holes [2]. Although it is still unclear what exactly causes the yips, most academics and practitioners believe that psychological (e.g., anxiety) and/or neurophysiological (e.g., focal dystonia) factors are largely responsible for this behavioural phenomenon [3].

Previous reviews of the yips [3, 4] have highlighted the general paucity of studies that have considered the underlying biomechanical mechanisms and processes that physically cause this debilitating affliction. The study of Marquardt attempted to redress this balance, but was only partially successful in achieving this aim. In this commentary, I highlight some of the main issues arising from the target article, how they impact on the study and what lessons can be learned and applied to future research in this area.

PROCESS- VERSUS PRODUCT-ORIENTED APPROACHES TO THE YIPS

The apparently novel feature of the study of Marquardt was that kinematic analyses were used for the first time to describe putter motions of golfers who were apparently affected by the yips (however, see [5]). Although the SAM PuttLab system is a very impressive measurement tool that is capable of producing a plethora of useful variables related to the 3-D motion of the putter, it is debatable how informative these variables are in the context of the current study. Rather unsurprisingly, the main findings of this study were that golfers who supposedly had the yips tended to exhibit greater error and variability in their putting strokes for a number of key variables compared to those golfers who do not have the yips and that this error and variability apparently increased with the severity of the yips. While this data may be of interest to a point, the emphasis on describing outcomes generally fails to inform us about the underlying mechanisms and processes that cause the outcomes. It is clear that for substantive progress to be made in this area, product-oriented research designs need to be superseded by process-oriented research designs [6, 7]. Future experimentation needs to focus on explaining the 3-D motion of the putter *in relation to* changes in joint couplings, grip forces and muscle activation parameters of upper body limb motions. Only then will the physical mechanisms causing the yips be revealed and inferences about the underlying neurophysiological processes be made.

USE OF BIOMECHANICAL ANALYSES IN THE DIAGNOSIS OF THE YIPS

Although measuring the kinematics of putter motions for specific golfers might be useful in the diagnosis of the yips, relying *solely* on these measures, as Marquardt did, is potentially dangerous and could further adversely affect putting performance. Just because the golfers studied by Marquardt exhibited yip-like symptoms, it does not necessarily mean they had the yips, especially considering the following evidence:

(i)   The literature suggests that the yips tends to manifest during very short putts - typically in the 2-6 ft range [2, 8] that golfers expect to hole. However, in the study of Marquardt, all putts were struck from a distance of approximately 13 ft.

(ii)   The general consensus among academics and practitioners is that the yips tend to manifest under pressurised situations when the golfer is likely to be feeling anxious [3, 4]. As the golfers in the study of Marquardt were only requested to strike a series of putts on a practice green under what appeared to be a low pressure situation, anxiety was unlikely to be a major factor during performance. The absence of any substantial anxiety appears to suggest that the movement artefacts displayed by the golfers were unlikely to be the yips. This point also appears to contradict Marquardt's suggestion that the yips is not a neurophysiological disorder, therefore, by implication, it must be a psychological disorder.

(iii) The majority of golfers who suffer from the yips tend to be professionals or low handicap players [3, 4], not higher handicap players like those who participated in the study of Marquardt (average handicap 16.6 strokes). Marquardt also claimed to have witnessed in other data collection sessions many novices who exhibited severe yips.

(iv)   Perhaps most tellingly, Marquardt remarked at various junctures during the target article that a number of golfers with mild and severe yips were not aware that they had a problem. Considering the abundance of anecdotal reports describing the yips as 'jerks', 'tremors', 'spasms' and 'twitches' [e.g., 1], it would be remarkable and surprising if golfers could not distinguish between what was simply poor technique and the yips. With this and the other points raised above in mind, it seems highly likely that golfers in the study of Marquardt were suffering from the former rather than the latter.

Clearly, to be able to diagnose whether a golfer has the yips with any degree of certainty, it is important that a battery of psychometric, biomechanical and neurophysiological tests are used. Suggesting that a golfer has the yips when there is no conclusive evidence is only likely to cause further anxiety leading to further deterioration of putting performance.

CONSTRAINTS ON MOVEMENT COORDINATION AND CONTROL IN PUTTING

Marquardt used information processing theoretical concepts (e.g., open loop control, motor programs, feedback, etc.) derived from cognitive psychology to explain movement control during putting and provided a rather unconvincing explanation of the yips claiming that "the original movement program is still active but is superimposed by a second and conflicting movement program" (p. 73). Furthermore, Marquardt had difficulty explaining the task-specific nature of the yips and how a slight change in the specific requirements of the task can have a large impact on movement dynamics.

A potentially more useful explanatory framework is offered by dynamical systems theory. Here, patterns of coordination and control are an emergent property of self-organising dynamics and the confluence of constraints impinging on the golfer [9]. It is well-established that small quantitative changes in, for example, task constraints can lead to large and significant changes in coordination and control [10], which could explain why the yips seem to disappear when the golf ball is occluded or fixed to the ground or if the hole is removed or replaced with a symbolic target like a tee.

The adoption of a dynamical systems theoretical framework could also be useful in helping to explain some of the physical phenomena related to the yips. For example, Adler et al. [11] reported 'abnormal' co-contractions in the wrist flexor-extensor muscles of yips affected golfers compared to normal controls. This finding was interpreted by the authors as being evidence of focal dystonia, but this need not be the case. Bernstein [12] famously referred to the process of "freezing" degrees of freedom during skill acquisition where joints are "rigidly, spastically fixed" (p. 108) through muscle co-contraction during the initial stages of learning so that they allow no or very little movement and, therefore, limbs become more controllable. As the learner progresses, there is a gradual release of the ban on the degrees of freedom enabling the performer to exploit passive motion-dependent forces and produce flexible and adaptive movement solutions. The recruitment or suppression of mechanical degrees of freedom is not uni-directional, but is dependent on the confluence of constraints on action [13]. Thus, the existence of muscle co-contraction might simply be a result of the intentional constraints of the golfer attempting to consciously control the putting action rather than some underlying pathology, especially considering that a greater internal focus of attention is typical in stressful situations [14, 15].

CONCLUSION

The study of Marquardt unfortunately failed to make a substantive contribution to the literature and our understanding of the yips. Future research needs to adopt a process- rather product-oriented approach, use a range of different analysis techniques to more conclusively diagnose the yips and also adopt a theoretical framework that could help explain the underlying causative mechanisms and processes.

REFERENCES

1. McDaniel, K.D., Cummings, J.L. and Shain, S., The "Yips": A Focal Dystonia of Golfers, *Neurology,* 1989, 39, 192-195.

2. Sachdev, P., Golfers' Cramp: Clinical Characteristics and Evidence Against it being an Anxiety Disorder, *Movement Disorder,* 1992, 7, 326-332.

3. Smith, A.M., Adler, C.H., Crews, D., Wharen, R.E., Laskowski, E.R., Barnes, K., Bell, C.V., Pelz, D., Brennan, R.D., Smith, J., Sorenson, M.C. and Kaufman, K.R., The 'Yips' in Golf: A Continuum Between a Focal Dystonia and Choking, *Sports Medicine,* 2003, 33, 13-31.

4. Kingston, K., Madill, M. and Mullen, R., Yielding to Internal Performance Stress? – The Yips in Golf: A Review with a Commentary from a Player's Perspective, in: Thain, E. ed., *Science and Golf IV: Proceedings of the World Scientific Congress of Golf,* Routledge, London, 2002, 268-283.

5. Filmalter, M., Noizet, P-A., Pöppel, E. and Murthi, B.P.S., Motor Strategy Disturbances in Golf: The Effect of 'Yips' on the Movement of the Putter Head, in: Crews, D., Lutz, R. eds., *Science and Golf V: Proceedings of the World Scientific Congress of Golf,* Energy in Motion, Inc., Mesa, AZ, 2008, 352-359.

6. Weinberg, R.S., Anxiety and Motor Performance: Where to From Here? *Anxiety Research,* 1990, 2, 227-242.

7. Gould, D., Greenleaf, C., Krane, V., Arousal-Anxiety and Sport Behavior, in: Horn, T. ed., *Advances in Sport Psychology* 2nd edn., Human Kinetics, Champaign, Illinois, 2002, 207-241.

8. Smith, A.M., Malo, S.A., Laskowski, E.R., Sabick, M., Cooney III, W.P., Finnie, S.B., Crews, D.J., Eischen, J.J., Hay, I.D., Detling, N.J. and Kaufman, K., A Multidisciplinary Study of the 'Yips' Phenomenon in Golf: An Exploratory Analysis, *Sports Medicine,* 2000, 30, 423-437.

9. Newell, K.M., Constraints on the Development of Coordination, in: Wade, M.G. and Whiting, H.T.A., *Motor Development in Children: Aspects of Coordination and Control,* Martinus Nijhoff, Dordrecht, 1986, 341-360.

10. Newell, K.M., On Task and Theory Specificity, *Journal of Motor Behavior,* 1989, 21, 92-96.

11. Adler, C.H., Crews, D., Hentz, J.G., Smith, A.M. and Caviness, J.N., Abnormal Co-Contraction in Yips-Affected but not Unaffected Golfers: Evidence for Focal Dystonia, *Neurology,* 2005, 64, 1813-1814.

12. Bernstein, N.A., *The Coordination and Regulation of Movements,* Pergamon Press, Oxford, 1967.

13. Newell, K.M. and Vaillancourt, D.E., Dimensional Change in Motor Learning, *Human Movement Science,* 2001, 20, 695-715.

14. Masters, R.S.W., Knowledge, Knerves and Know-How: The Role of Explicit Versus Implicit Knowledge in the Breakdown of a Complex Motor Skill Under Pressure, *British Journal of Psychology,* 1992, 83, 343-358.

15. Hardy, L. and Mullen, R., Performance Under Pressure: A Little Knowledge is a Dangerous Thing?, in: Thomas, P.R. ed., *Optimising Performance in Golf,* Australian Academic Press, Brisbane, 2001, 245-263.

The Vicious Circle Involved in the Development of the Yips:

A Response to Commentary

Christian Marquardt
Science&Motion Sports GmbH,
Schaefergasse 4, 65428 Ruesselsheim, Germany
E-mail: christian.marquardt@scienceandmotion.de

INTRODUCTION

I would like to thank Paul Glazier for his challenging commentary on my article about the development of the Yips, the aim of which was to introduce a method for objective measurement of the Yips by kinematic analysis of the putter movement and to then systematically identify the critical factors involved in the development and the establishment of the Yips. Based on our findings, we propose to understand the development of the Yips in a vicious circle where jerking (or focal dystonia) and choking (or performance anxiety) are not extremes of a continuum but rather different modules of a complex behavioural problem. In this understanding, the Yips is seen as a *learned* movement disorder, which over time can establish itself as an automated motor control program. This has significant consequences on treatment strategies for the Yips as well as for identifying Yips-related problems at early stages to avoid development of severe Yips.

THE DILEMMA OF THE CURRENT DIAGNOSIS OF YIPS

Glazier argues that the article contradicts a *common sense view* on the nature of the Yips where the Yips is symptomatically seen as a problem which can *per definition* only affect low-handicap golfers, golfers with a long history of golf, only occur under pressure situations and either has neuromuscular or psychological causes. Some of the Yips studies even recruit their participants only if they conform to the common definition of Yips, such as a low handicap or a long history of golf for being able to acquire focal dystonia [1, 2].

Controversial findings which do not fit the definition of focal dystonia or choking, but which could contribute to the understanding the problem are herewith neglected. Based on their practical work, most coaches will agree that the Yips also occurs on longer putts, in chipping, even in the full swing, in high-handicap golfers, in younger players, or during practice. In the data sample we tested, both high- and low-handicap golfers were affected by the Yips. Our data also showed that Yips is present at a distance of 10-12 ft, even if less pronounced. The assumption that the Yips *only* appears under pressure is one of the big myths about the Yips and has already been disproved by research [3]. Many studies investigated the Yips in a laboratory under no-pressure conditions [4]. The assumption that golfers who show severe involuntary jerking in "no-pressure" putts are not experiencing the Yips seems confusing. Sachdev [3] stated that anxiety has a modulating effect which is also known from other movement disorders. The Yips aggravates under pressure, but can also affect practice putts. These assumptions need to be systematically investigated in a future study in more detail.

A comparable dilemma arose from the definition of writer's cramp, another task-specific movement disorder, being diagnosed as a focal dystonia since the early 1980's [5] and seen as a consequence of excessive overuse of the writing hand (repetitive strain injury, RSI) [6], a mechanism which is also assumed to play an important role in the Yips. The common treatment approach for writer's cramp consisted of injections with Botulinum Toxin, an extremely poisonous drug, to destroy the neuromuscular end-plates of the most affected muscles. However, the mechanisms underlying task-specific focal dystonia are still not understood. Although RSI has been verified in the sensory cortex, a corresponding mechanism has not yet convincingly been shown for the motor cortex. In general, the prevalence of task-specific movement disorders (in the Yips up to 48% [1]) does not match at all to the prevalence of focal dystonia (3 per 10,000). Additionally, it seems unexplainable why even in patients with severe and long-lasting writer's cramp a simple change of the pen grip can immediately result in dramatic improvement of the affected writing movements if a substantial neurological dysfunction of the brain was the cause of the problem [7].

In contrast, Mai and Marquardt [8] interpreted writer's cramp as a learned behavioural disorder and suggested use of kinematic measures as an assessment tool for planning and evaluating training procedures. In general, the behavioral treatment approaches attempt to re-establish the old motor programs by systematic movement training under modified conditions. Mai and Marquardt [8] used preserved movement capabilities found under *simpler* conditions (i.e., circling) for retraining handwriting. Schenk et al. [7] used a modified pen grip to retrain handwriting. Other behavioral treatment approaches have used splints to immobilize the *compensatory finger* in musicians and then retrained the dystonic finger with simple sequential exercises [9, 10].

THE VICIOUS CIRCLE OF THE YIPS

Research on the Yips has not been able to provide substantial insight into the mechanisms involved in the Yips and the absence of systematic treatment approaches for the Yips is striking. The *common sense* view of the Yips is not based on systematic evaluation of the problem by means of external criteria, but is mostly based on self-estimation of *presumably affected* golfers. The recent research of the Mayo Clinic [1, 2] defining the Yips as a continuum from choking to focal dystonia introduced more confusion than clarification. Any golfer with *unexplainable* putting problems could now join this definition of Yips, as long as she or he meets some other criteria derived from the definition of focal dystonia and choking, which is playing for a long period of time or experiencing the problems under pressure. This common sense view of the

Yips culminates in Glazier's assumption that severe involuntary jerking found in high-handicap golfers, on longer putts, or in golfers not being in pressure situations could per definition not be attributed to the Yips and consequently needs to be interpreted as poor putting technique. In contrast, we suggest that these factors are connected to modules of the vicious circle, but are not preconditions for the Yips. In this understanding, a short putting distance will result in increased self-monitoring, a low handicap will allow the golfer to more precisely perceive putting problems, and pressure situations will increase the level of anxiety.

We propose to more precisely define the Yips based on objective measurement of the disturbed movements and to not mix up different aetiologies under the same notion. The Yips consists primarily of involuntary and inconsistent jerking at impact, which is modulated through over-control strategies, anxiety and perception. Consequently, other putting problems such as "freezing" or performance anxiety need to be distinguished from Yips.

Glazier assumes that we have difficulties in explaining the task-specific nature of the Yips with our model. The opposite is true, however: the task-specific nature of the problem is the key element of our model. We see difficulties in explaining the task-specific nature in the concept of focal dystonia. If a disturbed movement can be normally executed under a slightly modified condition, this needs to be explained. We normally use the same basic motor programs to execute similar movements also under slightly different conditions. For example, it can be shown that in normal handwriting, movements will be the same also if we write with a slightly modified pen grip. These findings clearly do not support the definition of task-specific focal dystonia as being a deterioration of basic motor control programs. It is not the basic motor program itself that is disturbed in the Yips, but rather the movement context, which is triggering other levels of motor control (i.e., feedback control processes) and which then results in an interference during movement execution. The disturbance of automated movements through elevated feedback control has also been shown for handwriting [11]. The intention to control the pen tip while writing can dramatically disturb automated handwriting movements.

A TOOL TO OBJECTIVELY MEASURE YIPS

Glazier recommends use of "a range of different analysis techniques to more conclusively diagnose the yips and also adopt a theoretical framework which could help explain the underlying causative mechanisms and processes" (p. 81). We think that this article does in fact present a smart method to objectively measure the Yips and we suggest using the derived information to systematically discuss the critical factors involved in the development of the Yips. Kinematic analysis of the putter movement provides information that is not adequately represented in previous studies of the Yips. Involuntary and inconsistent jerking of the hands or wrists is the major problem in the Yips. Glazier himself confirms that kinematic analysis can show that Yips-affected golfers "exhibit greater error and variability in their putting strokes for a number of key variables compared to those golfers who do not have the yips and that this error and variability apparently increased with the severity of the yips" (p. 80). It is debatable whether additional information on joint couplings, grip forces and muscle activation parameters of upper body limb motions can reveal the physical or neuro-psychological mechanisms *causing* the Yips.

Glazier's further criticism is that we fail "to inform about the underlying mechanisms and processes that cause the outcomes" (p. 80). We are convinced that the vicious circle proposed in our paper is an adequate model to better understand the underlying mechanisms in the Yips. Glazier himself mentions one of the crucial mechanisms of our model by stating that "the existence of muscle co-contraction might simply be a result of the intentional constraints of the golfer attempting to consciously control the putting action rather than some underlying pathology, especially considering that a greater internal focus of attention is typical in stressful situations" (p. 81), which is in fact described in our article. The question of whether we attach such a mechanism to dynamical systems theory or to theory of motor control and cognitive psychology seems philosophical to us.

Furthermore, we do not agree that our approach of identifying the Yips at early stages without yet recognition of the golfer is causing "further anxiety leading to further deterioration of putting performance" (p. 81). The chance to identify the Yips before outbreak is a powerful method to avoid development of severe Yips, which according to research of the Mayo Clinic is affecting up to 48% of the golfers [1].

DYNAMICAL SYSTEMS THEORY

In contrast to our approach based on kinematic analysis and cognitive psychology, Glazier promotes the dynamical systems theory as a potentially more powerful approach. We do not see this as a contradiction. Many of the models of motor control used in Neuropsychology are congruent with dynamical systems theory.

For example, the co-contraction involved with the Yips [4] could relate to early stages of learning, where according to Bernstein [12] a person needs to reduce the degrees of freedom by either keeping joint(s) or even the whole body "rigidly, spastically fixed" or by introducing rigid couplings between multiple degrees of freedom. As learning proceeds, there is a gradual release of the rigid control of degrees of freedom and the movement becomes more and more automated and efficient. As in the Yips, we find an obvious disturbance of the automated, open-loop movements and the co-contraction involved could be explained by the attempt to regain movement control by reducing the degrees of freedom.

The wrists would appear to be more involved in the Yips as compared to the elbow and shoulder joints. Beuter and Duda [13] investigated the effect of "high arousal" on the kinematics of movement and found that the distal joint movements are affected but not the proximal joints. They conjectured that "distal joints may be more susceptible to higher-order processing (such as cognitively trying to control the distal joint by aiming) or changes in movement strategies (e.g., going from an open skill to a closed skill mode of processing requiring more feedback)."

As a result, the automated smooth movements of the distal joints would come under "volitional control, which is less smooth and efficient". It needs to be noted that high arousal does not necessarily mean increased anxiety, as changes in movement strategy permanently occur in our daily life dependent on the task requirements and the consequences of potential failure; for example, in example in grasping a hot cup of tea (slow and with stiffened joints) as compared with grasping an empty plastic cup. In this understanding, the task of aiming the putter would intrinsically introduce high-order processing which would potentially result in a less smooth movement. If golfers feel their putting is like grasping a cup of hot tea, they could be prone to developing the Yips, because they would trigger an over-control strategy disturbing the smooth movement execution (interference), whereas golfers who putt like grasping plastic cups would not trigger the vicious circle.

LIMITATIONS OF THIS STUDY

A simple and precise method to measure the Yips is overdue and can serve as a basis for system analysis methods to identify the critical factors involved in the development of Yips, as well as for evaluating success of intervention in treatment studies. Unfortunately the current study is limited to analysis of the putting stroke and does not allow correlation of the data with the self-estimation of the golfers. The measurements were not systematically combined with a psychometric questionnaire. Therefore the question of whether golfers identified as mild Yippers were aware of any specific problems in their putting cannot be answered definitively. From my personal experience, these golfers often report that their putting is inconsistent and something might be *wrong* about their putting but they do not exactly know what. Most of them report that they would need more practice to enhance their poor technique. Consequently, a future study would need to combine both kinematic analysis to objectively identify involuntary jerking and questionnaires to assess the psychometric state.

CONCLUSION

Glazier indirectly confirms most of the assumptions made in our article. For example, he explains the task dependency of the Yips with a mechanism based on increased level of movement control rather than an underlying pathology, thus contradicting the classical definition of focal dystonia. Glazier also demands a method to objectively measure the Yips and for a derived explanatory framework which is meeting the main scope of this paper. Glazier also provided some helpful comments on the striking discrepancies between our findings and the common sense view of the Yips which we are convinced needs to be reconsidered.

REFERENCES

1.   Smith, A.M., Malo, S.A., Laskowski, E.R., Sabick, M., Cooney III, W.P., Finnie, S.B., Crews, D.J., Eischen, J.J., Hay, I.D., Detling, N.J. and Kaufman, K., A Multidisciplinary Study of the 'Yips' Phenomenon in Golf, *Sports Medicine*, 2000, 30 (6), 423-437.

2.   Smith, A.M., Adler, C.H., Crews, D., Wharen, R.E., Laskowski, E.R., Barnes, K., Bell, C.V., Pelz, D., Brennan, R.D., Sorenson, M.C. and Kaufman, K.R., The 'Yips' in Golf: A Contimuum between a Focal Dystonia and Choking, *Sports Medicine*, 2003, 33 (1), 13-31.

3.   Sachdev, A., Golfers' Cramp: Clinical Characteristics and Evidence Against it Being an Anxiety Disorder, *Movement Disorders*, 1992, 4, 326-332.

4.   Adler, C.H., Crews, D., Hentz, J.G., Smith, A.M. and Caviness, J.N., Abnormal Co-Contraction in Yips-Affected but not Unaffected Golfers: Evidence for Focal Dystonia, *Neurology*, 2005, 64, 1813-1814.

5.   Sheehy, M.P. and Marsden, C.D., Writer's Cramp – A Focal Dystonia, *Brain*, 1982, 105, 461-480.

6.   Byl, N.N., Merzenich, M.M. and Jenkins, W.M., A Primate Genesis Model of Focal Dysonia and Repetitive Strain Injury in Learning-Induced De-Differentiation of the Representation of the Hand in the Primary Somatosensory Cortex in Adult Monkeys, *Neurology*, 1996, 47, 508-520.

7.   Schenk T., Baur B., Steidle B. and Marquardt C., Does Training Improve Writer's Cramp? An Evaluation of a Behavioural Treatment Approach Using Kinematic Analysis, *Journal of Hand Therapy*, 2004, 17, 349-363.

8.   Mai, N. and Marquardt, C., Treatment of Writer's Cramp: Kinematic Measures as an Assessment Tool for Planning and Evaluating Training Procedures, in: Faure, C., Keuss, P., Lorette, G. and Vinter, A., eds., *Advances in Handwriting and Drawing: A Multidisciplinary Approach*, Europia, Paris, 1994, 445-461.

9.   Candia, V., Schäfer, T., Taub, E., Rau, H., Altenmüller, E., Rockstroh, B. and Elbert, T., Sensory Motor Retuning: A Behavioural Treatment for Focal Hand Dystonia of Pianists and Guitarists, *Archives of Physical Medicine and Rehabilitation*, 2002, 83, 1342-1348.

10.   Jabusch, H. and Altenmüller, E., Focal Dystonia in Musicians: From Phenomenology to Therapy, *Advances in Cognitive Psychology*, 2006, 2(2), 207-220.

11.   Marquardt, C., Gentz, W. and Mai, N., On the Role of Vision in Skilled Handwriting, in: Simner, M.L., Leedham, G. and Thomassen, A.J.W.M., eds., Handwriting and Drawing Research, IOS Press, Amsterdam, 1996, 87-97.

12.   Bernstein, N., The Coordination and Regulation of Movement, Pergamon Press, Oxford, 1967.

13.   Beuter, A. and Duda, J.L., Analysis of the Arousal/Motor Performance Relationship in Children Using Movement Kinematics, Journal of Sport Psychology, 1985, 7, 229-243.

A Biomechanical Investigation into Weight Distribution and Kinematic Parameters During the Putting Stroke

Paul Hurrion

Quintic Consultancy Ltd, PO Box 2939, Coventry, CV7 7WH, UK

E-mail: paul@quintic.com

ABSTRACT

This study examined the set-up position of 30 elite PGA professional golfers (2007 Season), in comparison with 30 amateur golfers (Handicap +3 to 9) while attempting the same putt of 25ft on a flat surface with a stimpmeter reading of 12. Video analysis at 50 frames per second was used to record kinematic parameters of the golfers' set-up and posture. All golfers performed their typical putting action while standing on an RSscan International 1.0 m x 0.4 m pressure platform. The RSscan Footscan® and Quintic Biomechanics 9.03 v14 software were synchronised to enable key positions of the putting stroke to be identified. Each golfer used their own personal putter. The main difference between the amateur and professional golfers was in set-up. This was found to be significant with amateurs' weight distribution 59.60% Right and 40.40% Left while the Professional Group was 48.34% Left and 51.66% Right, much closer to a balanced set-up. Students' t-test was used to compare the group means for each parameter with a level of significance set at $p < 0.05$. There is a trend to suggest that the wider the stance, the smaller the centre of pressure movement during the putting stroke. Although there was no significant difference in stance width, there was a significant difference in the total amount of centre of pressure movement ($p < 0.05$) between the two groups of golfers.

Key words: Centre of Pressure, Golf Putting, Weight Distribution

Reviewers: Jon Karlsen (Norwegian School of Sport Sciences, Norway)
T.J. Tomasi (PGA Center for Golf Learning and Performance, USA)

INTRODUCTION

Putting has been described as a game within a game on numerous occasions or even a 'black art'. It has caused much heartache in the search for the perfect stroke. Putting represents close to half the strokes most golfers would use in a full round of golf and is in many ways a miniature version of the full golf swing, yet perplexingly it remains the area of the game least taught.

The majority of coaching magazines, manuals, textbooks suggest 'feel' as the key to success, along with a 'good technique'. However the emphasis should be the other way – a good technique is required to create the confidence (feel) necessary to hole putts [1]. Pelz [2] describes the putting stroke as only one of several different types of golf swing and also iterates that that it accounts for nearly half of all swings made – it is easy to draw the inference that putting does not account for half of all tuition. However, what kinematic parameters constitute a good technique? The author believes putting is a strength exercise, the ability to create a stable posture and pivot point is essential if the putter is to be returned consistently from address to impact. It is often stated by golf professionals that it is best to stand comfortably at address and relaxed over the ball prior to hitting the putt. This creates a very individual style of putting. The two questions the author would like to pose are firstly, what constitutes a comfortable set-up? and secondly, is comfortable (for the individual) the optimal position to execute the putting stroke?

Cochran and Stobbs [3] state that the putter head, while actually in contact with the ball, behaves almost as though it were disconnected from the shaft. Research conducted at the Quintic laboratory with high-speed cameras filming at a frame rate of 15,000 fps has shown that the contact time for a medium putt (18 ft) is approximately half a millisecond. Half a millisecond is a miniscule period of time. If the putter head is opening and closing during the impact zone "2 inches before contact and 2 inches after impact" then the chances of finding the clubface square to the target line at impact is significantly reduced [2]. Therefore, it increases the need for the golfer to create a stable, balanced and solid base, along with a fixed pivot point in which to execute the stroke consistently. Successful putting is all about repeating the stroke mechanics under pressure and starting the ball on your intended line; without this ability, the ability to read the green becomes of secondary importance [1]. It is the opinion of the author that the address position is the first stage in developing a consistent and repeatable technique. In order to create a stable base and fixed pivot point for the shoulders to rotate around, static equilibrium is required. This is when the system of forces acting on a body produces no motion, the body is said to be in static equilibrium.

Putting is a strength exercise, but it does not require the body to produce explosive power, such as a weightlifter performing the clean and jerk. It requires stability and balance. The main focus of such balance within the body is as a result of proprioreceptors. These are receptors, which respond to stretch or pressure within the body and are widely distributed within our skin, tendons and skeletal muscles. Because of the abilities of these receptors to sense the amount of stretching our tendons and muscles are withstanding, the human body is able 'to know where its body parts are at any given moment'; subsequently this sensory information is reported to reflex centres of the central nervous system for interpretation and subsequent motor response.

Our ears are not only organs of hearing. They also help the body maintain balance. The position of your head is important during the putting stroke, not only will it influence distance perception and alignment, it is the first organ for detecting balance. Your inner ear consists of two sacs called the utricle and the saccule. Within these sacs are receptors called maculae. They are made of sensory hair cells covered by a gel-like cap with tiny crystals inside. Whenever you tilt your head, gravity causes the crystals to slide to one side, creating a pull on the gel and the sensory hairs. This triggers the hair cells to fire nerve impulses along the vestibular nerve to your brain. The rotational axis of your head can also influence balance. In addition, your eyes are also delivering important information about your body's position.

As previously stated, the ability to create a repeatable set-up position with the putter is crucial if unwanted manipulation of the putter face is to be limited during the putting stroke. The address position is the first stage in developing a consistent and repeatable technique. This article reports differences in set-up position between professional and amateur golfers attempting the same 25 ft putt on a flat surface. It studies weight distribution and balance, which are two variables that are vital if the golfer is to have a consistent impact position.

Due to the lack of research into the weight distribution and centre of pressure movement in putting, the purpose of the study was to describe these variables along with kinematic parameters of both amateur and professional golfers. Many players and coaches spend a considerable amount of time focusing on these technical areas without first having an understanding of the ranges professional and amateur golfers operate within.

METHODS
SUBJECTS
Thirty male PGA European Tour Golfers performed their typical putting action under the test condition for this study. A total of four out of the 30 professional subjects finished in the top 10 of the European PGA 2007 Order of Merit. Thirty male amateur golfers (handicap +3 to 9) also performed their typical putting action under the test conditions. All subjects were right-handed and given a number of practice putts with their own putter in order to familiarise themselves with the required putt. Each subject putted towards a hole positioned 25 ft away in a straight line with a stimpmeter rating of 12. Subjects wore their personal golf shoes and attire. The trials were all carried out in the Quintic Putting Laboratory over a period of six-month period during the competitive PGA European Tour 2007 season. The distance of 25 ft was chosen as the test distance, because this is the length of a medium to long demanding putt. Each subject used their own putter and used it until they were able to hole the putt. This was deemed to be a successful putt. Every participant holed six successful putts. An average of the six putts was created for each individual. Each golfer was encouraged to go through their normal pre-shot routine prior to each putt.

APPARATUS
A Footscan® pressure plate 1.0 m x 0.4 m, 4 sensors/cm^2 (8192 sensors total) with a sampling rate of 125 Hz was used to collect the data. The foot function was analysed

using RSscan Footscan 7.9 2nd generation software. The range of the Footscan®
pressure measurement system was 0.7 N/cm² – 155 N/cm². The cross in Figure 1,
represents the centre of pressure (COP) of the golfer at frame 1 (40 ms before the
beginning of the stroke – movement of the clubhead). The COP is the point on a body
where the sum total of the pressure fields acts, causing a force and no moment about
that point. The COP can move in two directions, medial/lateral and in the
anterior/posterior direction. In the example below, during the putting stroke the COP
moves towards the heels of the golfer. The cross enables the four quadrants to specify
the % weight distribution of the golfer at specific time intervals. For example in
Figure 1: Left Heel = 14.72% / Left Toe = 28.37 / Right Heel = 31.41% / Right Toe
= 25.50%.

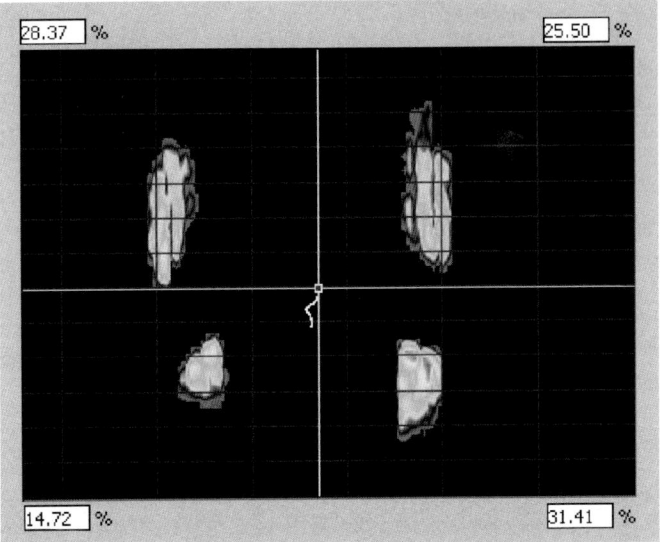

Figure 1. RSscan Pressure Platform Image of the Feet of a Right-
Handed Golfer

TEST PROCEDURE

The putting stroke was filmed using a standard digital video Sony TRV 900E
camcorder. The camcorder was placed at 90° to the path of the golf ball, level with
the putting surface. The RSscan Footscan® and Quintic Biomechanics 9.03 v14
software were synchronised using a 'key controller', a software package designed
specially to link the two software programs. This enabled the key positions of the
putting stroke to be identified and calculate the amount of COP movement for each
category.

All golfers used their normal putting stroke and personal putters. Digital video
film (50 Hz) was recorded giving the set-up, top of backswing, impact and follow
through. After processing, the film was analysed using a personal computer running
Quintic Biomechanics v14 video analysis software. Each video was calibrated in the
horizontal plane using the pressure platform in the video (1 m scale). All putting

strokes were digitised at a rate of 50 Hz. The putter head of each golfer was digitised and tracked using automatic tracking Quintic Biomechanics v14 and the resulting kinematic data smoothed using a low pass Butterworth filter (10 hz).

The students' t-test was used to compare the group means for each parameter and investigate if any were significantly different. The level of significance was set at $p < 0.05$.

RESULTS
WEIGHT DISTRIBUTION
For each of the 60 golfers, the weight distribution for the Left and Right feet at set-up along with the weight distribution of Heels and Toes were calculated (see Table 1 & 2). The values were obtained for set-up 40 ms prior to the club-head moving. The notion of 40 ms was used, because a number of golfers actually had a body movement away from the ball before the putter head even moved. In addition, the percentage of weight distribution in each quarter (Left Heel / Left Toe / Right Heel / Right Toe) was also calculated 40 ms before club-head movement.

Table 1. Weight Distribution at Set-Up for the 30 Amateur Golfers (S.E. = Standard Error)

					LEFT FOOT		RIGHT FOOT	
	LEFT	RIGHT	HEELS	TOES	HEEL	TOES	HEEL	TOES
Mean	40.40%	59.60%	47.70%	53.43%	19.57%	21.00%	27.17%	32.43%
± S.E.	3	5	4	4	3	3	4	3

Table 2. Weight Distribution at Set-Up for the 30 Professional Golfers (S.E. = Standard Error)

					LEFT FOOT		RIGHT FOOT	
	LEFT	RIGHT	HEELS	TOES	HEEL	TOES	HEEL	TOES
Mean	48.34%	51.66%	45.55%	54.45%	21.37%	26.97%	24.18%	27.48%
± S.E.	3	4	3	3	3	3	3	4

It is interesting to note that amateur golfers show a weight distribution at address of 60% right and 40% left, very similar to PGA recommended weight distribution for a long iron or even a driver at set-up [4]. This would justify the statement made in the introduction that putting in many ways is a miniature version of the full golf swing – with the majority of coaching suggesting feel and standing comfortable as the key to success. What is a comfortable set-up for the majority of golfers? Typically it is what they do the most of, i.e. practice the full swing. Only 5 amateur golfers had a set-up position of more than 50% weight on the left side. Interestingly, one amateur, a former international table tennis player had a set-up of 50% Left and 50% Right. This isn't that surprising given the nature of the game of table tennis, explosive reactions, both left and right, forward and backwards.

For the amateur group, there was a small bias in percentage favouring the toes at address 53%, again possibly reflecting the full-swing set-up posture. However, it should be noted that there was a considerable variation at set-up ranging from 10% to 90% weight distribution for the toes at address.

The professional golfers showed a more balanced weight distribution at address of 52% right and 48% left (Range 29% – 75% Right Side) to that of the amateur golfers. This was significantly different ($p < 0.05$) to that of the amateur golfers. Ten professionals had a slight bias towards the left side. However, the professional golfers at set-up exhibited an increase in percentage favouring the toes at address, 55% toes, ranging from 32% to 86%.

CENTRE OF PRESSURE MOVEMENT

For each of the sixty golfers, the centre of pressure movement was calculated for the total movement of the putt from start to finish (Mean Total Body COP movement). The putting stroke was broken down into three categories: 1) Start (40 ms before club-head movement), to the Top of Backswing; 2) Top of Backswing – Impact; and 3) Impact – Finish. The amount of COP movement was calculated for each category by synchronising the RSscan pressure platform with the Quintic video software program.

Table 3. Centre of Pressure Movement for the 30 Amateur and 30 Professional Golfers

	Mean Total COP Movement	Start – Top of Backswing	Top of Backswing – Impact	Impact – Finish
Amateur	83.10*	17.61*	12.23	53.26*
± S.E.	6	3	4	5
Professional	64.34	12.24	10.13	41.97
± S.E.	6	2	3	5

Centre of Pressure movement (mm); *Significant difference $p < 0.05$
SE = Standard Error

It is interesting to note that amateur golfers showed a significant increase in total amount of COP movement compared to the professionals. The amateur golfers on average moved 83.10 mm during the putting stroke. This compared to 64.34 mm of movement for the professional golfers. This was significantly different for the two groups of subjects at $p < 0.05$. In each section of the putting stroke, the average amount of movement was greater for the amateur group than for the Professional golfers. It is also interesting to note that the Start – Top of Backswing and Impact – Finish category were also significantly lower for the professional group.

It is the opinion of the author that the lower the amount of centre of pressure movement, the greater the stability and balance of the golfer during the putting stroke. The lowest total amount of COP movement (mm) during the whole stroke was 23 mm, with 18 mm of this movement coming after impact. It is interesting to note that this professional golfer had a 52% left and 48% right weight distribution with also an equal split heels and toes.

The highest amount of movement was recorded post impact to finish. The finish of the stroke was calculated as the moment the putter reached the furthest horizontal position from impact. The majority of this movement is a reaction to the impact as the head moves backwards (away from the target line). As a result, the putter head can often be seen to rise steeply after impact. A number of amateur golfers had movements of 75 mm during this phase of the stroke.

The professional group has an average stance width of 28.84 cm, 4 cm wider than that of the amateur group. This value may well explain some of the difference in COP movement. However, none of the kinematic parameters presented below in Table 4 were significantly different between the two groups at $p < 0.05$.

By means of comparison, the average amount of body movement for the same time length as performing a putt (2 seconds), when trying to stand still in a normal standing position was 24.28 mm of mean total body movement. Therefore it can be approximated that the notion of swinging a putter causes the Amateur group to increase their COP movement by 58.82 mm and the Professional group a further 40.06 mm.

KINEMATIC PARAMETERS

Table 4. Kinematic Parameters
SE = Standard Error

Parameter	Units	Pros		Amateurs	
		Mean	SE	Mean	SE
Stance Width	cm	28.84	3.24	24.21	3.45
Height: Sternum – Floor	cm	136	4.10	135	3.39
Stance Width / Sternum Height	%	21.29	3.84	17.98	2.68
Ball Position / Stance Width	%	71.11	5.76	63.24	6.28
Ball Position: Sternum	cm	2.51	2.55	2.63	2.44
Ball Position: Left Eye	cm	-0.57	2.87	0.68	1.90
Ball Position: Bottom of Arc	cm	109	3	88	5

Stance Width
Stance width was measured from inside the left heel to inside the right heel (see horizontal line in Figure 2)

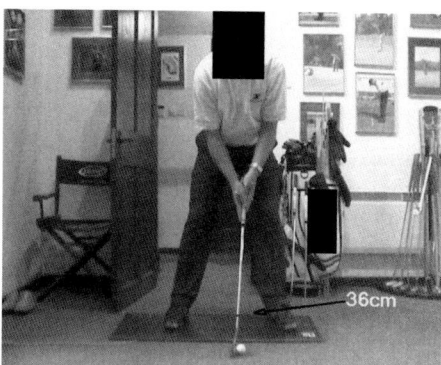

Professional Stance Width (cm)	
Average	28.84
S.E.±	3.24
Range	17 – 43

Amateur Stance Width (cm)	
Average	24.21
S.E.±	3.45
Range	15 – 37

Figure 2. Stance Width

Height: Sternum – Floor

This was the vertical distance measured from the sternum to the floor (see vertical line in Figure 3)

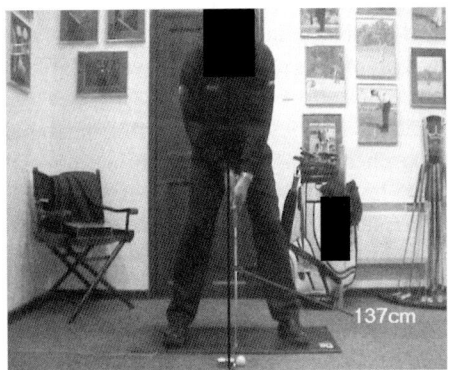

Professional Height: Sternum – Floor (cm)	
Average	136
S.E. ±	4.10
Range	125 – 144

Amateur Height: Sternum – Floor (cm)	
Average	135
S.D.±	3.39
Range	126 – 149

Figure 3. Sternum Height Above Floor

Stance Width/Sternum Height

For this measure, stance width was expressed as a percentage of sternum height. Both stance width and sternum height were measured in the manner above.

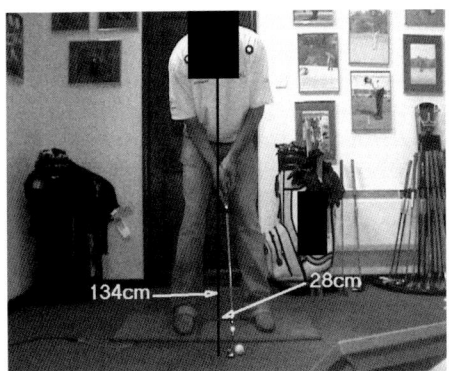

Professional Stance Width/Sternum Height (%)	
Average	21.29
S.E. ±	3.84
Range	10.71 – 33.07

Amateur Stance Width/Sternum Height (%)	
Average	17.98
S.E.±	2.68
Range	6.73 – 25.88

Figure 4. Stance Width 28cm / Sternum Height 134cm x 100= 20.90%

Ball Position/Stance Width (%)

Firstly, the horizontal distance between the inside right heel to the back of the ball was measured. See example in the photo below (Figure 5). This was then expressed as a percentage of the stance width (as measured above).

Professional Ball Position/Stance Width (%)	
Average	71.11
S.E. ±	5.76
Range	56 – 95

Amateur Ball Position/Stance Width (%)	
Average	63.24
S.E.±	6.28
Range	45 – 96

Figure 5. 24cm / 43cm x 100 = 55.81%
Note: A value of 100% means ball is positioned opposite left heel.

Ball Position: Sternum-Back of Ball
Figure 6 highlights the ball position in relation to the sternum. This is the horizontal distance between the bottom of the sternum and back of ball. A negative figure indicates that the ball is positioned behind the sternum and a positive figure indicates the ball is positioned in front of the sternum.

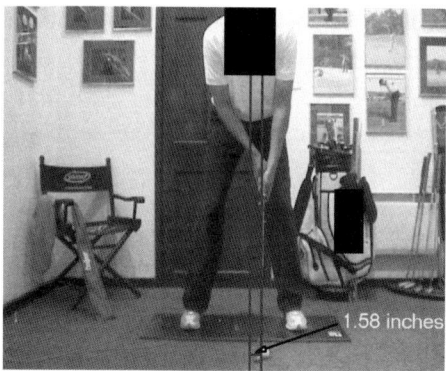

Professional Ball Position: Sternum-Back of Ball	Inches	cm
Average	0.95	2.51
S.E. ±	1.04	2.55
Range	-0.79 / + 3.54	-1 / + 9

Amateur Ball Position: Sternum-Back of Ball	Inches	cm
Average	1.12	2.63
S.E. ±	0.89	2.44
Range	-0.99 / + 3.91	-1 / + 10

Figure 6. Ball Position – Sternum

Ball Position: Left Eye-Back of Ball
Ball position was measured in relation to the left eye. The horizontal distance was measured between the middle of the left eye and the back of the ball. A positive value indicates the ball is positioned ahead of the left eye. A negative value indicates the ball is positioned behind the left eye (see Figure 7).

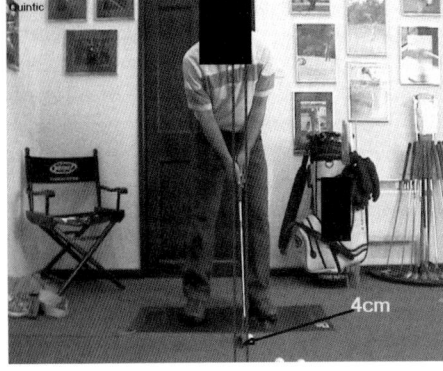

Professional		
Ball Position: Left Eye-Back of Ball		
	inches	cm
Average	-0.23	-0.57
S.E. ±	1.14	2.87
Range	-2.76 / +1.58	-7.00 / +5.00

Amateur		
Ball Position: Left Eye-Back of Ball		
	Inches	Cm
Average	0.36	0.68
S.E. ±	1.26	1.90
Range	-2.06 / +1.98	-6.35 / +6.78

Figure 7. Ball Position – Left eye

Ball Position:Bottom of Arc-Back of Ball

Finally, ball position was measured in relation to the bottom of the arc of the through-swing to the back of the ball (Figure 8). The bottom of the arc was determined from the digitisation data and subsequently was the lowest vertical point. A negative figure means that the bottom of the arc occurs in front of ball. It is interesting to note that this measure indicates that the bottom of the arc of the putting stroke does not always fall under the sternum, the figure of – 1.58 inches highlights this.

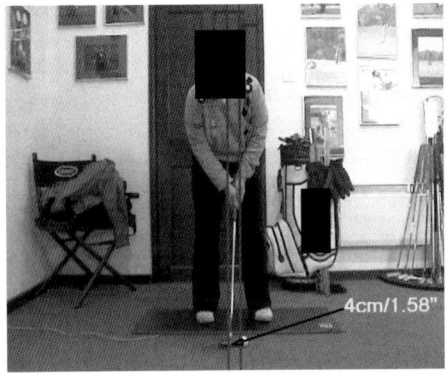

Professional		
Ball Position: Bottom Arc-Back of Ball		
	inches	cm
Average	2.35	5.97
S.E. ±	1.63	4.14
Range	-1.58 / +5.51	-4.00 / +14.00

Amateur		
Ball Position: Bottom Arc-Back of Ball		
	inches	cm
Average	2.05	5.57
S.E. ±	1.43	3.89
Range	-2.08 / +5.34	-4.56 / +13.65

Figure 8. Ball Position – Bottom of Arc

CONCLUSION

This paper has reported various differences in set-up position between 30 elite PGA professionals and 30 amateur golfers while attempting the same putt of 25 ft on a flat surface with a stimpmeter reading of 12. The main difference between the amateur and professional group was in set-up. This was found to be significant with amateurs approximately 60% Right – 40% Left while the professional golfers were much closer to 50% on both sides. There is a trend (p = 0.11) to suggest that the wider the stance width (professional), the smaller the centre of pressure (COP) movement during the putting stroke. Although there was no significant difference in stance width, there was a significant difference in the total amount of COP movement between the two groups. No significant differences were found between the kinematic parameters, most notably ball position and posture, between the amateur and professional golfers. The use of balance and pressure analysis is becoming more popular in the analysis of the golf swing, but there has been very little research into these parameters during the putting stroke. The pressure analysis enables the instructor to look at dynamics and body movement that the naked eye cannot see. Generally the instructor can see positional aspects of the golf swing such as address and top of backswing, but the balance/pressure software allows the instructor to critically review weight distribution and COP movement during the stroke. A good putting technique has the ability to create a stable posture and pivot point to allow the putter to be returned consistently from address to impact without manipulation. Standing comfortably at address and relaxed over the ball creates a very individual style of putting. However, in the author's opinion, "comfortably" and "optimum balance" (50% Toes / 50% Heels / 50% Left / 50% Right) are seldom the same position. None of the sixty golfers exhibited a set-up position with 25% of weight distribution in each of the four quadrants. Each individual had a bias to one or two particular quadrants. It is therefore the opinion of the author that it is possible for all golfers analysed during this study to obtain a more stable and balanced position for the putting stroke. Future research should focus on the effect of COP movement on performance and the importance of balance and weight distribution in reducing body movement during the putting stroke.

REFERENCES

1.   Hurrion, P., Putting on Fast Greens, *Golf International*, 2008, March, Issue 78.

2.   Pelz, D., *Dave Pelz's Putting Bible: The Complete Guide to Mastering the Green*, Doubleday, New York, 2000.

3.   Cochran, A. and Stobbs, J., *The Search for the Perfect Swing*, Heinemann, London, 1968.

4.   Professional Golfer Association of Great Britain and Ireland, *PGA Training Manual*, PGA National Training Centre, The Belfry, UK, 2006.

A Biomechanical Investigation into Weight Distribution and Kinematic Parameters During the Putting Stroke:

A Commentary

Jon Karlsen
Norwegian School of Sport Sciences,
PO Box 4014, Ullevål Stadion, 0806 Oslo, Norway
E-mail: jon@putting.no

INTRODUCTION

Paul Hurrion has done a descriptive analysis of set-up parameters including weight distribution and centre-of-pressure (COP) movement. He has also compared elite professionals with good amateurs. I would like to commend Hurrion for using highly skilled elite players in his study. Quantifying and understanding the kinematics and kinetics of the best players is an important step of gaining knowledge about how to perform putting technique at its best.

I find the study relevant. The set-up is important for making a good and consistent putting stroke, because the biomechanics of the set-up dictates how the body can move during the stroke.

A further and even more important step is to relate kinematic parameters to technique performance, which is how consistent a player can start the ball in the direction the putter face is aimed at address, and how consistent a player can start the ball with the intended speed.

Is it so that a player will start the ball more consistent if the stance is wider, if the weight distribution is 50/50, or if there is less lateral movement? To me it seems likely, and I use these as preferences in my teaching, but we still need more scientific studies to prove it.

DO AMATEURS USE A FULL SWING SET-UP IN PUTTING?

The main difference Hurrion found between the amateurs and professionals was that amateurs had a weight distribution at set up that was closer to what we see in the full swing with about 60% of the weight on the right foot. It corresponds with what I have experienced from teaching elite juniors, especially those who have not received much teaching in basic putting technique. Very often these juniors have more like a full-swing set-up, which is characterized by a 'full-swing grip' compared to a 'putting grip' which is placed in between the palms of the left hand, a 'full-swing posture' compared to a 'putting posture' where the cervical spine is close to horizontal, and the upper body more forward tilted. In addition, I often find straighter elbows in these juniors, compared to a putting set-up where the upper arms are tucked into the body, and the lower arm follows the shaft when viewed in the saggital plane.

What I above call a 'putting set-up' refers to my teaching preferences for technique. Interestingly, they seem to correspond very well with Hurrion's [1]

PUTTING TECHNIQUE IN PERSPECTIVE

On the importance of putting technique for putting performance, I seem to disagree with Hurrion; i.e., "Successful putting is all about repeating the stroke mechanics under pressure and starting the ball on your intended line, without this ability, the ability to read the green becomes of secondary importance" (p. 90). From research we have done, and through practical teaching, I find green reading to be far more important than putting technique for putting performance. In one study of highly skilled players, we found that green reading explained almost twice as much of the distance variability than putting technique (60 vs. 34 %) [2]. In another study, we concluded that the putting stroke only had a minor influence on the direction variability in putting [3]. For example, we found that the stroke of an average European Tour player was consistent enough to hole 95% of all putts from 4 meters. Even though this was calculated from repeated putts, it indicates the minor influence of the technique, and thus the high importance of green reading.

CONCLUSION

In my view, this underlines the importance of not losing perspective of what putting is about when we are discussing technical details. The fact that coaches, players and researchers like to discuss technical details to an extent that does not match its importance in determining performance can be explained by the fact that technique is easier to describe, picture, present and discuss compared to the mental processes related to green reading. However, it will still be important to learn more about the technical details of putting, and I will encourage Paul Hurrion and others to continue their excellent work in this field.

REFERENCES

1.   Hurrion, P., How to Putt Like a Tour Pro, *Golf International*, 2007, December, http://www.paulhurrion.com/77_Putt.pdf

2.   Karlsen, J. and Nilsson, J., Distance Variability in Golf Putting: The Role of Green Reading, *Annual Review of Golf Coaching*, 2008, 2, 71-80.

3.   Karlsen, J., Smith, G. and Nilsson, J., The Stroke has Only Minor Influence on Direction Consistency in Golf Putting Among Elite Players, *Journal of Sports Sciences*, 2008, 3, 243-250.

A Biomechanical Investigation into Weight Distribution and Kinematic Parameters During the Putting Stroke:

A Commentary

TJ Tomasi
PGA Center for Golf Learning and Performance,
PGA of America Golf Schools,
8565 Commerce Center Pkwy,
Port St. Lucie, FL 34986, USA
E-mail: pblion@aol.com

INTRODUCTION

This paper is original in that while there are many studies using force plates and special video software, most target the full golf swing and do not deal with the center of pressure (COP) of putting.

It is clear from the results that the professional golfers set up differently than the amateurs in terms of foot-pressure distribution and that there is less movement of the COP in the professional than the amateur group during the putting motion. What is not clear, since no objective measurement was made of the 60 subjects to determine who were good putters, is what the differences between the groups have to do with good putting.

Since the goal of the study was to compare weight distribution and key kinematic parameters between amateurs and professional to identify any statistically significant differences, I believe the goal was achieved. However, it is all too easy for the reader to make the jump from 'the pros do it this way' to 'and so should you' a jump fueled by the implicit assumption promoted by the author that 'if you are a tour pro, you are a good putter.'

BASE LINE OF PUTTING EXCELLENCE

While it is the author's perogative to limit the scope of the study, this implicit assumption and its ramifications should be noted. I believe the scope of the study would be much expanded had, in addition to the pro/am groups, the author established a base line of putting excellence for the entire field.

One way to do this would be to identify the 30 most successful putters and the 30 least successful putters by recording who holed six 25 footers in the least amount of attempts and, by extension, the 30 least successful putters as the 30 who needed more attempts. Or perhaps the top 20 versus the worst 20, with the middle 20 eliminated from the final comparisons.

Since a record must have been kept of each attempt until the subject made six putts, it would have been very simple to record the total number of attempts (e.g., subject #5 took 45 attempts to make six 25-foot putts, subject #8 took 15 attempts to make six 25-foot putts, etc.) and then to calculate the percentage of successful putts. Armed with this baseline, relationships between weight distribution and COP could be firmed up so that in addition to 'here's what the professionals and amateurs did differently,' you'd have 'here's what the best putters did differently from the worst putters'.

SWAY

The author equates changes in COP with sway with the implication that sway is to be avoided (p. 94). While 'sway', as normally used in golf, should be avoided, should pressure shifts also be avoided? In the normal usage, golf sway is not identical with pressure shifts so to yoke the two concepts, one benign and one detrimental, is to further muddle the issue.

I believe that certain magnitudes of change in pressure that are recorded while putting may not be detrimental to good balance nor directly related to swaying. In fact, they may be part of a sway-prevention mechanism; i.e., part of the body's natural system of balance necessary to effectively perform a motor activity. Perturbations to a body at rest cause palliative counterbalance responses and it may be only when these shifts in COP are unduly restrained that true imbalance occurs. To follow this line of reasoning; the very act of trying to stand stock still – with frozen head, your lower body anchored in cement – increases stress, because natural correctional systems are interfered with. Performance will decline, with the ultimate being the yips where the subject tries to stay so still that they literally 'can't move' until a sudden explosion of imbalance sends the body flailing and the ball flying.

So I would be hesitant, without any research to the contrary, to subscribe to the logic that "the lower the amount of centre of pressure movement, the greater the stability and balance of the golfer during the putting stroke" (p. 94) with the implication that this makes for better putting.

There is no reference in Hurrion's study to foot pressure measurements on the inside or outside rims of the feet (only heel and toe and right and left). Rim pressure would seem to be an important factor in terms of measuring sway and if it is not, then it should be identified as such.

OPTIMUM BALANCE

Hurrion's opinion is that "optimum balance" in the putting set-up is 50% toes/50% heels/50% left /50% right" (p. 99). However, in the absence of any research to the contrary, when 60 golfers (100% of the subjects in Hurrion's study) don't match the "optimum balance" in set-up, it may be that the 50/50/50/50 is not optimum at all since no one does it. Posing it another way: if you did a study to test the hypothesis that there was no optimum balance set-up with a sample size of 60 golfers composed of 30 tour pros and 30 amateurs with handicaps less than ten, and the results were that none of the subjects used the optimum balance set-up, you might conclude that your hypothesis was correct; i.e., there is no optimum balance set-up.

CONCLUSION

Hurrion's study is impressive in that the technology is state of the art, and it involves a large number of high-level players, but it might have been interesting to fill out the amateur field with a few middle and high handicaps.

A Commentary on R.S. Sharp's "On the Mechanics of the Golf Swing"[1]

Alan Turner

School of Engineering and Design,
University of Sussex, Falmer,
Brighton, BN2 6SQ, UK
E-mail: a.b.turner@sussex.ac.uk

INTRODUCTION

When I first saw the above title as an article in the *Proceedings of the Royal Society A*, over 19 pages long, I thought that this must really be something; it is quite an honour to have something published by such a prestigious journal. However, as I read it I realised that it was largely misconceived and not of much value to the practicing golfer.

TRANSITION FROM BACKSWING TO DOWNSWING

The author presumes that the golfer is stationary at the top of the backswing and he starts his simulations from there: this has led him to several misconceptions. The real golfer is not stationary at the start of the downswing and I am convinced that it is far better to start any simulations from the start of the backswing – the address position. I am not quite sure what the author means by "it is not uncommon for the club to reverse its motion after the arms and body". As the real backswing is finishing, the legs and hips start the downswing while the arms and club are momentarily still going back and the arms start down while the club is still going back. Is the author confusing backswing momentum with a deliberate further movement backwards after the club has stopped at the top? Read Jack Nicklaus' [1, p. 99] description of what is called 'the transition', "No stop at the top".

THE TWO-LINK MODEL

The article goes to great lengths to show that the two-link model (arms-club) cannot simulate the real swing properly. Why? We all know this; it was demonstrated years ago. The author gives Jorgensen's [2] erroneous two-link model a generous but unjustified long discussion.

SHAFT FLEXIBILITY

The author doesn't seem to know of Milne and Davis's [3] mathematically elegant

---

[1]Sharp, R.S., On the Mechanics of the Golf Swing, *Proceedings of the Royal Society A*, 2009, 365, 551-570.

work on shaft flexibility, which nailed once and for all the myth that the shaft springs forward from the top of the backswing to be straight at impact and that a fast swinger should therefore have a stiff shaft. In reality, the shaft is straight well before impact and fast swingers need a stiff shaft because the centre of gravity of the clubhead is behind the line of the shaft and a high 'centrifugally driven torque' on the head would otherwise close the face too much. See also the paper by Horwood [4] for a discussion of shaft flex.

WRIST TORQUE

In discussing the review paper of Penner [5], the author perpetuates the confusion surrounding wrist torque near impact (p. 554). He states "golfers use hold back torque to delay the release, some of them maintaining that torque up to impact". Why should a golfer want to do this? It is simply not true, and strain-gauge shaft measurements of a freely swinging golf club with no applied torques show that it is the off-set centre of gravity of the head and the 'centrifugally driven torque' described above that bends the shaft forward near impact – as though a 'hold-back torque' is being applied by the golfer.

TORQUE CHANGES AT TOP OF BACKSWING

The author states "the downswing should start with positive shoulder torque and negative arm and wrist torques" (p. 555). This is not true from a standing start as the videos described below demonstrate experimentally: whether some golfers actually think they do this (the right hand exerting a strong force on the left thumb for example), I don't know. And anyway, in a real swing the evidence of a net positive wrist torque on the club shaft is in the flex it has at the top – look at any still photographs of the club shaft at the top of the backswing, it is flexed backwards indicating that a positive torque is being applied to slow the club down and start the downswing, all in a smooth transition. I'm sure the negative arm and wrist torques in this simulation come about because of the false initial conditions taken from the photographic data. The author says that the initial motion is a rigid-body rotation around the hub – well this is almost right, and was an excellent coaching thought of Ben Hogan, but that very first part of the downswing is with the arms and club still moving backwards slightly from the backswing, closing up the angles. A fast swinger like Hogan and most modern pros generate considerable backswing momentum in the club which is taken out in the transition as the torques change from negative to positive before the top of the backswing is reached. Still, the author is correct in stating that you don't start down with the arms or hands. See the video on You Tube [6] in which Hogan explains the transition from backswing to downswing.

WRIST LIMIT STOP

I am confused by the term 'wrist limit stop'. What can this be but muscular and ligament force exerted by the right hand and the left thumb? However, the whole point about not hitting hard too soon with the hands is correct and this has been shown by many studies. The benefit to long hitting of having an acute angle between the left arm and the club shaft at the point in the downswing when the left arm is horizontal was shown by Robinson [7].

EMPIRICAL DATA

The author (p. 559) starts to fit the models to real swings, but why he took such old sparse data I don't know: the Cochran and Stobbs [8] data was a revelation in 1968 but there is some excellent photogrammetric data around now. This would immediately have shown him the need to simulate the swing from start to finish (and I'm sure his numerical tools could do this admirably). See, for example, the work of Mann and Griffin [9] and the associated CD which shows a composite (android) average of fifty odd pros swinging several clubs.

INERTIA OF THE RIGHT ARM

The author goes on to discuss 'Optimal Swings' and I can't think that this is of much value, because the arm inertia (and shoulder motion) is not modelled correctly. The inertia of the right arm is not discussed and this is important as it increases tremendously in the real swing. The mass of the right forearm has its radius increased in the downswing and is one of the main reasons that the right hand has to drive forward, and to hit (exert a torque on the shaft, not too early – agreed), in the downswing for the shaft and arm to align (almost) at impact. If the right hand didn't apply a forward force like this the conservation of angular momentum would cause the arm-shaft line to straighten far too early. This increasing arm inertia has a big effect and was one of the reasons why Turner and Hill [10] didn't see the point in refining torque profiles in their model. It was demonstrated at Institute of Physics lectures that in a Shoulder, Arm, Club model, making a small change to the arm inertia equivalent to simply removing a watch causes the ball to be missed! It was concluded that the human golfer is a multi-variate negative feedback system of considerable complexity.

LENGTH OF BACKSWING

The author (p. 569) suggests that the problem of hitting from the top becomes more likely as the backswing length increases. Experience of playing with teaching pros suggests that exactly the opposite is true: many faults are cured by taking a full shoulder turn and a full backswing. Modern thinking is that for any given person it is the synchronisation of all torques that gives a well-timed hit. The author's "optimal strategy" of hitting first with the shoulders while "holding back with the arms" is true, but rather too simple – is he perhaps thinking of Dr Murray's *The Golf Secret* [11] "move the left shoulder down and then move it vertically up"? For high-handicappers this is good advice, but in the modern swing the shoulders do not move in plane with the arms; they move in a fairly flat plane in the backswing almost perpendicular to the spine angle and then at the start of the downswing the left shoulder initially moves vertically upwards as the legs and hips drive forwards (with the hands moving almost vertically down for a good 12 inches). In a good swing, the shoulders are more or less aligned with the target line at impact with the hips open. How would the author explain Jack Nicklaus' [1, p 112] 'Hold your shoulders until last'?

A SIMPLE EXPERIMENT

To support the statements above – i.e., i) from stationary, from the top of the backswing a negative 'hold-back' torque is not needed at the start of the downswing;

and ii) the effect of arm inertia is crucial to arm-club alignment at impact and renders any torque profile analysis irrelevant if not simulated correctly – two videos were made of a physical, simple arm-club model. A real club was hinged to an old table leg and driven by strong luggage elastic with a car sponge providing the wrist torque. A white ruler was screwed to the arm to show the shaft position. All the videos (paused and then viewed frame by frame) showed that the arm-shaft angle became more acute at the start of the downswing without any need of a negative 'hold-back' torque. If a golfer feels that he holds the club back against a "wrist stop", then that is simply a feeling. The physical evidence is that the net torque on the shaft is positive. One run was made with normal arm inertia and this showed that with no continuous arm driving torque, the shaft aligned with the arm well before impact. A second set-up was made with high arm inertia (a sheet of lead taped around the end of the arm) to simulate the effect of the right arm coming in. The shaft-arm alignment now was right at impact but with no pushing forward with the right hand the club still overtakes the hands.

CONCLUSION

To finish on an encouraging point, perhaps the author should keep the interest of the Royal Society; obtain some good photographic data (perhaps from Ralph Mann) and simulate the whole swing including the hips, body and both arms. To have two *Procedings of the Royal Society A* articles on golf mechanics would be a real achievement!

REFERENCES

1. Nicklaus, J. and Bowden, K., *The Full Swing in Photos*, Golf Digest, Trumbull, CT, 1984.

2. Jorgenson, T.P., *The Physics of Golf*, 2nd edn., American Institute of Physics, Melville, NY, 1999.

3. Milne, R.D. and Davis, J.P., The Role of the Shaft in the Golf Swing, *Journal of Biomechanics*, 1992, 25(9), 975-983.

4. Horwood, G., Flexes, Bend Points and Torques, in: Cochran, A.J., ed., *Golf: The Scientific Way*, Aston Publishing, Hemel Hempstead, UK, 1995, 103-108.

5. Penner, A.R., The Physics of Golf, *Reports on Progress in Physics*, 2003, 66, 131-171.

6. http://www.youtube.com/watch?v=QL_6M_xZvq0&feature=related

7. Robinson, R.L., A Study of the Correlation Between Swing Characteristics and Club Head Velocity, in: Cochran, A.J. and Farrally, M.R., eds., *Science and Golf II: Proceedings of the World Scientific Congress of Golf*, E & FN Spon, London, 1994, 84-90.

8. Cochran, A.J. and Stobbs, J., *The Search for the Perfect Swing*, Heinemann, London, 1968.

9. Mann, R. and Griffin, F., *Swing Like a Pro*, Broadway Books, New York, 1998.

10. Turner, A.B. and Hills, N.J., A Three Link Mathematical Model of the Golf Swing, in: Cochran, A.J. and Farrally, M.R., eds., *Science and Golf III*, Human Kinetics, Champaign, IL, 1998, 3-12.

11. Murray, H.A., *The Golf Secret*, rev. 6th edn., Elliot Right Way Books, Kingswood, UK, 1956.

A Commentary on R.S. Sharp's "On the Mechanics of the Golf Swing"[1]

Robert Neal

Golf BioDynamics Pty Ltd,
c/o Jim McLean Golf School, Doral Resort & Spa,
4400 NW 87th Ave, Miami, FL 33178, USA
E-mail: r.neal@golfbiodynamics.com

INTRODUCTION

This article is a well-written scientific piece examining different mechanical models of the downswing. It is not meant for "general consumption" and contains enough Greek letters and equations to scare off all but the ardent consumer of this information. The descriptions of the models that were used are quite clear and Dr. Sharp has been quite meticulous in his presentation of the results. The basis of his modeling and simulations is on the work done by previous scientists and engineers and he cites most of the key papers that have appeared over time in scientific journals.

FROM SIMPLE TO COMPLEX MODELS

One of the excellent aspects of this article is that it starts with a relatively simple model for the downswing (planar, double pendulum), develops the geometry and then describes results obtained with it. Careful cross-checking of the output from this model are compared to empirical data and other published works. This step in model building is crucial and gives the reader confidence that subsequent results of complex models are believable. This process of beginning with the known and moving toward the unknown is a convincing and logical step.

Dr. Sharp presents results from two basic models: i) a double pendulum model (similar to the one used by many previous authors including Williams [1], Lampsa [2] and Jorgensen [3]; and ii) a three-segment model that includes a body to represent the upper torso (which he calls the shoulder), the arm (upper limb), and the club. He has a few variations within these models including: a) the treatment of the club shaft as non-rigid over its entire length by putting a joint in the shaft at the base of the grip so that the hands and grip are one body and the rest of the club shaft and club head are another one; b) a resistive force on the club due to air drag; and c) gravitational field effects.

It is interesting to note that despite the changes in complexity of the models, the simple two-segment one, when optimized, can give very similar output data to the

---

[1]Sharp, R.S., On the Mechanics of the Golf Swing, *Proceedings of the Royal Society* A, 2009, 365, 551-570.

more complex ones. Part of the reason for these similarities is the choice of the parametric data selected (e.g., mass-inertia properties of the bodies, maximum torques that can be applied at the joints, the form of the torque functions, and the initial conditions). He also demonstrates that the effects of fluid drag on the golf club and the gravitational field are so small that they can be ignored in this type of model.

THREE-SEGMENT MODEL

Sprigings and Neal [4] developed a three-segment model for the downswing in golf that included a segment running from the sternum to the left shoulder (right handed golfer), an arm segment representing the entire left upper limb, and a club segment. Furthermore, the pivot point of the first segment (upper torso) was capable of translating horizontally. This model is actually a very realistic one for the levers of the golfer. Scant reference is made to it, yet results from the simulations run by Sprigings would have been excellent ones with which to make comparisons with Sharp's model outputs.

MOTION ANALYSIS DATA

3D kinematic data are relatively easy to collect these days with real-time motion tracking systems. Data on some modern player, rather than data obtained from old records of players from the 1960's, would have made the model and empirical results more meaningful. Peak clubhead speeds around 60 m/s (134 mph) would have been unheard of in days gone by yet there are quite a number of touring professionals whose swing speed approaches this value. Long-drive champions (perhaps a fairer comparison since their key criterion for success is clubhead speed) have clubhead speeds around 155 mph (69 m/s) and Jason Zuback's clubhead speed at one time was 163 mph (73 m/s). Thus, while the optimization models give results that are consistent with those of touring professionals, they are still short of the types of speeds that the long-drive champions obtain.

TORQUE MODELS

The torque models used by Sharp were either constant (i.e., they could only reach a maximum and then stay constant) or linear (with a pre-set maximum). This type of model for torque application is not consistent with the way in which muscle forces can be produced. In mammalian muscle, there are two underlying mechanical properties of muscles that have a huge effect on the possible kinematics available to an athlete; the force-length and the force-velocity relationship. Of these two, the force-velocity relationship is the dominant one in fast movement of multiple body segments. Sprigings and Neal [4] used a hybrid torque model in which the torque that could be applied at the joint was dependent on the joint angle and the joint angular velocity. This step gave the model an increased level of complexity, but also made it much closer to reality!

PEAK TORQUE VALUES

The peak torque values that could be obtained at the various joints in the model were much higher than one would typically see in golf. While Sharp mentions this fact, he maintains that the effect of the changed magnitudes is minor (in terms of speed), but that the time for the downswing is increased if smaller peak values are used. Interestingly, the time for the downswing in the Sprigings model was consistent with the values seen in high-level tour players yet the maximum torques were substantially less than those of Sharp.

CONCLUSION

I did like the dimensional analysis that was done at the end of the paper! It gave a brief but useful insight into why even small players can hit the ball a long way compared to their long-levered counterparts. According to Sharp, a 20 per cent difference in height (e.g., comparing a person who is 160 cm with someone who is 190 cm and assuming that they scale linearly on all dimensions) would only lead to a 10 per cent difference in clubhead speed. This difference, while substantial, is probably not as great as most people would think.

REFERENCES

1.   Williams, D., The Dynamics of the Golf Swing, *Quarterly Journal of Mechanics and Applied Mathematics*, 1967, 20, 247-264.

2.   Lampsa, M.A., Maximizing Distance of the Golf Drive: An Optimal Control Study, *ASME Journal of Dynamics Systems, Measurement, and Control*,1975, 97, 362-367.

3.   Jorgenson, T., *The Physics of Golf*, 2nd edn., Springer, NY, 1999.

4.   Sprigings, E. J. and Neal, R. J., An Insight into the Importance of Wrist Torque in Driving the Golf Ball: A Simulation Study, *Journal of Applied Biomechanics*, 2000, 16, 356 – 366.

A Commentary on R.S. Sharp's "On the Mechanics of the Golf Swing":[1]
A Response to Commentaries

Robin Sharp
Department of Mechanical, Medical and Aerospace Engineering,
Faculty of Engineering and Physical Sciences,
University of Surrey, Guildford, GU2 7XH, UK
E-mail: robinsharp@waitrose.com

INTRODUCTION

Arising from my article "On the Mechanics of the Golf Swing", Proceedings of the Royal Society, Series A, 2009, 365, 551-570, first published on-line in November, 2008, the editor of the *Annual Review of Golf Coaching* kindly invited me to write this article. The main aim is to interpret my article for people who are interested in golfing technique but who are not expert in mechanics.

In my younger days, I played golf with passion. I was Bedfordshire Amateur Champion in 1966 and, for some years, held the course record of 67 for my home course at the Bedfordshire Golf Club, Biddenham. I greatly enjoyed playing for a very successful Bedfordshire County team for a few years until synovitis in my right wrist forced me to stop playing. I used to play consistent but not spectacular golf, since my best drives would carry only about 170 m in still, warm air. My bad form almost always involved hooking and I usually tried to counter my tendency to hook with geometrical alterations, like weakening my grip and swinging in a more upright plane, with little success. I had the experience of consulting a professional golfer about my hook, only to find that I could only hit straight shots when trying to show him the problem. In my case, these things stimulated my curiosity.

Of course, I did not learn to play by first studying the mechanics of the swing. I guess that I used "reinforcement learning", which involves trying something almost at random and, if it works, trying to do it again. If it does not work, one tries something else. When a magazine tells you that your game will be transformed in one hour, you should be sceptical. You can be fairly sure that the person telling you learned over years of serious application.

ABOUT MY ARTICLE

Unless an author is willing to pay substantial fees, the Royal Society limits papers to

---

[1]Sharp, R.S., On the Mechanics of the Golf Swing, *Proceedings of the Royal Society A*, 2009, 365, 551-570.

20 pages. Appendices can be made available as electronic supplements, which are made freely available over the Internet, without length limits. My article occupies the full 20 pages and has important appendices. It is necessary to read all of the article to get the full story. It is not the case that one can include everything one can think of. The material has to be selected. It is rather easy to think of other interesting things to do and to say but it is all hypothetical, if the allowable space is already filled.

My article engages with the following main question: When a golfer hits the best (long) shot of which he/she is capable, how does he/she employ his/her muscular resources? Secondary questions that arise are: Does the answer depend on the length of the swing, the stature of the golfer etc? To what extent does gravity contribute to clubhead speed and is there advantage in swinging in an upright plane to gain more from gravity? If the arm swing or wrist-cock angles are increased from conventional values and it is assumed that muscle capabilities will not be affected, will the swing be more or less powerful if it is re-optimised? Is aerodynamic drag on the clubhead significant? If a driver is advertised as having wind-tunnel-developed low-drag properties, should one buy it? Is there any potential advantage in using a driver with a relatively stiff or flexible shaft? Is it feasible to design clubs matched to each other to the extent that, accepting that the more lofted clubs will have shorter shafts, they will give perfectly-timed shots when swung with a common strategy?

The method used to try to find answers is to set up and exercise computer simulations of golf swings. Such simulations are based on Newton's laws of motion. Basically, if a mechanical system has known geometric and mass properties and it is acted on by known forces, we can find its motions by solving the Newton equations, which are an elaborate form of Force = Mass * Acceleration. In the case of a golfer, it will often be the case that we know the motions from high-speed photography, bio-mechanical motion-measurement systems etc., and we know something of the golfer's geometry and mass properties from biomechanical data-books (we cannot take him/her to pieces and measure the parts, as one may do with a bicycle, say). Then we need to solve the inverse-dynamics problem, given the motions, find the forces acting.

In the well-known and highly-rated book *Search for the Perfect Swing*, action sequences at 10 ms intervals giving wrist and clubhead positions for the Ryder-Cup golfers Bernard Hunt, Geoffrey Hunt and Guy Wolstenholme are shown. Guy Wolstenholme's data are shown in Figure 1.

A well-established model for the swing is the planar double-pendulum, in which the arms rotate around a fixed point, the base of the neck, driven by a torque, and the wrists are represented by a free hinge. A limit-stop at the wrist joint is needed, to stop the club "cocking" beyond the feasible range, at the start of the downswing. In simple terms, the basic geometry of a sensible golf swing can be seen as involving the establishment of a "folded-up" configuration at the top of the backswing, to minimise the inertia that has to be rotated by the torque on the arms, followed by a "release" phase. In the release, the wrist action takes place and much of the momentum that has been built up in the arms is transferred to the clubhead, where it is useful. Due to the way the wrist joint operates, the clubface moves from "open" to "closed" as the wrists uncock and, to some extent associated with "conservation of angular momentum" – a consequence of Newton's laws, the clubhead will be moving at its fastest roughly

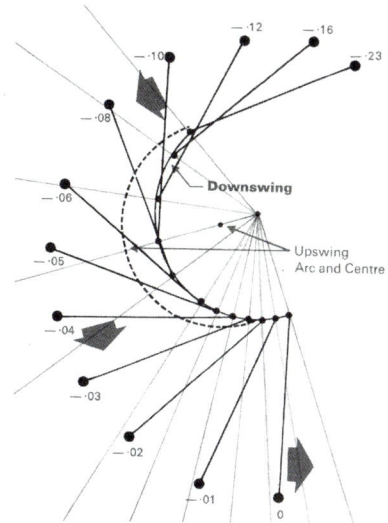

Figure 1. Wrist and Clubhead Position Data for Guy Wolstenholme
from *Search for the Perfect Swing* [1]

The construction lines are the author's own.

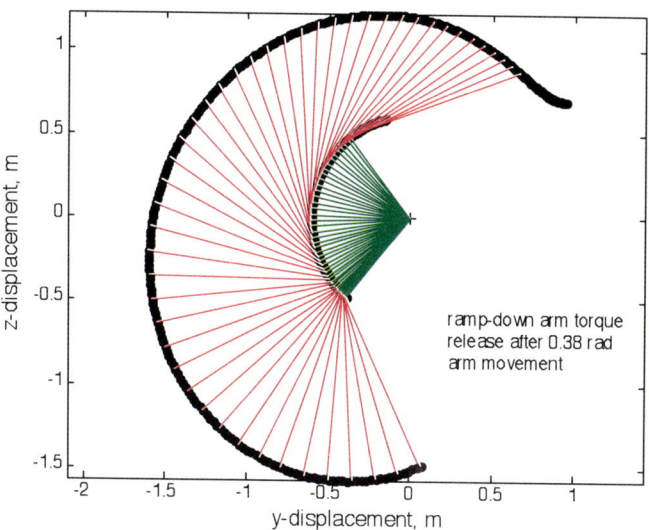

Figure 2. An Arm/Club Swing in which the Arm Torque is Applied
Early and Then Diminishes

The arms are shown in green rotating around the fixed hub. The club shaft is shown
in magenta. The club releases, that is, the wrist limit-stop contact ceases, after only
22° of motion from the start of the downswing. The hit is much too early and the
clubhead is way past its peak velocity when it reaches the ball. The clubface will be
very much closed at this point. The bottom of the arc is way behind the ball, which
could only be hit cleanly if it were on a high tee. The arms, in green, and the club, in
magenta, are not shown until the wrist-release occurs.

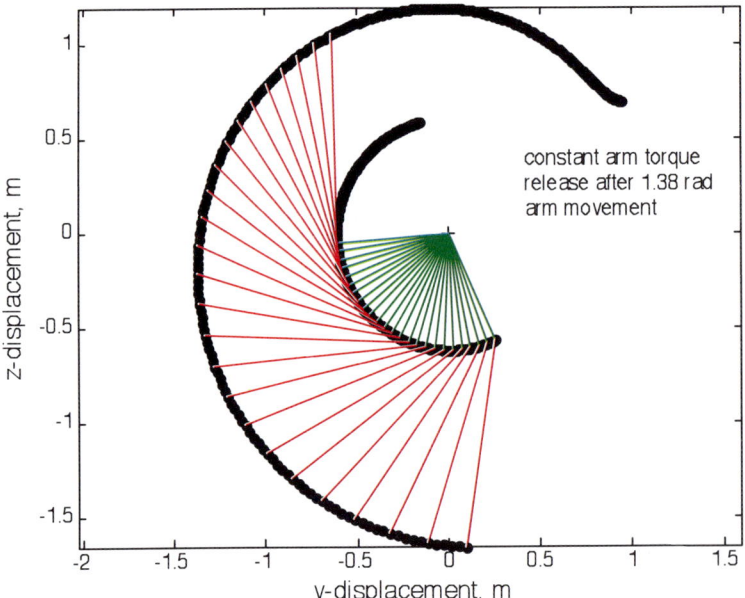

Figure 3. An Arm/Club Swing in which a Constant Arm Torque is Applied

The arms are shown in green rotating around the fixed hub. The club shaft is shown in magenta. Release occurs after 80° of arm rotation from the start of the downswing. This is looking like a proper iron-club swing, with the approach of the clubhead to the ball coming from above, but the clubhead will not yet have reached its maximum speed. The release is a little late for a shot with a driver especially. Again the arms, in green, and the club, in magenta, are not shown until the wrist release occurs.

when the arm and club are aligned with each other. Thus, there are two good reasons for the timing of the wrist action to be important; 1) we want the clubface to be square to the line of travel when it reaches the ball; and 2) we want it to be travelling at its fastest at that point. We can use the double-pendulum model, with a free wrist joint, to show the influence of distributing the arm torque variously on the timing of the release, see Figures 2 to 4.

There is a vital lesson here. It is that the distribution of effort in the golfer's arm action has a substantial influence on the timing of the wrist action, when the wrists simply provide a free hinge. If the effort is too early, the release comes too soon, the clubhead is slowing down when it gets to the ball, the approach to the ball is from below and the clubface will be closed. If the arm effort is too late, the converse happens.

Now, we observe that the arm/club or double pendulum swing does not really do justice to a real golf swing. Taking the view of a right-handed player, the shoulders rotate around the top of the spine, while the straight left arm rotates around the left shoulder joint. The torso muscles drive the shoulders and there exists another limit-

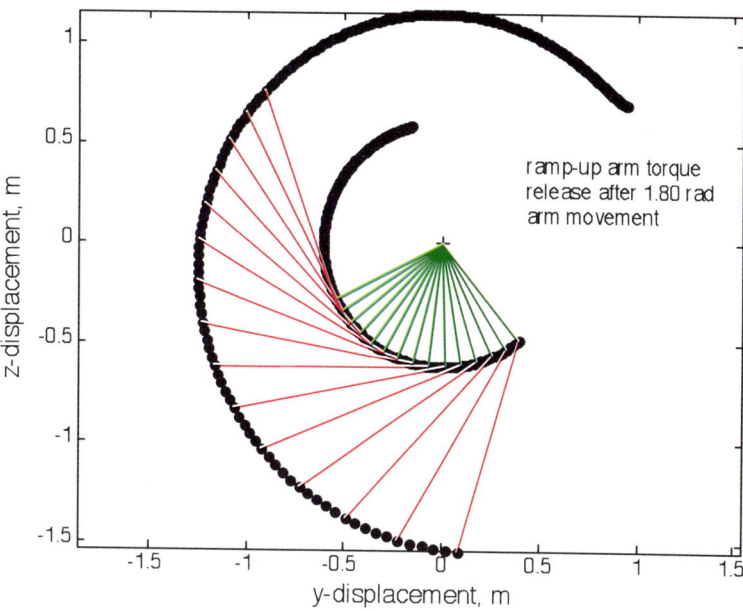

Figure 4. An Arm/Club Swing in which the Arm Torque Starts Small
and Ramps Up

The arms are shown in green rotating around the fixed hub. The club shaft is shown
in magenta. The release now occurs at an arm travel angle of 103° and the hit is too
late by some margin. The steep approach of the clubhead to the ball may make this
timing suitable for hitting from a seriously poor lie. As in Figures 2 and 3, the arms, in
green, and the club, in magenta, are not shown until the wrist release occurs.

stop that prevents the arms from rotating too far relative to the shoulders. There is a
set of muscles that drive the arms, but react on the shoulders; and similarly the wrists
have muscles associated with them. Each set of muscles can hold back or drive
through, according to what is found effective in the learning process. Also, gravity is
acting in a real swing, the clubshaft is flexible to an extent that can be easily measured
and there will be some aerodynamic drag on the clubhead and shaft, which is not so
hard to estimate. If we really want to know what makes for our best shot, we had
better use such a model, at least, to try to find out.

Suppose now that we have such a model. To make it simulate a swing, we need to
specify the geometry and mass details for the golfer and club, we need to define his
starting position and we need to decide on the muscular torques that the golfer applies
through time. The geometry and mass data are standard in biomechanics, largely from
the US NASA program, so that if our golfer is assumed to be 1.83 m tall and to have
mass 90 kg, we can use bio-data to estimate his joint positions, mass centre locations,
inertias, etc. We can measure any club, so that we know it precisely. We do not know
the golfer's muscle strengths, but we do know his motions with a driver – if he is

Bernard Hunt, Geoffrey Hunt or Guy Wolstenholme. Therefore, in those cases, we can solve the inverse dynamics problem to find what torques they applied in the recorded swings. This solution is obtained by describing the driving torques parametrically. What this means is that we can (judiciously) choose a few parameters which describe the general form of the torques applied. We then assume a set of parameters and run the simulation repeatedly, with the parameters being altered by an optimiser, until we find those parameters that give a best match between the simulation results and the motion data. Figure 5 shows the parameters that describe the various torques.

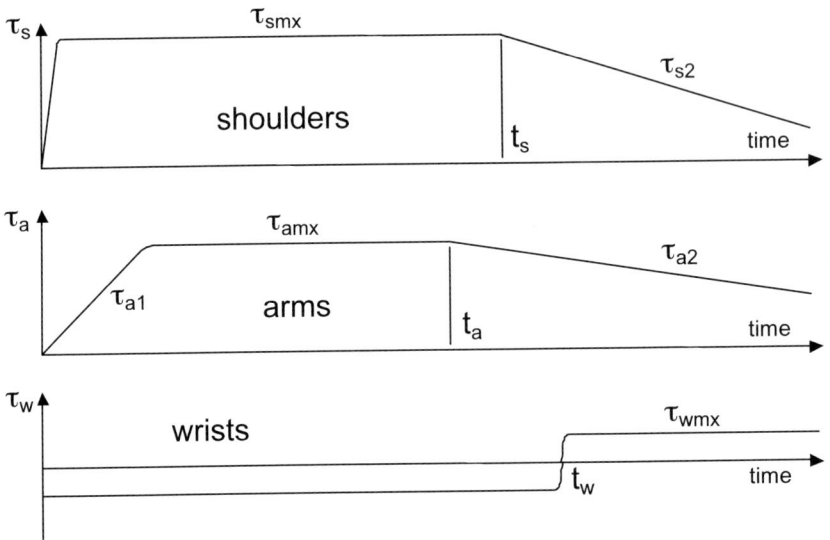

Figure 5. Shoulders, Arms and Wrist Torques

In the swing model, the shoulder torque is described by the parameters τ_{smx}, τ_{s2} and t_s. τ_{smx} is the maximum torque available from the torso, τ_{s2} is the rate at which the torque drops off after time t_s. The shoulder torque builds up from zero at the start of the downswing at a defined (non-variable) rate. The arm torque is similarly represented, except that the rate of build up is variable, given by τ_{a1}. The wrists either hold back or drive through with their full capability, τ_{wmx}, depending on the value of the switch-time parameter t_w. In fact, t_s, τ_{s2}, t_a and τ_{a2} are seldom used in the optimal fitting trials.

Figure 6 shows how the best-fit simulated swing matches the motion data in respect of Guy Wolstenholme. Figure 7 shows the torques applied in the simulated swing. The original article contains the corresponding results for the other two golfers.

The shoulder rotation is depicted in red by a line joining the fixed hub to the left shoulder joint. The left arm is shown in green, the club grip in blue and the club shaft in magenta. The club flexibility is concentrated at the joint between grip and shaft.

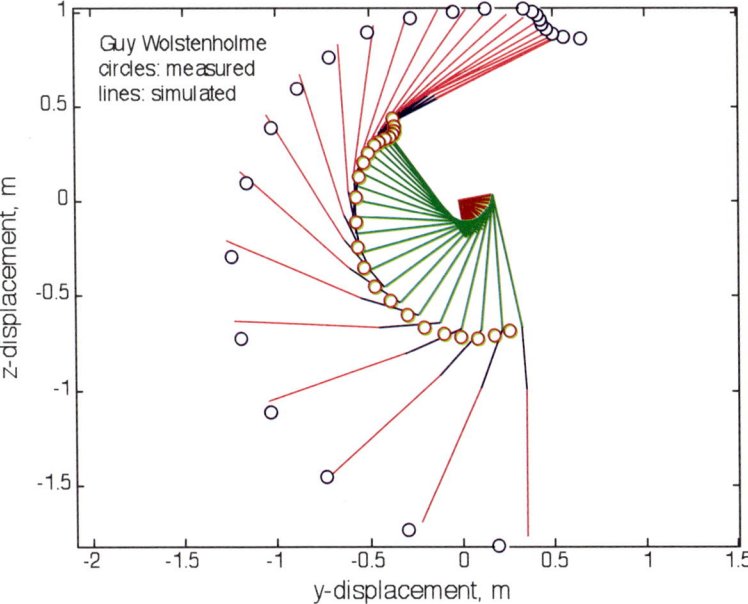

Figure 6. Comparison of Measured and Simulated Hand and Clubhead Position Data for Guy Wolstenholme

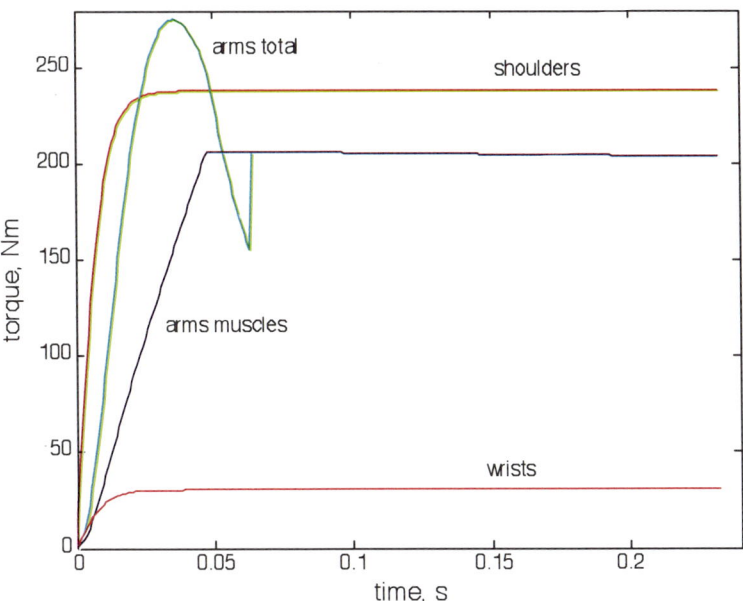

Figure 7. Shoulder, Arm and Wrist Torques in the Guy Wolstenholme Best-Fit Swing

The shoulder torque in Figure 9 builds to its maximum and stays there. The arm torque builds at a rate which implies that the arm limit-stop drives the arms until the time from the start of the downswing reaches 0.06s. Then the arms release and they continue at their full torque capacity up to impact. The wrists hit through all the time, although this does not imply that the wrists release at the beginning of the downswing (see figure 6). The club is driven towards the ball by the wrist limit-stop in the early stages of the downswing, whatever the wrist muscles do. Before the arms release, they are driven by the arm to shoulder limit stop. The torque provided by the limit stop is represented by the difference between green and blue lines.

It is highly significant that the best-fit results for Bernard and Geoffrey Hunt, whose swings are very different from those shown, demonstrate exactly the same pattern of torques as for Guy Wolstenholme, strongly suggesting that a good golf swing involves two releases. The initial part of the downswing involves the arms and wrists remaining at their top-of-the-backswing relative positions. After about one-fifth of the downswing duration, the arms should release and, with this timing, the wrists will release at the correct time for an effective shot. Once the wrist release has commenced, the wrists drive through to make the club come to the ball as quickly as possible. The faster the wrist release phase can be made by virtue of the wrists driving through, the later it can start, for a well-timed shot. The later it starts, as long as it is not too late for a proper impact situation, the more efficient is the swing, in the sense that more of the golfer's work gets into the clubhead at impact.

The swing simulation can now be used to answer a new question, since we now know, or at least we think we know, how strong the shoulders, arms and wrists are. The question is: Could our golfer have done better? The simulation can be run in a new mode, to maximise the clubhead speed at impact. We accept the top-of-the-backswing position, the golfer's geometric and mass properties and assume strength capabilities that come out of the optimal fitting simulations, see Figure 7 for Guy Wolstenholme. In the new optimisations the parameters, t_s, t_{s2}, t_a and t_{a2} are omitted, since they were so seldom used in the optimal fitting trials.

The result is shown in Figure 8, demonstrating a very reasonable 7.2% gain in clubhead speed, as compared with the recorded swing. Corresponding results are given in the original article for Bernard and Geoffrey Hunt, with similar gains in speed at impact relative to best-fit swings. The torque-utilisation pattern is very similar to the previous one, see Figure 9.

The speed at impact is 7.2% greater than that in Figure 6, where the objective was optimal fitting to the experimental data. The shoulder rotation is depicted in red by a line joining the fixed hub to the left shoulder joint. The left arm is shown in green, the club grip in blue and the club shaft in magenta. The club flexibility is concentrated at the joint between grip and shaft.

As in the previous case of Figure 7, the shoulder torque builds to its maximum and stays there. The arm torque builds at a slightly faster rate than before, while the wrists again drive through, once the wrist release has commenced at about 0.15s into the downswing. The difference between the green and the blue curves shows the torque applied by the arm limit-stop.

These simulated swings are altered imperceptibly by omitting the aerodynamic drag on the clubhead. Gravity has a small, noticeable influence, but this is too small to affect the golfer's preference for swinging flat or upright.

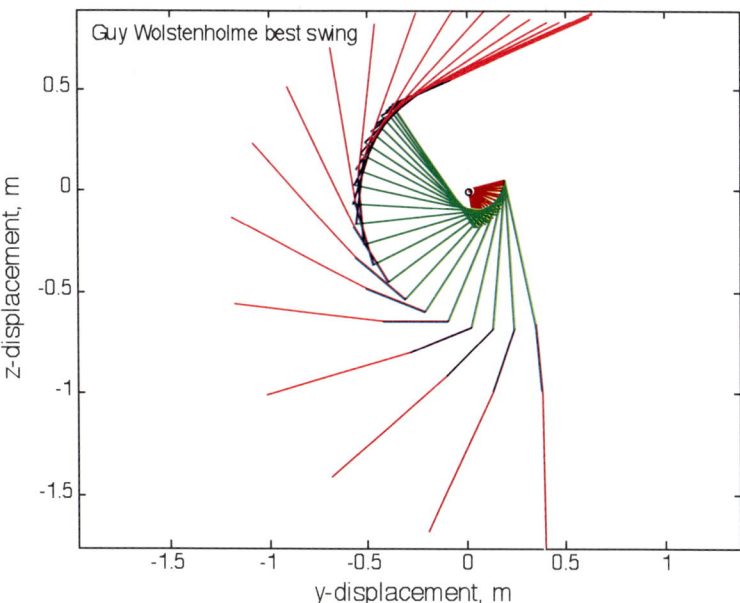

Figure 8. Simulated Swing for Guy Wolstenholme in which the Objective is Maximum Clubhead Speed at Impact

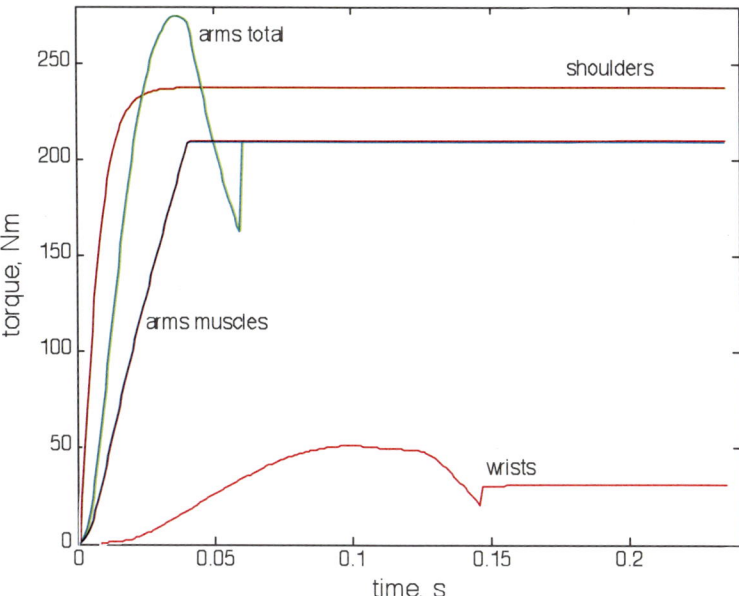

Figure 9. Driving Torques Applied to Shoulders, Arms and Wrists in Guy Wolstenholme's Best Swing, Shown in Figure 8

I have calculated some energies since the original paper was written. Again for Guy Wolstenholme, but for no special reason, they are given in Figure 10. The shoulder kinetic energy (energy of motion) is given by 0.5 * moment of inertia * (angular velocity)^2, the arm, grip and shaft kinetic energies are of the form 0.5 * {mass * (mass centre velocity)^2+ moment of inertia * (angular velocity)^2}, while the shaft potential energy is of the form 0.5 * stiffness * (angular deflection)^2.

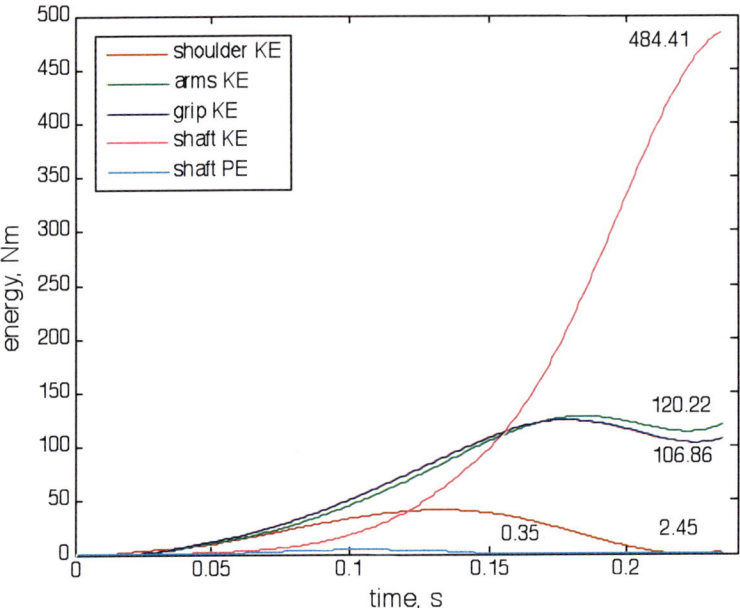

Figure 10. Energies Through Time for Guy Wolstenholme's Best Swing, Figure 8

67.8% of the total energy expended is in the clubhead at impact. The calculations draw attention to the fact that the golfer has to do work to move his own limbs and the energy stored in their motion at impact is not useful. The ideal golfer is both strong and light. The strain energy stored in the clubshaft and released, the shaft potential energy term, is so small with a standard shaft that it is not worth much discussion.

HOW DOES THE PROBLEM SCALE?

In applying the findings generally, we need to know what happens if the golfer is half as muscular. If the patterns change radically according to the golfer's strength, we would need a new approach for each category from weight lifters to jockeys. Changing the driving torques through a range 60% to 140% of their "fitted" values, and repeating the swing optimisations on a maximum-clubhead-speed-at-impact basis shows that the swing geometries are virtually unaltered. With each driving torque reduced by a factor of x, the swing is slower by a factor of $\sqrt{x}$, and the clubhead speed at impact is lower by a factor of $\sqrt{x}$. Ben Hogan's very late hand action is not a result of Ben Hogan being strong or weak in every respect, but rather testifies to his wrists being very strong in relation to his arms and shoulders. This is what enables him to leave his wrist release so late and still get to the ball in time. Compared with more nearly standard swingers, his arm release must also be relatively late to get the timing that, for him, was perfect. The point is illustrated in Figure 11, where a standard swing, with maximum shoulder torque, τ_{smx} = 190 Nm, maximum arm torque, τ_{amx} = 170 Nm and maximum wrist torque, τ_{wmx} = 20 Nm, is compared with one involving τ_{smx} = 161.5 Nm, τ_{amx} = 144.5 Nm and τ_{wmx} = 50 Nm. For the "strong wrist" case, the arm swing is slower and the transfer of momentum into the clubhead after the wrist release is more effective. The swing is more efficient than the standard one.

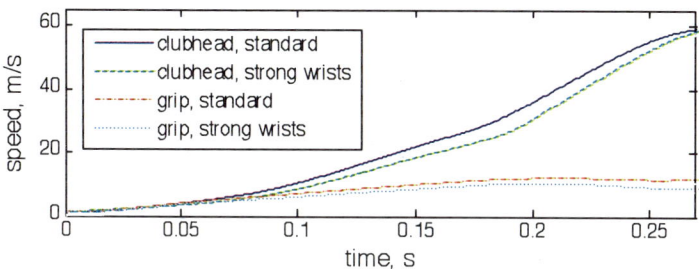

Figure 11. Speeds of Hands and Clubhead for a Standard Swing with τ_{wmx} = 20 Nm and a "Strong-Wrist" Swing with τ_{wmx} = 50 Nm

In the latter case, shoulder and arm torques are reduced to 85% of their standard values to make the clubhead speed at impact about the same as in the standard case. The "strong-wrist" swing takes slightly longer to impact than standard.

Using dimensional analysis to examine the scaling problem more completely, demonstrates that a 21% bigger player, with every dimension increased similarly, will get only 10% more clubhead speed. However, here I must confess that the argument in the original article was not completed. The larger golfer's clubhead will be bigger by 21% and heavier by 77%. Using relations given in *Search for the Perfect Swing* [1], this implies that the ball's initial velocity will be 19% greater; not far off proportional to the scale factor. Small golfers who hit the ball very hard are indeed remarkable.

INFLUENCES OF SWING AND CLUB VARIATIONS

Swing and club variations are studied in Appendix D of the original article. A change from the standard configuration is specified and the swing re-optimised to accommodate the change. The process is like that of a golfer who buys new clubs and then has to tune his swing to them, insofar as they are different from his/her old ones. Significant advantages in clubhead speed at impact came from: 1) a four-times more compliant clubshaft (2.52% gain); 2) a 5.7° larger shoulder-turn angle (1.28% gain); 3) a 5.7° larger arm-turn angle (1.95% gain); 4) a 5.7° larger wrist-cock angle (1.19% gain); 5) halving the driver's shaft mass (2.32% gain); and 6) lengthening the driver shaft by 10 cm (2.02% gain). The first of these variations appears to be especially interesting, since an eight-times more compliant shaft gets worse again. The optimal swing with the four-times more compliant shaft is shown in Figure 12. Careful scrutiny of this figure will reveal that the clubshaft does bend noticeably in the middle section of the downswing and then it straightens coming to the ball. However, it remains the case that the strain energy stored in the shaft is very small compared with the other energies involved. The advantage from the flexible shaft probably comes from it effectively contributing to a bigger wrist-cock angle. The gain is likely to be greater for those golfers whose wrist-cock angle is relatively small.

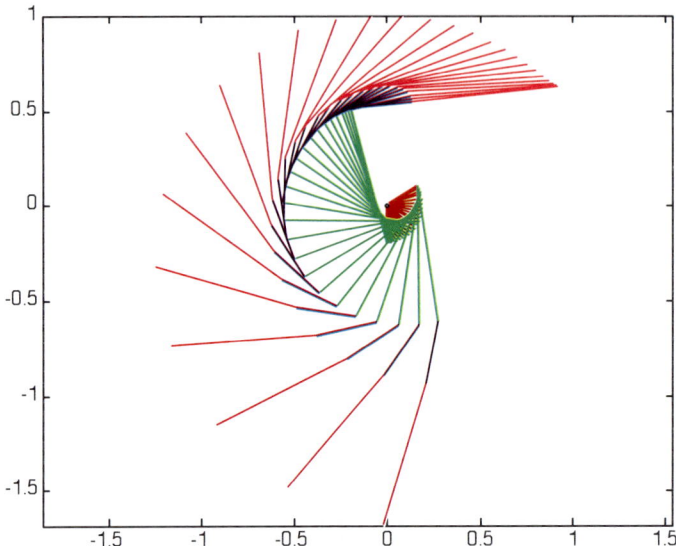

Figure 12. A Standard Golfer's Swing Optimised for a Driver with One Quarter of the Standard Shaft Stiffness, Showing a 2.52% Gain in Clubhead Speed at Impact

The shoulder rotation is depicted in red by a line joining the fixed hub to the left shoulder joint. The left arm is shown in green, the club grip in blue, and the club shaft in magenta. The club flexibility is concentrated at the joint between grip and shaft.

Historically, clubs have been matched to each other by adjusting their swing weights. Other bases have also been tried, for example, frequency matching. There seems to be little fundamental justification for any particular matching criterion. It is only reasonable to accept that the more lofted clubs will have shorter shafts, to accommodate the changing balance between the need for power and the need for accuracy as one approaches the target. Also, for the same reasons, the swing a golfer uses will shorten as the clubs get shorter. 3-iron and 9-iron simulated swings show that the same swing durations would result from making a 3-iron head a little heavier than normal and a 9-iron head much heavier than normal. Probably, if they were advantageous changes, the process of continuous improvement, or evolution, would have discovered it already. No other obvious basis for matching clubs to each other seems to be available. Evidently, the golfer must adapt to the club being used, in the same way that he/she must adapt to the lie of the ball, etc. Every competent golfer must appreciate that he/she should practice with each and every club to become proficient with them. Expertise with a driver only is insufficient.

CONCLUSION

Aerodynamic drag on the clubhead and shaft of a golf club are negligible. Gravity has only a small influence, with no practical implications with respect to swinging flat or upright.

The distribution of effort driving the arm swing is vital to controlling the timing of the wrist release. If too much driving torque is applied to the arms too early, the wrist release will come too soon, the clubhead will be slowing down coming to the ball, the approach of the clubhead to the ball will be from below, and the face will probably be closed. This will occur notwithstanding what the golfer does with his/her wrists, since the wrists are not strong enough to overcome deficiencies in the timing of the effort into the arm swing. Conversely, if the effort into driving the arms is too late, the clubhead will not have reached its maximum speed and the face will most likely be open at impact. Again the wrists have a very limited capability to provide corrective action. It is likely that the best distribution of effort will result from having an arm release point in the swing. This seems to correspond with Tony Jacklin's 1, 2, 3 rhythm; i.e., 1, start the downswing with the shoulders keeping the arms and wrists fully cocked; 2, release the arms but keep the wrists fully cocked; 3, release the wrist action, in the end, hitting with everything available. Keeping the arms cocked from the start of the downswing for the first several tens of milliseconds seems to be the feature that amateur golfers do not always learn. To some extent, it is counter-intuitive, that if one holds back the effort, the clubhead speed at impact will be greater, but that seems to be the truth of it.

In the region of normal clubshaft flexibilities, the flexibility is not so influential but it is likely that a significant gain in clubhead speed at impact is available if a relatively very flexible shaft is employed. It is curious that even greater flexibility does not bring greater advantage. There appears to be an optimum flexibility for any particular golfer.

Swinging longer, if possible, in respect of shoulder, arm and wrist cock, is advantageous in terms of power and the light shaft of the modern driver is significantly useful. Using a longer driver will also help with clubhead speed at impact, given that the necessary re-optimisation is accomplished.

Matching clubs to each other to make a set according to some objective criterion is probably not justifiable on a fundamental basis. Rather, it should be accepted that the golfer needs to adapt to the club. Adapting to clubs with smooth and continuous variations as one goes from driver to sand-iron will naturally be easier than adapting to randomly related clubs. Apparently, clubs should be matched in this sense in all respects, shaft-length, weight, mass centre location, shaft-stiffness, etc.

The common practice of examining photographic sequences of expert golfers and basing advice to learners on what one can see in such photographs appears not to properly recognise the dynamic nature of the golf swing. I wish to argue that the golfer controls his/her muscles and not the motions directly and he/she wants to know what to do with the muscle commands. The idea that the distribution of effort through the downswing is a central consideration is most important and it should lead to golfers, on the practice ground, trying early hits and late hits and thinking in terms of an arm release in addition to a wrist release, as opposed to continually adjusting their geometry in an effort to find their best form.

REFERENCE

1.   Cochran, A. and Stobbs, J., *Search for the Perfect Swing: The Proven Scientific Approach to Fundamentally Improving Your Game*, Triumph Books, Chicago, IL, 2005.

Injury Prevention: Avoiding One of Golf's More Painful Hazards

David M Lindsay[1], Theo H Versteegh[2] and Anthony A Vandervoort[2]

[1]Sport Medicine Centre, University of Calgary,
2500 University Dr NW, Calgary, AB, Canada, T2N 1N4
Email dlindsay@ucalgary.ca
[2]School of Physical Therapy, Faculty of Health Sciences,
University of Western Ontario, London, Ontario, Canada

ABSTRACT

Although the sport of golf may be mistakenly perceived as a benign physical activity, there are in fact patterns of problems such as strains to the upper limb and low-back pain that have the potential to interfere with the professional golfer's livelihood and recreational golfer's enjoyment. In this article, a summary of the literature has been provided outlining the nature and extent of common musculoskeletal injuries that golfers deal with as well as some of the risk factors that may increase injury susceptibility. A detailed overview of prevention strategies to minimize the risk of suffering a golf injury has also been provided. Since many injuries arise from poor swing biomechanics, taking instruction with a knowledgeable golf instructor can be an important first step towards injury prevention. However, if a golfing client already has an injury which originated or is aggravated by playing or practicing, then the personalized help of a physician or physiotherapist experienced in golf biomechanics is also warranted. Proper attention to prevention will ensure a lifetime of enjoyable golf "par"ticipation.

Key words: Flexibility, Golf Swing Biomechanics, Low-Back Pain, Overuse Injuries, Posture, Risk Factors, Warm-Up

Reviewers: Rob Mottram (Golf Health & Performance Center, USA)
Harvey Newton (Newton Sports, USA)
Michael Voight (Belmont University, USA)

INTRODUCTION

Many non-golfers regard the sport as a rather benign activity. [1] This perception may partly be due to the seemingly effortless appearance of an elite tour professional's swing or perhaps to the fact the sport can be played by individuals of almost any age. This latter point is supported by research showing that while activity participation in general declines with age, activities such as walking, gardening and golf show increased participation rates around retirement age. [2] However, while golf may be a sport for all ages, research is also showing that golf injuries can occur at surprising frequencies whether one is a young professional or senior recreational player. [1, 3, 4]

While a well executed golf swing may not appear overly stressful, many body parts are moving at high velocity and through extreme ranges of motion (ROM). The magnitude and complexity of these motions has led some to regard the full golf swing as one of the more difficult biomechanical motions to execute. [5] Mastering these motions, as demonstrated by elite amateur and touring professionals, requires dedicated practice where these powerful movements may be repeated several hundred times per day. The subsequent and cumulative stresses on the limb and spinal joints associated with such practice may lead to the development of overuse injuries. [6, 7] Furthermore, since swing mechanics may contribute to injury susceptibility [8], the less efficient and inappropriate movement patterns demonstrated by less skilled recreational golfers may further increase injury susceptibility.

Epidemiological research has shown that golf injuries are quite common. Professional Golf Association (PGA) tour players average two injuries per year with half of these injuries limiting the ability to play for an average of five weeks. [1] Recreational players, on average, lose approximately four weeks of playing time per injury. [6] In terms of injury location, the lower back would appear to be the most commonly affected body part, [1, 4, 6, 7] although shoulder, elbow and wrist injuries are also common. [4, 6, 9] In terms of severity, most golfers regard their injury as minor (approximately 51%) as compared to moderate (27%) or major (22%) severity. [6] McCarroll reported that 54% of professional golfers and 45% of amateur players categorize their injury as chronic. [1] The prevalence of chronic minor injuries amongst golfers is supported by a report that as many as one third of elite touring professionals are playing injured at any given time. [10]

The best approach to minimizing the risk of injury from playing golf is through injury prevention, which requires a combination of good technique, sound judgment as well as proper education and awareness. The purpose of this paper is to review and discuss, from an evidenced-based perspective, some of the factors contributing to injury susceptibility from golf. The paper also attempts to integrate scientific evidence with a practical guide on how to minimize or eliminate such injury risks in the hope of avoiding a lot of unnecessary pain, frustration and time away from the course.

RISK FACTORS

OVERUSE

Overuse has been identified as the leading cause of golf-related injury [1, 6], which is not surprising given the hours of practice many golfers perform in order to improve their skill level. The gradual onset of overuse injuries is thought to be associated with the cumulative stress placed on the tissue over time. [11-14] Kumar [11] reported that workers who developed low back pain were found to have consistently worked for more hours over their lifetimes than their pain-free colleagues. It is believed that prolonged exposure to repetitive and static tasks results in a decline in the tolerance levels of tissues to withstand stress over time particularly when combined with insufficient rest. Professional golfers or dedicated amateurs who undertake extensive practice may thus be jeopardizing their health as the result of these cumulative stresses.

For example, it has been shown that performing the golf swing creates 6100 ± 2,413N of spinal compressive force in amateurs and 7,584 ± 2,422N of force in professional golfers or equivalent to eight times a person's body weight. [15, 16] Considering professional golfers will perform the swing upwards of 2,000 swings per week [17], it is no wonder why professional golfers and dedicated amateurs are prone to repetitive strain or overuse type injuries. In fact, Gosheger et al. [6] found in their study that of the nearly 40% of amateurs and 60% of professionals who experienced golfing injuries, over 80% of these injuries were due to overuse. The most common sites of overuse injuries were the back, the shoulder, the knee, the elbow and the hand and wrist.

TECHNIQUE FACTORS

There are few more contentious things in golf than what constitutes the ideal swing. However, there is increasing evidence that differences in technique factors even amongst-elite players may predispose golfers to injury. Lindsay and Horton [18] in their investigation of spinal kinematics using a device known as a lumbar motion monitor were able to show that elite golfers with low-back pain (LBP) tended to address the ball with more spinal flexion and used more left side-bend during their backswing. The golfers also tended to use considerably more rotation ROM during the follow-through than the maximum rotation ROM that these same players were able to demonstrate in a clinical setting from a neutral posture and controlled speed. The authors suggested that spinal irritation and pain could result from this relative over-rotation of the spine while performing the golf swing. Furthermore, Grimshaw et al. [19] in a case study of a professional golfer with LBP was able to eliminate this pain by altering his technique and improving muscle conditioning. Conditioning exercises targeted the transverse abdominis and multifidus muscles while technique changes focused on increasing the amount the pelvis turned on the backswing resulting in a decrease in spinal motion and hence a decrease in low-back stress. Another technique shown to decrease the stress on the lower back is to shorten the backswing. Bulbulian et al. [20] looked at kinematic and electromyographic (EMG) recordings of various trunk and shoulder regions during a full recoil backswing compared to a modified short backswing. Results showed that shortening the backswing by 46.5 ± 24.7 degrees (or approximately 20%) corresponded with a decrease in trunk muscle activation levels, but had no effect on stroke accuracy and no significant reduction in club-head velocity.

Although more research needs to be done, these preliminary studies would seem to indicate that controlling spinal movement while promoting more hip turn and shortening the backswing would help decrease the stress on the lower back. However, the approach of limiting spinal motion during the golf swing to help protect the back is in contrast to current golf coaching philosophies of increasing the 'X-factor' or increasing the angle between the imaginary lines bisecting both shoulder and the hip joints to improve performance. There is biomechanical evidence that higher skilled golfers tend to incorporate a larger "X-factor" (i.e., more spinal rotation) at the top of the backswing than less skilled players. [21, 22] Additionally, better players tend to increase their "X-factor" by a further 19% during the initial phase of the downswing, compared to only 13% for their less-skilled counterparts. [23] Tiger Woods, arguably the best golfer of the day, would appear to incorporate a large amount of spinal rotation or 'X-factor' in his full swings. However, most recreational golfers, as well as a lot of elite players, simply do not have the necessary ROM required to emulate Tiger's swing safely [18], hence predisposing themselves to injury.

When dealing with injury prevention of the knee, one factor to consider is the external adduction or varus moment associated with the lead knee. A high adduction moment is associated with increased compression on the medial compartment, which is the most common site of osteoarthritis (OA) of the knee. [24] Lynn et al. [25] showed there was a decrease in the knee external adduction moment of the lead leg when an externally rotated or 'toed out' lead foot position of approximately 20 degrees at set up was adopted. Therefore it is recommended for golfers with known OA of the lead leg or those that wish to minimize medial knee stress to set up with the lead leg toed out towards the direction of the target.

Some of the common shoulder problems that occur with golf are acromioclavicular joint disease, subacromial and rotator cuff impingement and posterior glenohumeral instability of the lead shoulder. [26] All of these conditions are irritated by full horizontal adduction and internal rotation of the shoulder, the position the lead arm is in at the top of the backswing. The technique modification suggested in the literature is to shorten the backswing or the follow-through, depending on what is the aggravating position of the involved shoulder. [9, 17] Strengthening the rotator cuff muscles, particularly on the lead side, may also offer additional protection against shoulder injury. [17]

Wrist injuries are another health issue facing golfers and may relate to the fact this region is associated with a very high rotational velocity, exceeding 1000 m/s [27], and large amplitude ROM [28] as the wrists "release" immediately before and through impact. Excessive repetition of the high-velocity, large amplitude wrist release likely produces considerable stress on the wrist structures and increases injury susceptibility, particularly among professional players. [6, 10] This stress may be amplified if the player uses an inappropriate grip at the set-up or swings at the ball using an overly steep descending swing path. [29] Furthermore, Cahalan et al. [28] showed that golfers with hand and wrist pathology displayed decreased wrist ROM and strength compared to non-symptomatic golfers.

It would appear from the above that in addition to correcting any grip or swing faults, stretching and strengthening the wrist and forearm muscles may be important for injury prevention. It may also be appropriate for some "less conditioned" golfers to refrain from mimicking the large amount of wrist cocking that most elite players use to help generate maximum clubhead speed. [30]

Stretching and strengthening the muscles of the forearm may also be appropriate for injury prevention of the elbow. This is because medial and lateral epicondylitis, the most common elbow injuries in golf [31], also typically involve the wrist flexors and extensors but at the muscle origin rather than at the insertion – which is the site of common hand and wrist pathologies in golfers. Weakness or premature fatigue of these muscles may diminish the ability of these muscles to control the stress to the elbow at impact. [32] From a technique perspective, excessive grip pressure is thought to play a role in increasing the eccentric load on the wrist extensor (lead) and flexor (trail) muscles as the clubhead makes contact with the ball and ground at impact. This potentially excessive muscular loading may result in cumulative micro-tearing at the common origin of the wrist extensor and flexor muscles (lateral and medial epicondyles respectively) and result in subsequent pain. A preliminary investigation into grip pressures by Broker and Ramey [33] showed that less-skilled amateur golfers tended to grip the golf club with greater force than highly skilled players. This may partially account for the almost six-fold increase in elbow injuries among recreational golfers compared to professional players. [34]

PREVENTION STRATEGIES
CARDIOVASCULAR ACTIVITY PROGRESSION

Walking the golf course equates to approximately a 10 kilometer hike and requires reasonable cardiovascular endurance. It has been calculated that during a typical round of 18 holes, a male golfer burns about 1500 calories. [35] Carrying clubs adds about another 10-15% to these numbers. [36] When heart rates were monitored in a study of European recreational golfers, the women in the study tended to reach a peak of about 80% of their maximum heart rate while walking some of the uphill fairways. For the men in this sample, the peak intensity reached was about 70% of their maximum heart rate, depending on the age of the golfer and whether the terrain was level or uphill. [37]

While the above numbers may not seem excessive, they are associated with a moderate degree of cardiovascular stress. For example, a Finish study examined the effects of walking and playing golf 2-3 times a week over a 20-week period. Fifty-five healthy sedentary male subjects aged 48 to 64 years participated in the study. The researchers found that the subjects who played golf (walking the course) significantly increased cardiovascular fitness, decreased body fat and improved cholesterol levels in comparison to a control group which did not golf. [38]

In order to better meet the physical challenges of golf, thus preventing injuries from excessive fatigue, it is important for golfers to map out a plan to gradually increase their cardiovascular exercise tolerance. In terms of cardiovascular fitness, this could be as simple as going on a reasonable walk 3-4 times per week. Golfers should be instructed to try and gradually increase the distance and intensity of these walks in the first few weeks leading up to the start of the golf season.

MUSCULOSKELETAL ACTIVITY PROGRESSION

While the cardiovascular demands of golf are not always recognized and can be mitigated if necessary by riding in a power cart, the considerable biomechanical stresses on the musculoskeletal system have received more extensive research attention. [39] The golf swing is a unique dynamic movement involving powerful patterns of coordinated muscle contractions. Touring professionals often repeat these powerful movements several hundred times per practice sessions that are frequent during competition phases, resulting in considerable stresses being generated and dissipated throughout the body structures during each of these sessions. [9]

When the area of spinal stress is studied, it is clear that the golf swing produces a complex loading pattern involving shear, compression, and torsional stresses compounded by rapid changes in the direction of these forces. Hosea et al. [16] found the average peak shear load on the spinal column for amateurs and professionals to be 596 N and 329 N respectively. In comparison, peak shear loads in the spine of male rowers have been calculated to be approximately 848 N. As mentioned previously, the compression loads associated with vigorous golf swings equaled approximately eight times body weight in both amateur (6100 N) and professional (7584 N) golfers which is approximately 2 ½ times higher than the spinal compression forces produced from running. [15] Additional cumulative loading on the spine has also been attributed to the flexed posture associated with putting (most golfers prefer a relatively short-handled putter), as well as from walking while carrying clubs. [6, 36]

It is also of interest to examine hip and knee stress during a golf swing. For example, Stover et al. [40] calculated that the lead hip experienced a much greater rotational torque than the trail hip during the downswing – an observation that may partly explain the asymmetrical deterioration of golf superstars Jack Nicklaus's and Tom Watson's hips (both have undergone total joint arthroplasty procedures on their lead hip). Gatt et al. [41] noted the fact that the magnitude of forces on the knee during a golf swing was at least equal to those generated from running or side-cutting motions. However, these were asymmetrical with the lead knee being subjected more to an internal rotation, posterior, and varus force on the downswing while the trail side experienced an external rotation, anterior, and valgus stress.

Muscle function during the golf swing has also been studied extensively by using electromyography. For example, Pink et al. [42] analyzed muscle activity in eight shoulder muscles of both the right and left arms during the golf swing, and concluded that although golf was not a strenuous arm activity, it did require high synchronous activity of the rotator cuff muscles in order to protect the glenohumeral complex. They also reported that all of the right-handed golfers seen at their local orthopedic clinic for shoulder problems had left-sided rotator cuff problems.

Kao et al. [43] examined the activity of the scapular muscles in the upper back region (levator scapulae, rhomboid, trapezius, serratus anterior) during the golf swing. Their data indicated that the upper, middle, and lower trapezius all work together to help retract the scapula during different parts of the swing, with activity in the trailing arm occurring primarily during takeaway whereas activity in the leading arm occurred during acceleration. The lead-side levator scapulae and rhomboid muscles also played a key role in helping to elevate and retract the scapula on the downswing.

Pink et al. [44] also studied the activity patterns of the trunk muscles (erector spinae and abdominal obliques) in amateur golfers. Relatively high and constant activity in the oblique muscles was recorded throughout most parts of the swing (note that they did not distinguish between external or internal abdominal oblique muscles).

In a similar study using professional golfers, Watkins et al. [45] measured muscle activity in the erector spinae, gluteus maximus, abdominal oblique, and rectus abdominis and established that all trunk muscles were relatively active during the acceleration phase of the golf swing. Among this group of muscles, the trail side abdominal obliques showed the highest relative activity. Other authors have found a higher relative contribution from the lead internal oblique compared to the trail external oblique on the downswing [46, 47], with both muscles contracting before the club reached the top of the backswing. High levels of bilateral erector spinae activity on the downswing are thought to help stabilize the spine during the powerful trunk flexion and rotation forces produced by the abdominal muscles. [44, 45]

For further understanding of the contributions from the lower limb, Bechler et al. [48] studied the activity patterns of the gluteus maximus, gluteus medius, adductor magnus, biceps femoris, semimembranosus, and vastus lateralis muscles in competitive golfers. They noted that it was the extensors and abductors of the trail hip, in conjunction with the lead adductor magnus, which contracted powerfully to initiate pelvic rotation during the downswing. Concurrently, the lead vastus lateralis and the hamstrings acted to stabilize the knee joints during this pelvic rotation.

As can be seen from the above, swinging a golf club aggressively puts considerable stress on certain parts of the body such as the lower back and lead arm. As a result, it is important when returning to golf after a long lay-off or after an injury to gradually introduce and progress movements that replicate and ultimately mirror these same stresses. Also, since impact with the ground is where a large component of the stress associated with the golf swing occurs, golfers must be instructed on ways to control these forces. This would include instructing golfing clients to only hit off grass or very soft mats during the initial ball striking component at the start of each golf season.

There is very little scientific evidence demonstrating what an ideal golf-specific activity build-up program should look like. The present authors have used the following guide with good anecdotal success:

- Gently swing a medium iron (i.e., a 7-iron) in the backyard for 5–10 minutes once or twice per day. Don't use a full swing to start. Do this for one week.
- During the second week, gradually build up the length and speed of these backyard practice swings. Attaching a small weight (e.g., taping a golf ball to the club-face) can make the exercise a little bit harder. One or two practice sessions per day, each lasting 5-10 minutes is still appropriate.
- Starting the third week, progress to hitting a small bucket of balls (i.e., about 30) at the driving range or practice facility. Start with very gentle swings and progress to half or three-quarter swings, using only short irons. Make sure you warm-up first (see *Warm- up Prior to Playing* section). Hit the ball off a tee, very soft mat, or lush grass — and take frequent breaks. Don't hit balls more than two days in a row.
- As the week progresses, slowly increase the length and speed of the swings as well as the number of balls hit (e.g., up to about 50 balls).
- Starting the fourth week, continue to practice every second day but start to introduce the long irons and finally the woods. By the end of this fourth week (meaning you've been hitting balls for two weeks), you might be able to hit 100

balls (including gentle warm-up shots) per session, but be careful. There may be days when you have to back-off or rest completely.

Obviously the timeframes outlined in this guide will vary considerably depending on the skill level of the individual, their fitness level, and whether they are still recovering from any previous injuries. However, it still provides a useful structured plan that most golf clients will benefit from before starting a new golf season or when returning after an injury or long lay-off. As outlined, a player will typically be ready to fully return to golf approximately one month from when they started swinging a club in the back yard. When the player is ready to start golfing again, they should be instructed to start off with 9 holes before taking on the full 18. They should also be educated on proper warm-up procedures and to allow a full day's rest between rounds. They should also be advised to apply ice for 15 minutes to treat any pain associated with their return to activity.

STRENGTH AND FLEXIBILITY ENHANCEMENT
The ideal golf swing requires considerable joint ROM and muscle strength from virtually all parts of the body, but particularly in the rotation directions. Without adequate flexibility, not only does the swing become more inefficient, it may also be unsafe. A player lacking strength and flexibility is working under a physical handicap which not only affects his or her score, but also increases the likelihood of suffering an injury. Outlining an appropriate stretching and strengthening exercise program for golf is beyond the scope of this paper, and readers can refer to Smith [49] for a recent review, as well as Newton [50]. It is worth noting that stretching and strengthening the wrist and trunk may be particularly important for golfers as previous studies have shown associations between wrist ROM restriction and weakness in golfers with wrist pain [28] as well as trunk rotation ROM restriction [18] and weakness [51] in golfers with LBP. From a performance perspective, it would appear as though improvements in strength generally correlate better with increases in clubhead speed than flexibility improvements. [52]

SET-UP POSTURE
The golf swing is a very challenging activity. Much of what happens during the swing is determined by how the body is positioned at set-up. While it is unlikely that one set-up posture is ideal for all golfers, the athletic posture adopted by many professionals is a good starting point due to its stable appearance that allows efficiency of motion particularly around the trunk region.

The turning motion of the body to get to the top of the backswing and finish position comes from the hips and spine. The hip joints are very large and strong joints. The spinal joints on the other hand are smaller and more complicated and as a result are easily injured. The most efficient position for the spine is to keep it relatively straight during the set-up. This means the hips should provide the forward tilt of the trunk that allows the arms to hang comfortably in front of the body when gripping the club. Flexing the spine rather than the hips not only prevents the spine being able to rotate properly during the backswing, but may make it more difficult to use the abdominal muscles to generate power on the downswing. [18]

As previously mentioned, controlling extreme spinal rotation ROM during the top of the backswing and at the follow-through may help reduce the stress to the lower back. One way of achieving this is to have the player increase the amount they turn out or *open* their feet at set-up. Keeping the trail foot too straight or square tends to restrict the amount of pelvic or hip turn during the backswing which may cause excessive rotation of the spine away from the target (i.e., to the right for a right-handed swing) as the player compensates in an attempt to reach the top-of-backswing position. Similarly, over-rotation of the spine at the end of the follow-through (i.e., to the left) may result if the lead foot is not sufficiently turned out or if an excessively spiked shoe is used to anchor the lead foot to the ground. Turning out the lead foot has also been shown to decrease stress at the medial knee, which is the area of the knee most often affected by knee osteoarthritis. [25]

Keeping the knees too straight is one reason the spine may be forced to flex excessively at set-up. Most golfers know that when attempting to lift a heavy object it is important to bend the knees, rather than put excessive strain on the back muscles. The golf swing, which also involves very powerful back muscle contractions, is no different. A knee bend of about 25 to 30 degrees is recommended. A simple maneuver to find the correct amount of knee bend is achieved by standing up straight and side-on to a mirror. While looking in the mirror, the knees are then bent just enough until the front of the kneecaps are just over the ball of the foot (front part of the arch). This angle represents the desirable knee position when the golfer addresses the ball. It will still be necessary to bend forward at the hips about 25 to 30 degrees, while maintaining a neutral spinal curve, in order to help balance the upper body above the feet as the club is brought down to the ball.

In summary, if the golfer has assumed the correct set-up posture, both feet will be turned out 25 degrees, both knees will be flexed 25 degrees, and the trunk will be tilted forward at the hips 25-30 degrees while keeping the spine relatively straight. Finally, the body weight should feel comfortably stable and balanced over the middle parts of the feet.

Figure 1. Balanced Athletic Posture for the Set-Up of the Golf Swing

EQUIPMENT FACTORS

Two key equipment factors that may influence injury susceptibility in golf are whether the golf club is properly matched to the golfer and the type of surface used by the golfer to hit balls from when practicing.

Golf clubs represent the critical link between the human body and the golf ball. When a golfer uses clubs which are not well suited to their particular physical dimensions or swing characteristics, their body is forced to compensate. These compensations make it more difficult to swing efficiently and consistently and increase the risk of injury. For males, the standard club length is designed for someone 70 in. or 178 cm. For women the numbers are 64 in. or 163 cm.

Neal et al. [53] reported on the effects of using an inappropriately matched golf club on spinal swing mechanics. They demonstrated that using a club with a shaft that was 2 inches (5 cm) shorter than the recommended length resulted in approximately 4 degrees less spinal rotation at the top of the back-swing, and 8 degrees more flexion at impact. However, these numbers were not part of a specific scientific investigation and were based on a single golfer. Lindsay et al. [54] completed an investigation comparing spinal mechanics among elite golfers using a driver and 7-iron. The purpose was to investigate the changes in set-up posture and spinal motion during the swing caused by the different length clubs. The 7-iron is approximately 18 cm shorter than the driver.

The address position flexion angles recorded in Lindsay et al.'s [54] study using the 7-iron (35.1 ± 12.8 degrees) were significantly higher (p = 0.02) than the driver results (28.9 ± 10.9 degrees). During the actual swing, significantly greater maximum flexion and left side bend ROM occurred when using the 7-iron (p < 0.05). The explanation for increased left side bending when swinging the 7-iron may relate to club shaft length and its associated influence on swing plane. Swing plane refers to the oblique plane the golf club is moved through during the swing. The shorter length 7-iron typically requires the ball to be positioned closer to the body than the driver. This necessitates a more vertical orientation of the 7-iron shaft during the set-up as well as during the actual swing, compared to the driver. As the club is accelerated, the forces associated with a more vertical or steeper swing plane will tend to drive the hips and trunk laterally resulting in an increase in thoraco-lumbar side bend motion. The results in Table 1 show greater left- and right-side bend motions during swings with the 7-iron, but only the former was significant. Side bending of the spine during the golf swing has been postulated by others as a contributing factor to low back injury. [55, 56] Rotation ROM towards the target (left rotation) was also noticeably greater for the longer club, although the magnitude of this difference fell just outside statistical significance (Table 1). The higher left rotation ROM may be explained by the higher left rotation velocity achieved by the driver on the downswing (Table 2) resulting in greater momentum pushing the spine into super-maximal left rotation. These results suggest golfers must warm-up properly before swinging aggressively, especially with longer clubs such as a driver, otherwise injury from over-exertion could occur.

The only significant findings for spinal velocities during golf swings with a driver and 7-iron were for right side bending (p = 0.02), with the 7-iron producing the higher values [54]. This was somewhat surprising as the club head speed achieved by the driver is typically much higher than the 7-iron. It would therefore seem logical that the velocity of the trunk at impact would also be greater for the driver.

In summary, the findings from Lindsay et al.'s study [47], showing that different clubs produce different spinal motion characteristics, offer valuable information for clinicians and teachers. They may also have implications for club fitting (especially shaft length) as well as the prevention or control of low-back pain (LBP). Indeed, a shorter golf club requires additional flexion when setting up and hitting golf balls. Furthermore, the shorter club produces greater amounts of spinal side bending during the swing. A high degree of side bend has been implicated as a contributing factor in the development of LBP among golfers. Players with back pain should be properly educated about: the use of equipment (e.g., shaft length) that is appropriately matched to body size, proper warm-up prior to playing, addressing the ball with good posture, and not over-swinging.

Table 1. Maximum Spinal ROM Means (degrees) and SD for the Golf Swing

	Flexion	Extension	Left Side Bend	Right Side Bend	Right Rotation	Left Rotation
Driver	45.6 ± 9.7	2.8 ± 9.9	7.1 ± 6.0	26.3 ± 5.2	37.0 ± 8.4	44.5 ± 10.5
7-iron	51.0 ± 9.9	3.0 ± 8.9	9.8 ± 5.9	27.9 ± 4.8	34.8 ± 8.8	40.4 ± 10.1
	$p = 0.01$	$p = 0.88$	$p = 0.03$	$p = 0.13$	$p = 0.24$	$p = 0.06$

Table 2. Average Maximum Spinal Velocities (deg/sec) During the Golf Swing

	Flexion	Extension	Left Side Bend	Right Side Bend	Right Rotation	Left Rotation
Driver	60.9 ± 33.7	137.9 ± 47.3	38.4 ± 14.9	109.2 ± 25.3	88.2 ± 20.5	194.8 ± 54.6
7-iron	57.5 ± 32.6	138.3 ± 43.7	40.7 ± 13.5	121.7 ± 24.8	83.5 ± 20.1	180.3 ± 50.8
	$p = 0.63$	$p = 0.97$	$p = 0.46$	$p = 0.02$	$p = 0.28$	$p = 0.20$

As mentioned, hitting off hard artificial surfaces such as driving range mats is another possible contributing factor to upper-limb stress from golf activity. Players typically contact the turf before, during or after ball impact, thereby creating high resistance loading on the upper limbs. Repetitive and excessive loading may contribute to injuries such as wrist tendonopathy, elbow epicondylitis and rotator cuff strain. [7, 26] While a number of manufacturers produce simulated turf mats, there are typically two different types installed at practice facilities. One type is a solid mat that typically has a thin layer of a durable synthetic turf that is implanted onto a 30mm thick base comprised of dense foam. The other common mat consists of a pliable brush-like surface comprised of closely packed vertical strands of nylon fibers (approximately 40 mm long) set into a hard polymer base (Figure 2).

Figure 2. Brush Fibre Mat

Recently, Lindsay et al. [57] conducted a study to compare the perceived impact forces, upper-limb stress, quality of shots and similarity to hitting from grass between these two common types of hitting mats. Results from their study showed that perceptual differences clearly exist in how different types of practice mats affect upper-limb stress and the quality of golf shots. The results from Table 3 most strongly reflect subjects' overall preference for the brush fiber mat as subjects could only select one type of mat for each of the 5 questions. Results showed that a minimum of 80% of the study participants selected the brush fiber mat over the solid mat in each of the categories. The largest perceived difference between mats pertained to upper-limb stress, with almost 91% of subjects stating they felt the brush fiber mat produced the least stress during impact. When subjects were specifically asked which mat they preferred to hit balls from, 81% selected the brush fiber mat. Regarding why they preferred the brush fiber mat, subjects typically stated; "better simulated a real golfing experience," "allowed for better ball contact," and "felt like I could mis-hit without discomfort." Participants who preferred the solid mat stated that this mat was "smoother and lighter to hit off," and "(its) firmness made it easier to hit from."

Table 3. Comparison of Perceived Shot Performance between Different Driving Range Mats

Question	Subject Preference (%) (n = 23)	
	Brush Fiber Mat	Solid Mat
1. Which mat best absorbed the impact of your club hitting the ground?	85.7	14.3
2. Which mat resulted in the least upper limb stress during ball contact?	90.5	9.5
2. Which mat permitted the best quality of ball contact?	80.0	20.0
4. Which mat best simulated hitting off a lush fairway?	81.0	19.0
5. Which mat do you prefer hitting off?	81.0	19.0

WARM-UP PRIOR TO PLAYING

As mentioned, the golf swing is a very complex asymmetrical movement involving powerful muscle contractions and extreme ranges of motion. Owing to the considerable physical demands associated with the full golf swing, it would seem logical that an adequate warm-up routine be performed prior to playing or practicing. The purpose of the warm-up is to enhance performance by physiologically and psychologically preparing the body for competition while at the same time reducing the risk of injury. The performance and injury prevention benefits are likely related to the increased body temperature associated with the warm-up activities. [58] An elevation in body temperature is reportedly associated with an increase in the speed and force of muscle contractions due to: increases in nerve conductivity, improved blood flow to and through the active tissues, and enhancement of localized metabolic processes such as the release of oxygen from hemoglobin and myoglobin. [59] Furthermore, increased temperature results in the reduction of the tissue's internal viscosity. [58, 60] The reduction in viscosity creates less intramuscular resistance (i.e., the tissue is less stiff) which is postulated to not only improve the quality of the muscle contraction, [58] but also help reduce the mechanical overload on muscle fibres, and consequently reduces the risk and severity of muscle injury. [59, 61]

While the benefits of warming up are reasonably well documented, it would appear from the literature that most golfers do not perform an adequate warm-up. Palmer et al. [62] examined the typical warm-up habits of a convenience sample of male and female Canadian golfers with an average age of 70 years. The large majority of this group of 100 recreational players utilized a very short warm-up and stretching period of five minutes or less – only 8% of the total sample would be considered as having adequately stretched. Fradkin et al. [63], in a survey of 304 golfers in the United States, found that only 18% of the sample performed an adequate warm-up. These authors also reported that golfers who did not adequately warm-up were 1.3 times more likely to have suffered a golf related injury. Gosheger et al. [6] also reported that only 19% of golfers surveyed in their European study warmed up appropriately, and that these golfers reported 60% less injuries than the golfers who did not warm-up.

There has been very little scientific investigation into what constitutes the ideal warm-up for golf. As a result, we have attempted to incorporate an evidence-based approach to help outline an appropriate pre-activity warm-up strategy for the typical player. An appropriate warm-up should last a minimum of 10 minutes [9, 63] and can be broken down into four sections:

General Body Warm-Up. An effective method for initiating the warm-up is by low-intensity activity that uses as many of the large muscle groups as possible. Muscle contractions produce heat that in turn is transported by the blood vessels to other parts of the body resulting in an increase in body temperature. Examples of good warm-up exercises are: brisk walking, climbing a flight of stairs, or simply placing a club behind your back and carefully rotating from side-to-side for a few minutes. One very good tip for golfers is to park at the far end of the parking lot when they arrive at the golf course. This longer walk to the clubhouse will help start the warm-up process.

Stretching. Pre-activity stretching remains a controversial topic among research scientists and medical and fitness practitioners. Shrier [64], in his systematic review of the effects of stretching on performance, reported that most studies investigating acute static stretching show no immediate beneficial effects and in one case stretching had a detrimental effect on jumping performance. However, he did acknowledge that regular stretching appeared to have desirable long-term performance and injury prevention effects. In a similar review, Thacker et al. [59] concluded that there was insufficient evidence to suggest that warm-up stretching would equate to increased performance and injury protection. However, the authors conceded that warm-up stretching did appear to improve flexibility which in turn should have some desirable health benefit. Meanwhile, Neuberger et al. [65] reported that performance in a number of sporting activities involving strength and speed improved when vigorous stretching related to the activity was undertaken as part of the warm-up.

Woods et al. [58] reported that the controversy surrounding the protection benefits of pre-activity stretching may relate to the type of injury that is being studied. Amako et al. [66] found that, although the warm-up stretching had no significant effect on bone or joint injuries, it did decrease the incidence of muscle-related injuries. Bixler and Jones [67] in a study of football injuries, also found that while stretching and warm-up had no significant effect on overall injury rate, there was a statistically significant reduction in musculotendinous injuries in the quarter of the game immediately following the stretching intervention.

Investigation into the health and performance benefits of static stretching immediately prior to golfing activities is quite limited. Fradkin et al. [68] compared clubhead speed in a group of ten golfers who performed static stretching as the main part of a warm-up routine with a matched control group of golfers who did not perform warm-up exercises. Results showed that the group performing the warm-up stretches clearly demonstrated immediate and longer term improvements in clubhead speed compared to the control group that did not warm-up. To date there have not been any golf-specific studies that have directly investigated the influence of static stretching on injury prevention, but a survey of 304 golfers by Fradkin and colleagues [63] revealed that golfers who did not adequately warm-up were 1.3 times more likely to have suffered a golf related injury.

As mentioned previously, pre-activity stretching remains controversial. However, it is the opinion of these authors that based on the literature that is currently available on this topic, there is insufficient evidence to eliminate stretching from the warm-up routine. Perhaps the most reasonable approach to take until additional research is completed is to avoid excessive, vigorous stretching immediately prior to playing. Stretching may be broken down into two types, static and dynamic. Dynamic stretching has been included in the next section.

Static stretching should occur within the 15 minutes immediately preceding an activity in order to have the optimal lengthening benefit of the stretch. [58] The key muscles used in the golf swing should be targeted. This would include muscles of the back, hip, groin, hamstrings, quadriceps, calves, neck, shoulders and forearms. Incorporating a rotational element to the stretch would help mimic some of the more apparent golf swing motions. Each stretch should be gently held for 10 to 20 seconds. Pain should not be experienced. Pre-game stretching exercises for golf can be found at www.fitforegolf.com.

Golf-Specific Dynamic Stretching. The aim of this portion of the warm-up is to further increase body temperature while at the same time help reduce tissue resistance associated with the specific motion of the golf swing. These repetitive movements are believed to help improve the quality of movement while also reducing the risk of injury. [69] Dynamic stretching should start with gently swinging a short iron back and forth. Gradually build up the tempo until you feel loose, and then add resistance by gently swinging two clubs at once. Since elite golfers tend to demonstrate asymmetrical side-to-side trunk rotation flexibility and strength [18, 51], it is important, from a muscle balance, coordination and injury prevention perspective, that warm-up swings be performed *both* left- and right-handed.

Practice. If a driving range or hitting area is available, take time to practice your shots. This further helps loosen-up the golf muscles, and helps improve timing and consistency. Start with a short club such as a wedge and only hit 20-yard shots to begin. Build up to longer shots and add longer clubs.

MAINTAIN PROPER FLUID HYDRATION

Water is an essential nutrient and our bodies are comprised of over 60% fluid. It only takes about a 3% loss in body weight from dehydration before performance is affected. [70]

The primary function of body water is to act as a coolant. Sweating allows us to cool off, but if the fluid lost is not replaced, the amount of sweat produced gradually decreases and causes us to overheat. As we become dehydrated, our blood thickens causing the heart to work harder as it tries to maintain circulation. This results in premature fatigue and poor performance. These effects are further compounded the older we get due to the natural decrease in the body's fluid volume that occurs with age [71]. This can even progress to serious symptoms of heat stroke if appropriate fluid intake is not maintained. It is worth noting that alcoholic beverages are not recommended for hydration maintenance or replenishment due to their diuretic properties. [70]

ROLE OF PRE-SEASON ASSESSMENTS

There is much interest, yet minimal scientific investigation, into the role of pre-season fitness assessments in preventing injury. These assessments, typically performed by physical therapists or fitness personnel with golf biomechanics training, involve a number of strength and flexibility tests to key parts of the musculoskeletal system. Elite athletes in particular use these assessments to help identify physical deficiencies that if left untreated may compromise performance or potentially cause injuries. As mentioned, prospective studies have yet to be completed on the effectiveness of pre-season assessments in preventing injuries. However, Evans et al. [72] recently conducted a prospective study investigating a number of potential musculoskeletal risk factors for low-back pain (LBP) in a population of elite golfers. The authors found that golfers who demonstrated a side-to-side difference of greater than 12 seconds in the ability to hold a static side-bridge position and those with tight hip flexor muscles were more likely to report LBP in the season following the pre-season assessment. It was postulated that if the golfers had corrected the hip flexibility and trunk endurance deficiencies through exercise, they may have avoided LBP.

KNOW YOUR LIMITS

The old saying "no pain no gain" remains one of the largest misconceptions in sport medicine. Pain is part of the body's incredibly important and valuable warning system. It alerts us when tissue damage is occurring so we can take evasive action and hopefully avoid serious injury. Thus, there are several key patterns of discomfort that represent signals to which golfers should pay attention. The first is sudden onset (called acute) pain. Pain that occurs quite suddenly and persists in an area is a key indicator that something has gone wrong and to take appropriate action before the situation gets worse (e.g., sudden back pain immediately after taking a swing).

A second important pattern is severity. The more it hurts, the more likely a serious injury has occurred. A good rule of thumb is if a golfer is grimacing from the pain, then he or she should not continue playing. Finally, one of the trickiest patterns to decipher is intermittent or recurring pain. We have all experienced "nagging" injuries which come and go. In fact, this is a common pattern with many golf injuries. A good guide is if mild pain returns consistently with activity and is in the same general location, golfers should pay attention and take some appropriate action (e.g., warm-up properly, apply ice after activity, have their technique checked). However, if the pain seems to grow in intensity with lesser amounts of effort or comes on earlier in each round; it is time to stop and have it properly investigated.

SEEK PROFESSIONAL GUIDANCE

Poor swing mechanics are a common cause of injury amongst recreational golfers. [8] Examples of differences in swing techniques demonstrated by less-skilled golfers include: less left shoulder horizontal adduction and right shoulder external rotation ROM at the top of the backswing; more left elbow flexion and less forearm supination at impact, and a reduced shoulder-to-hip separation throughout the swing. [22] Since proper technique that is appropriately matched to the physical characteristics and abilities of the individual may help reduce injury susceptibility, taking a lesson from a certified golf professional can be an important first step towards injury prevention. It is interesting to note that a study by Theriault et al. [9] showed that players reporting golf-related injuries attended significantly fewer golf lessons than the subgroup of uninjured players.

If a golfing client already has an injury which originated or is aggravated by golf, it is also time to see a physician or physiotherapist experienced in golf biomechanics who can provide personalized advice on appropriate treatment remedies for specific problems. Ideally, golf educators and healthcare providers should work collaboratively when working with an injured client. This is becoming more common-place with elite level players across North America, Europe and Australia and is starting to filter down to the recreational player.

CONCLUSION

It is important to recognize that injuries from golf are quite common and that many of these injuries can become chronic. As such, injury prevention is extremely important for all golfers irrespective of skill. Golfers need to be proactive in preparing their body properly, having their swing checked to ensure they are using equipment and an appropriate technique that is suited to their physical characteristics, and listening to their body to recognize "when to say when". If there is a problem, they should seek the advice of a health-care professional experienced in golf biomechanics. Proper attention to prevention will ensure a lifetime of enjoyable golf "par"ticipation.

REFERENCES

1. McCarroll, J.R., The Frequency of Golf Injuries, *Clinics in Sport Medicine*, 1996, 15, 1- 7.

2. Cameron, C., Craig, C.L., Stephens, T. and Ready, T.A., Physical Activity Monitor: Increasing Physical Activity: Supporting an Active Workforce. 2001, Canadian Fitness and Lifestyle Research Institute, http://www.cflri.ca/pdf/e/2001pam.pdf, Website Accessed on March 17, 2009.

3. Cann, A.P., Lindsay, D.M. and Vandervoort. A.A., Optimizing the Benefits versus Risks of Golf Participation by Older People, *Journal of Geriatric Physical Therapy*, 2005, 28, 85-92.

4. Fradkin, A.J., Windley, T.C., Myers, J.B., Sell, T.C. and Lephart, S.M., Describing the Epidemiology and Associated Age, Gender and Handicap Comparisons of Golfing Injuries, *International Journal of Injury Control and Safety Promotion*, 2007, 14, 264-266.

5. Nesbit, S.M. and Serrano, M., Work and Power Analysis of the Golf Swing, *Journal of Sports Science and Medicine*, 2005, 4, 520-533.

6. Gosheger, G., Liem, D., Ludwig, K., Greshake, O. and Winkelmann, W., Injuries and Overuse Syndromes in Golf, *American Journal of Sports Medicine*, 2003, 31, 438-443.

7. McHardy, A., Pollard, H. and Luo, K., Golf Injuries: A Review of the Literature, *Sports Medicine*, 2006, 36, 171-187.

8. McCarroll, J.R., Rettig, A.C. and Shelbourne, K.D., Injuries in the Amateur Golfer, *The Physician and Sportsmedicine*, 1990, 18, 122-126.

9. Thériault, G. and Lachance, P., Golf Injuries: An Overview, *Sports Medicine*, 1998; 26, 43-57.

10. McCarroll, J.R. and Gioe, T.J., Professional Golfers and the Price They Pay, *The Physician and Sportsmedicine*, 1982, 10, 64-70.

11. Kumar, S., Cumulative load as a risk factor for back pain. *Spine*, 1990, 15, 1311-1316.

12. Norman, R., Wells, R., Neumann, P., Frank, J., Shannon, H. and Kerr, M., A Comparison of Peak vs. Cumulative Physical Work Exposure Risk Factors for the Reporting of Low Back Pain in the Automotive Industry, *Clinical Biomechanics*, 1998, 13, 561-573.

13. Miranda, H., Viikari-Juntura, E., Heistaro, S., Heliövaara, M. and Riihimäki, H., A Population Study on Differences in the Determinants of a Specific Shoulder Disorder versus Nonspecific Shoulder Pain Without Clinical Findings, *American Journal of Epidemiology*, 2005, 161, 847-855.

14. Waters, T., Yeung, S., Genaidy, A., Callaghan, J., Barriera-Viruet, H. and Deddens, J., Cumulative Spinal Loading Exposure Methods for Manual Material Handling Tasks. Part 1: Is Cumulative Spinal Loading Associated with Lower Back Disorders?, *Theoretical Issues in Ergonomics Science*, 2006, 7, 113-130.

15. Hosea, T.M., Gatt, C.J., Galli, K.M. and Gertner, E., Biomechanical Analysis of the Golfer's Back, in: Stover C.N., McCarroll J.R. and Mallon W.J., eds., *Feeling up to Par: Medicine from Tee to Green*, F.A. Davis Co., Philadelphia, 1994, 97-108.

16. Hosea, T.M., Gatt, C.J., Galli, K.M. et al., Biomechanical Analysis of the Golfer's Back, in: Cochran, A.J., ed. *Science and Golf*, Chapman & Hall, London, 1990, 43-48

17. Jobe, F.W. and Pink, M.M., Shoulder Pain in Golf, *Clinics in Sports Medicine*, 1996, 15, 55-63.

18. Lindsay, D.M. and Horton, J.F., Comparison of Spine Motion in Elite Golfers With and Without Low Back Pain, *Journal of Sports Sciences*, 2002, 20, 599-605.

19. Grimshaw, P.N. and Burden, A.M., Case Report: Reduction of Low Back Pain in a Professional Golfer, *Medicine and Science in Sports and Exercise*, 2000, 32, 1667-73.

20.   Bulbulian, R., Ball, K.A. and Seaman, D.R., The Short Golf Backswing: Effects on Performance and Spinal Health Implications, *Journal of Manipulative and Physiological Therapeutics*. 2001, 24, 569-575.

21.   McTeigue, M., Lamb S.R., Mottram R. and Pirozzolo, F., Spine and Hip Motion Analysis During the Golf Swing, in: Cochran, A.J. and Farrally, M.R., eds., *Science and Golf II: Proceedings of the World Scientific Congress of Golf*, E & FN Spon, London, 1994, 50-58.

22.   Zheng, N., Barrentine, S.W., Fleisig, G.S. and Andrews, J.R., Kinematic Analysis of Swing in Pro and Amateur Golfers, *International Journal of Sports Medicine*, 2008, 29, 487-493.

23.   Cheetham, P.J., Martin, P.E., Mottram, R.E. and St. Laurent, B.F., The Importance of Stretching the X-factor in the Downswing of Golf, in: Thomas, P.R., ed., *Optimizing Performance in Golf*, Australian Academic Press Pty. Ltd., Brisbane, 2001, 192-199.

24.   Baliunas, A.J., Hurwitz, D.E., Ryals, A.B., Karrar, A., Case, A.P., Block, J.A. and Andriacchi, T.P., Increased Knee Joint Loads During Walking are Present in Subjects with Knee Osteoarthritis, *Osteoarthritis and Cartilage*, 2002, 10, 573-579.

25.   Lynn, S.K., MacKenzie, H. and Vandervoort, A.A., Frontal Plane Knee Moments During the Golf Swing: Effect of Target Side Foot Position at Address, in: Lutz, R.S., and Crews, D.S. eds., *Science and Golf V. Proceedings of the Fifth World Scientific Congress of Golf*, Energy in Motion, Mesa, AZ, 2008, 13-20.

26.   Kim, D.H., Millett, P.J., Warner, J.P. and Jobe, F.W., Shoulder Injuries in Golf, *American Journal of Sports Medicine*, 2004, 32, 1324-1330.

27.   Nago, M. and Sawada, Y., A Kinematic Analysis of the Golf Swing by Means of Fast Motion Picture in Connection with Wrist Action, *Journal of Sports Medicine*, 1977, 17, 413-418.

28.   Cahalan, T.D., Cooney, W.P. III, Tamai, K. et al., Biomechanics of the Golf Swing in Players with Pathologic Conditions of the Forearm, Wrist, and Hand, *American Journal of Sports Medicine*, 1991, 19, 288-293.

29.   Dalgleish, M.J., Vicenzino, B. and Neal, R.J., Swing Technique Change and Adjunctive Exercises in the Treatment of Wrist Pain in a Golfer: A Case Report, in: Thomas P.R., ed., *Optimizing Performance in Golf*, Australian Academic Press, Brisbane, 2001, 200-223.

30.   Hume, P.A., Keogh, J. and Reid, D., The Role of Biomechanics in Maximising Distance and Accuracy of Golf Shots, *Sports Medicine*, 2005, 35, 429-449.

31.   McCarroll, J.R., Overuse Injuries of the Upper Extremity in Golf, *Clinics in Sport Medicine*, 2001, 20, 469-479.

32.   McHardy, A.J. and Pollard, H.P., Golf and Upper Limb Injuries: A Summary and Review of the Literature, *Chiropractry and Osteopathy*, 2005, 13, 1-7.

33.   Broker, J.P. and Ramey, M.R., Understanding Golf Club Control Through Grip Pressure Measurement, in: Lutz, R.S. and Crews, D.S., *Science and Golf V: Proceedings of the World Scientific Congress of Golf*, Energy in Motion, Mesa, AZ, 2008, 52-59.

34.   Kohn, H.S., Prevention and Treatment of Elbow Injuries in Golf, *Clinics in Sports Medicine*, 1996, 15, 65-83.

35.   Sell, T.C., Abt, J.P. and Lephart, S.M., Physical Activity-Related Benefits of Walking During Golf, in: Lutz, R.S. and Crews, D.S., eds., *Science and Golf V. Proceedings of the Fifth World Scientific Congress of Golf*, Energy in Motion, Mesa, AZ, 2008, 188-194.

36.   Wallace, P. and Reilly, T., Spinal and Metabolic Loading During Simulations of Golf Play, *Journal of Sports Science*, 1993, 11, 511-515.

37.   Broman, G., Johnsson, L. and Kaijser, L. Golf: A High Intensity Interval Activity for Elderly Men, *Aging Clinical and Experimental Research*, 2004, 16, 375-381.

38.   Parkkari, J., Natri, A., Kannus, P. et al., A Controlled Trial of the Health Benefits of Regular Walking on a Golf Course, *American Journal of Medicine*, 2000, 109, 102-108.

39. Lindsay, D.M, Mantrop, S. and Vandervoort, A.A., A Review of Biomechanical Differences Between Golfers of Varied Skill Levels, *Annual Review of Golf Coaching*, 2008, 2, 187-197.

40. Stover, C.N., Wiren, G. and Topaz, S.R., The Modern Golf Swing and Stress Syndromes, *The Physician and Sports Medicine*, 1976, 4, 42-47.

41. Gatt, C.J., Pavol Jr, M.J., Parker, R.D. et al., A Kinetic Analysis of the Knees During a Golf Swing, in: Farrally, M.R. and Cochran, A.J., eds., *Proceedings of the World Scientific Congress of Golf. Science and Golf III*, Human Kinetics, Champaign, IL, 1999, 20-28.

42. Pink, M., Jobe, F.W. and Perry, J., Electromyographic Analysis of the Shoulder During the Golf Swing, *American Journal of Sports Medicine*, 1990, 18, 137-140.

43. Kao, J.T., Pink, M., Jobe, F.W, et al., Electromyographic Analysis of the Scapula Muscles During a Golf Swing, *American Journal of Sports Medicine*, 1995, 23, 19-23.

44. Pink, M., Perry, J. and Jobe, F.W., Electromyographic Analysis of the Trunk in Golfers, *American Journal of Sports Medicine*, 1993, 21, 385-388.

45. Watkins, R.G., Uppal, G.S., Perry, J. et al., Dynamic Electromyographic Analysis of Trunk Musculature in Professional Golfers, *American Journal of Sports Medicine*, 1996, 24, 535-538.

46. Lim, T.Y., Lower Trunk Muscle Activities During the Golf Swing – Pilot Study, *Proceedings of the third North American Congress on Biomechanics*, Waterloo, August 14-18, 1998.

47. Horton, J.F., Lindsay, D.M. and MacIntosh, B.R., Abdominal Muscle Characteristics of Elite Male Golfers With and Without Chronic Low Back Pain, *Medicine and Science in Sports and Exercise*, 2001, 33, 1647-1654.

48. Bechler, J.R., Jobe, F.W., Pink M. et al., Electromyographic Analysis of the Hip and Knee During the Golf Swing, *Clinical Journal of Sport Medicine*, 1995, 5, 162-166.

49. Smith, M., Physical Preparation for Golf: Strategies for Optimising Movement, *Annual Review of Golf Coaching*, 2007, 1, 151-164.

50. Newton, H., Effective Strength Training for Golf: What's the Right Approach? *Annual Review of Golf Coaching*, 2007, 1, 135-140.

51. Lindsay, D.M. and Horton, J.F., Trunk Rotation Strength and Endurance in Healthy Normals and Elite Male Golfers With and Without Low Back Pain, *North American Journal of Sport Physical Therapy*, 2006, 1, 80-91.

52. Thompson, C.J., Effect of Muscle Strength and Flexibility on Club-Head Speed in Older Golfers. in: Thain, E., ed., *Science and Golf IV. Proceedings of the Fifth World Scientific Congress of Golf*, Routledge, London, 2002, 35-44.

53. Neal, R.J., Sprigings, E.J. and Dalgleish, M.J., How has Research Influenced Golf Teaching and Equipment?, in: Thomas, P.R., ed., *Optimizing Performance in Golf*, Australian Academic Press, Brisbane, 2001, 175-191.

54. Lindsay, D.M., Horton, J.F. and Paley, R.D., Trunk Motion of Male Professional Golfers Using Two Different Golf Clubs, *Journal of Applied Biomechanics*, 2002, 18, 366-373.

55. Morgan, D., Cook, F., Banks, S., Sugaya, H. and Moriya, H., The Influence of Age on Lumbar Mechanics During the Golf Swing, in: Farrally, M.R. and Cochran, A.J., eds., *Science and Golf III: Proceedings of the World Scientific Congress of Golf*, Human Kinetics: Champaign, IL, 1999, 120-126.

56. Sugaya, H., Tsuchiya, A., Moriya, H., Morgan, D.A. and Banks, S.A., Low Back Injury in Elite and Professional Golfers: An Epidemiologic and Radiographic Study, in: Farrally, M.R. and Cochran, A.J., eds., *Science and Golf III: Proceedings of the World Scientific Congress of Golf*, Human Kinetics, Champaign, IL, 1999, 83-91.

57. Lindsay, D.M., Hadi, W., Wright, I. and Vandervoort, A.A., Comparison of Perceived Golf Shot Performance, Upper Limb Stress and Ball Flight Characteristics Between Solid and Brush Fiber Hitting Mats, in: Lutz, R.S. and Crews, D.S., eds., *Science and Golf V. Proceedings of the Fifth World Scientific Congress of Golf*, Energy in Motion, Mesa, AZ, 2008, 335-343.

58.   Woods, K., Bishop, P. and Jones E., Warm-Up and Stretching in the Prevention of Muscular Injury, *Sports Medicine*, 2007, 37, 1089-1099.

59.   Thacker, S.B., Gilchrist, J., Stroup, D.F. and Kimsey Jr., C.D., The Impact of Stretching on Sports Injury Risk: A Systematic Review of the Literature, *Medicine and Science in Sports and Exercise*, 2004, 36, 371-378.

60.   Versteegh, T.H., Vandervoort, A.A., Lindsay, D.M. and Lynn, S.K., Fitness, Performance and Injury Prevention Strategies for the Senior Golfer, *Annual Review of Golf Coaching*, 2008, 2, 199-214.

61.   Sarfran, M.R., Seaber, A.V. and Garret, W.E., Warm-Up and Muscular Injury Prevention: An Update, *Sports Medicine*, 1989, 8, 239-249.

62.   Palmer, J.L., Young, S.D., Fox, Lindsay, D.M. and Vandervoort, A.A., Senior Recreational Golfers: A Survey of Musculoskeletal Conditions, Playing Characteristics and Warm-Up Patterns, *Physiotherapy Canada*, 2003, 55, 79-85.

63.   Fradkin, A.J., Windley, T.C., Myers, J.B., Sell, T.C. and Lephart, S.M., Describing the Warm-up Habits of Recreational Golfers and the Associated Injury Risk, in: Lutz, R.S. and Crews, D.S., eds., *Science and Golf V. Proceedings of the Fifth World Scientific Congress of Golf*, Energy in Motion, Mesa, AZ, 2008, 112-119.

64.   Shrier, I., Does Stretching Improve Performance? A Systematic and Critical Review of the Literature, *Clinical Journal of Sports Medicine*, 2004, 14:267-273.

65.   Neuberger, T., What the Research Quarterly Says About Stretching, *Journal of Physical Education, Recreation and Dance*, 1969, 40, 75-77.

66.   Amako, M., Oda, T., Masuoka, K. et al., Effect of Static Stretching on Prevention of Injuries for Military Recruits, *Military Medicine*, 2003, 168, 442-446.

67.   Bixler, B. and Jones, R.L., High-School Football Injuries: Effects of a Post-Halftime Warm-Up and Stretching Routine, *Family Practice Research Journal*, 1992, 12:131-139.

68.   Fradkin, A.J., Improving Golf Performance with a Warm Up Conditioning Programme, *British Journal of Sports Medicine*, 2004, 38, 762-765.

69.   Weerapong, P., Hume, P.S. and Kolt, G.S., Stretching: Mechanisms and Benefits for Sport Performance and Injury Prevention, *Physical Therapy Reviews*, 2004, 9, 189-206.

70.   Wilmore, J.L., Costill, D.H. and Kenney, W.L., *Physiology of Sport and Exercise*, 4th edn., Human Kinetics, Champaign, IL, 2008.

71.   Lindsay, D.M., Horton, J.F. and Vandervoort, A.A., A Review of Injury Characteristics, Aging Factors and Prevention Programs for the Older Golfer, *Sports Medicine*, 2000, 30, 89-103.

72.   Evans, K., Refshauge, K.M., Adams, R. and Aliprandi, L., Predictors of Low Back Pain in Young Elite Golfers: A Preliminary Study, *Physical Therapy in Sport*, 2005, 6, 122-130.

Sport Psychology, Hypnosis and Golf

Simon Jenkins
Carnegie Faculty of Sport and Education,
Leeds Metropolitan University, Leeds, LS6 3QS, UK
E-mail: S.P.Jenkins@Leedsmet.ac.uk

ABSTRACT

Hypnosis has received relatively little attention in the academic and professional sport psychology literature and concerns have been expressed about its use. Nevertheless, there are numerous websites advertising products and services related to hypnosis and golf. The purpose of this article is to provide a resource for practitioners to reflect on their provision of services related to hypnosis. Hypnosis has been highly controversial since the 18th Century when a medical student by the name of Mesmer learned of how a Jesuit priest successfully cured his patients with magnets applied to their bodies. In the 19th Century, the notion that hypnosis involves a different state of mind; i.e., hypnotic trance, became established in science and it was not until the 1940s that this notion was seriously questioned by scientists. In this article, alternative theoretical viewpoints of hypnosis are presented with particular reference to the stage hypnosis and NLP work of Paul McKenna.

Key words: Beliefs, History of Hypnosis, Mind Control, NLP, Paul McKenna, Self-Hypnosis, Stage Hypnosis, Trance

INTRODUCTION

The aim of this target article is to encourage practitioners in golf psychology (or sports psychologists/hypnotherapists who work with golfers) to reflect on how they use the term 'hypnosis' and how they inform their clients about their use of hypnosis. In doing do, it is hoped that practitioners will be able to provide case studies/anecdotes that shed light on the myths, misconceptions, expectations and fears about hypnosis. It also aims to stimulate experts in ethics to provide insights about issues related to hypnosis. The article is based on the thesis that an understanding of hypnosis needs to be historical and theoretical. The dominant, alternative theoretical viewpoints are presented with regard to stage hypnosis and, in particular, the career of Paul McKenna when he faced a legal challenge from a man who believed that his schizophrenia was triggered by McKenna's stage hypnosis show.

HYPNOSIS, MIND CONTROL AND SELF-BELIEF

Tony Jacklin found it difficult to cope with his 'defeat' to Lee Trevino in the 1972 British Open. On occasion, he used valium to help him sleep. He was so desperate about his state of mind before one tournament in 1977 that he subjected himself to hypnosis from a doctor in London:

> "He sat me in a chair, told me to shut my eyes, relax, and imagine I was doing something nice that I enjoyed. He said, 'it's a lovely day, your're cutting the grass in a straight line, your wife has got a nice cold lager waiting for you' – but none of it worked." [1, p. 60]

Jacklin attributed his problems to poor putting:

> "I got to the point that when I was over a six inch putt I visualised muffing it, I couldn't knock the ball in smoothly. Every single part of every game was an effort because I had a conflict between a will to want to do it and an almost bigger will not allowing me to do it." [1, p. 83]

Jacklin then sought a woman called Rene Kurunsky, a scientologist, who had helped him in the mid-1960s when he was suffering from poor putting in South Africa. Following a recommendation by Kurunsky, Jacklin and his wife spent a few days of 1977 at the College of Scientology in East Grinstead (England, UK) in order to be 'audited'. In scientology, auditing is a form of counselling which is designed to detect and remove 'engrams' – the "subconscious residues of traumatic experiences, accumulated during reincarnations, which hinder the spirit from expressing its unadulterated goodness" [2]. Jacklin found auditing to be an infuriating but enjoyable experience: "Although the woman drove me bananas at times and it pissed me off the hours I spent, I enjoyed it because you use your own mind." [1, p. 84].

Scientology, founded by science-fiction writer Ron Hubbard, has been regarded as a religious cult. During the first few weeks of joining a cult, a person typically enjoys a honeymoon phase and is treated like royalty. [3, p. 50] It appears that Jacklin was treated in this way:

> "While we were at the College, we weren't allowed to drink and you're supposed to have seven hours' sleep a night and never go hungry. I felt fantastic after five hours' auditing a day for four days, not just about my problem, but I was so aware of everything…" [1, p. 84]

Jacklin described Scientology beliefs and explained his putting problem as follows:

> "The belief in Scientology is that we're all a spirit first. Rene always reckons I've got a fantastic spirit which makes me what I am. Your spirit is your soul – a thetan – and it goes on, and has gone on forever. … The spirit is the person and the mind can get in the way. …
> "The problem is that sportsmen need to be more childlike because there's no fear in children. The same as if I want to throw something I throw it

naturally, I don't have to think about it, I let it go. When we're childlike and let it happen rather than make it happen, that's when it will happen right. My reaction to what had been fed into my mind had affected my thinking, my clarity, but I benefited immediately when I admitted I was negative."
[1, p. 85]

The Church of Scientology was an outgrowth of a movement that came into being with the incorporation of the Hubbard Dianetic Research Foundation in 1950. [4, 5] Dianetics has been described as a "melange of Eastern mysticism, Freudian psychoanalysis, and a fair amount of pseudo-science" [6]. As a brief illustration of the Eastern influence, it has been argued that Scientology's notion of 'thetan' is similar to Buddhist notions of spirit or self. With regard to Freud, it has been argued that through hypnotism, Hubbard believed that he had confirmed Freud's idea that earlier trauma holds later trauma in place. [4] In the quotation above from Jacklin, there is reference to 'clarity'. An individual who has successfully completed Dianetic auditing is called a 'Clear', because engrams have been purged from the 'reactive mind'. Engrams are only recorded during periods of physical or emotional suffering, during which the 'analytical mind' shuts off and the 'reactive mind' is turned on. [7] The 'analytical mind' is that part of the mind which enables problems to be perceived and solved in an effective manner. The 'somatic mind' is directed by either the analytical mind or the reactive mind, and places solutions into effect on the physical level. [7]

As stated above, Scientology has been regarded as a religious cult. While some religious cults are based on the bible or Eastern religion, others are based on the occult or (like Scientology) on the ideas of their leader. Cult mind control is a system that disrupts an individual's identity. Personal identity includes beliefs, thoughts, emotions and behaviours. Mind control involves the use of hypnotic processes (e.g., repetition of words/behaviour and forced attention) in combination with group dynamics and behaviour modification (e.g., conformity and obedience to authority) to break a person down and then indoctrinate that person with new ideas.[1]

The individual is deceived and manipulated into accepting the beliefs of the cult and to conform to a certain type of personality. [3, p. 54; p. 67; p. 179]

It is ironic that Tony Jacklin may have unwittingly have exposed himself to hypnotic processes in Scientology that were potentially more powerful than those he

---

[1]It has been claimed that Hubbard wrote a manual on brainwashing and offered to sell his brainwashing techniques to the FBI. [4] It should be noted, however, that 'mind control' is not the same as 'brainwashing'. The term 'brainwashing' was first used in 1951 to describe how American servicemen captured in the Korean War suddenly reversed their values and allegiances, and believed they had committed fictional war crimes. [3, p. 55] Mind control involves little or no overt physical abuse, but brainwashing is typically coercive. [3, p. 55] In 1974 a small hippy terrorist cult called the Symbionese Liberation Army (SLA) kidnapped Patty Hearst, grand-daughter and heiress of the newspaper multi-millionaire William Randolph Hearst. When kidnapped, Patty Hearst was locked for weeks in a dark closet. She was starved, raped and brainwashed into becoming an active member of the cult with a new identity. The cult convinced her that the FBI was hunting her. The SLA was founded by student activists in San Francisco and was dedicated to overthrowing what it saw as the 'police state' in America. Under her new identity, Hearst participated in a bank robbery, for which she was convicted and served a jail term despite claiming that she had been brainwashed by the SLA. [3, p. 55] She served two years of a seven-year sentence, after which President Jimmy Carter intervened to commute her sentence. [8]

was earlier exposed to in a medical context before the Uniroyal tournament in 1977. In either case, Jacklin's account suggests that he is not one of the estimated 10-20% of the population that is highly hypnotisable. While there is evidence that Jacklin subscribed to some of Scientology's beliefs, it does not appear that his personal identity was terribly disrupted:

> "At the end they tried to get me to go on another course, but I thought, look out, they're getting their claws into you. I'm a pro golfer not a Scientologist, so I didn't want to get involved. ... But I really enjoyed digging into my mind – I got a natural high from it. ...
> Ron Hubbard is incredible. The millions of words he has written mean he's putting down in black and white the finer feelings that I would have. He's using all the right words, that I wouldn't begin to know... I'm not a religious person, but Scientology is as close as anything I've come to that I would believe in concerning the spirit that is in every individual. ...
> Everybody needs to believe in something. If they haven't got a strong belief in themselves, they need something else to hang on to. ... I believe in something – maybe it's me, and someone will say, you selfish bastard. Well, I'm sorry, but that's the way I am." [1, p. 85-87]

HYPNOSIS IN SPORT

Taylor et al. [9] stated that: "the topic of hypnosis in general, and applied to the sports domain in particular, should be approached critically and with caution":

> ...hypnosis is a valuable, powerful, and possibly dangerous tool for professionals in applied sport psychology. The potential benefits may be significant and, at the same time, the potential harm may be profound. As a result, extensive preparation should be required including coursework, training and supervised experience in preparation for use of hypnosis. [9, p. 73]

In contrast to Taylor et al.'s [9] cautionary tone, the Centre for Sports Hypnosis™ defines hypnosis as "a deep state of relaxation, similar to what you might experience in day-dreaming":

> During hypnosis you are still aware of everything around you, but it doesn't interfere with what you're focusing on like it does in a normal wakened state. You're in complete control all of the time, so *you can't be made to do or say anything you don't want to*, and you can come out of it any time you wish. It's a very relaxing feeling, so most people really enjoy the experience. [10, italics added]

From conducting interviews with six sport psychology consultants, "who each possessed training and experience related to hypnosis" [11, p. 368], Jason Grindstaff and Leslee Fisher tackled a number of "guiding questions": i) hypnosis training and experience; ii) stereotypes and misconceptions related to hypnosis; iii) utilizing hypnosis as a performance enhancement technique; iv) advantages and disadvantages of using hypnosis with athletes; and v) cultural considerations related to using hypnosis. [11, p. 372] Three of the themes were: a) whether or not to use the word "hypnosis" in practice with athletes; b) how consultants assessed whether or not to utilize hypnosis; and c) inappropriate use of hypnotic techniques.

While some practitioners used the term "hypnosis" with athletes, others avoided using it. One of the practitioners who tended to avoid using it explained that "when I used the word hypnosis I had to spend a whole session on misconceptions and stuff" [11, p. 376]. Citing the American Psychological Association (APA) and Association for the Advancement of Applied Sport Psychology (AAASP) Ethical Codes of Conduct, Grindstaff and Fisher conclude that "consultants who do not inform clients of the full nature of the consultation process and do not respect client autonomy in the decision-making process are potentially walking an ethical line" [11, p. 377].

Practitioners appeared to vary in the extent to which they might regard hypnosis as being contraindicated in particular cases. For example, one practitioner stated trauma during childhood such as physical abuse would be a contraindication for use of hypnosis.

The theme of "inappropriate use of hypnotic techniques" was regarded as rather serious by the authors; and, in fact, one of the practitioners began to use hypnotic techniques on Grindstaff during the interview without his consent and with no explanation as to why he or she was doing it! [11, p. 382]. Grindstaff and Fisher state:

> Offering unsolicited hypnotic services to an individual who has not entered into mutually agreed upon terms could present a potentially unethical situation; however, a number of practitioners discussed how they often will not inform the athlete that hypnosis is being incorporated into the session. Reasons for not being candid about hypnosis were related to the second guiding question and centered on avoiding the time required to dispel myths and misconceptions regarding hypnosis. [11, p. 381]

In view of the discussion above of Tony Jacklin, it is worth pointing out that one of the practitioners indicated that religion was a factor in his decision-making process about hypnosis with athletes; expressing the belief that some religious groups are "anti-hypnosis": "I tend to think they're the ones that are often seen as very controlling, right wing religions or very much won't allow control over people".[2]

SELF-HYPNOSIS

Some sport psychologists, such as Robert Nideffer, have emphasized self-hypnosis in psychological skills training. Nideffer defines self-hypnosis as "a self-induced state of relaxation that enhances your ability to respond to your own suggestions" and as "a tool to increase your ability to get immersed in what you attend to" [13, back cover]. His reasons for teaching self-hypnosis rather than hetero-hypnosis are:

---

[2]Paul Durbin states that: "Today, most religious groups accept the proper ethical use of hypnosis for helping people. Exceptions are Christian Science, Seventh-Day Adventist and some individuals of various churches. In recent years, the Seventh-Day Adventist have lessened their resistance by using relaxation therapy and suggestion theory." [12]

1. Many people have a stronger belief in hypnosis to help them than they do in relaxation in mental rehearsal. It's also possible that *the word hypnosis carries with it an aura that captures the interest* and helps them focus on their images.
2. With self-hypnosis, you grow to accept control and responsibility. ...the problems about trust and dependency that can develop in relationships with other people (e.g., a hypnotist) are less likely to occur.
3. Self-hypnosis emphasizes that becoming immersed is a skill that you can develop.
4. Self-hypnosis is easily structured so that you can give yourself post-hypnotic suggestions[3] that will facilitate the transfer of your feelings and experiences in the hypnotic state to the actual performance situation.
    [13, p. 86-87; italics added]

Nideffer clearly feels that it is beneficial to couch mental training in a context of hypnosis, even if only 'self-hypnosis'. It is thus interesting to study a book – not dealing specifically with sport – called *Mind Power: Getting What You Want Through Mental Training* by Bernie Zilbergeld and Arnold Lazarus. The authors use the term 'mental training' as a euphemism for self-hypnosis and avoid using the term 'hypnosis' because many Americans are suspicious of hypnosis [14]:

> The essence of mental training is a state called trance, a natural human capacity consisting primarily of a state of focused attention in which we are more receptive than usual to suggestion. This state often comes about spontaneously, where it is used for ends both positive and negative. Practice with the methods in this book will give you control over the state, so that you can enter it at will to achieve goals you desire. [14, p. 18]

Subjects require motivation to practice daily in order to develop self-hypnosis skills, but it is difficult to achieve without guidance from a hypnotist or at least use of tape-recorded suggestions. [14, p. 85; 15, p. 11; 16, 17]

INNER MENTAL TRAINING

An exemplar of self-hypnosis in sport psychology is Lars-Eric Uneståhl's "Inner Mental Training" (IMT), which was developed between 1975 and 1979 [18, 19]. IMT involves the use of three audio-cassettes in order to learn relaxation, positive suggestion, concentration, goal programming, anxiety reduction, self-confidence and assertive training, mental rehearsal of competition, and activation and psyching-up. Athletes are encouraged to engage in mental training five days a week, with 10 to 25 minutes per day. The basic programme (using the first two cassettes) involves three months of training, which is recommended to be done during the non-competitive season. Before starting IMT, the athlete reads a booklet that describes the background to it. The third cassette may be used in preparation for competition, but it is recommended that most of the programmes on it should only be used if needed.

---

[3]A post-hypnotic suggestion is a suggestion that is made during hypnosis, but acted upon at some time after hypnosis.

IMT begins with four weeks of relaxation training. The technique used is Edmond Jacobson's Progressive Relaxation [20]. Jacobson hypothesised that if the muscles of the body are relaxed, then anxiety and tension will be dissipated. Progressive relaxation involves systematically tensing and relaxing specific muscle groups in a predetermined order. Once this has been learned, the subject can proceed to relax the muscle without pre-tensing them. IMT also involves elements of autogenic training, which has been widely used by athletes in Europe. [21] Often described as a self-hypnotic technique, autogenic training [22] is most readily associated with Johannes Schultz, who was a German physician. Schultz's interest in the practical application of hypnotic techniques was stimulated by the work in the 1890s of the psychologist Oscar Vogt (see Appendix) at a time when hypnosis was applied to problems such as drug addiction and constipation. [23]. Autogenic training may involve the following self-statement steps:

1. Heaviness in the arms and legs (beginning with the dominant arm or leg)
2. Warmth in the arms and the legs (again, beginning with the dominant arm or leg)
3. Warmth in the chest and perception of a reduced heart rate
4. Calm and relaxed breathing
5. Warmth in the solar plexus area
6. Sensation of coolness on the forehead [24]

It has been suggested that athletes learn each stage before progressing to the next stage. [24] If athletes are having difficulty feeling the appropriate sensation, sometimes learning can be facilitated by having them physically experience the sensation; e.g., immersion in heated water to generate feelings of warmth.

After the first two weeks of IMT, visual imagery is introduced. The athlete creates his own "mental room" in which there is a blackboard for suggestions and a film screen for visualisation. It is assumed that a word or image has much more impact if it is combined with deep relaxation. In the fifth week, the athlete makes positive suggestions with associated imagery. This is called the "conditioning of C (competition) words" (calm, committed, concentrated, confident, and consistent). The sixth week involves "dissociation and detachment training" in which relaxation techniques, in particular the mental room, are used as a way of dealing with distractions. The seventh and eighth weeks involve "ideomotor training", of which one of the applications is for programming goals, using either suggestions or images. The ninth and tenth weeks involve problem-solving techniques such as cognitive restructuring and systematic desensitisation in order to create new and positive experiences of situations, which previously have been associated with failure, during deep relaxation. The eleventh week is self-confidence and assertive training. It is based on the premise that negative expectations about performance are best changed by changing a person's self-image and this can be done in a "dissociative state where reality testing and analytical thinking is put aside". Unesthal uses the traditional view of hypnosis that the subconscious (where the self-image is 'housed') can be influenced by "ego-strengthening suggestions". The twelfth week involves concentration training; specifically, developing two 'triggers'. A trigger is something you do or think in order to produce an effect, which cannot be created directly. In the third week of IMT, the athlete will have learned a trigger for rapid induction of relaxation (making a fist of the left hand, taking a deep breath and then exhaling). For concentration training, 'Trigger 1' is a movement or act, which is part of the athlete's normal pre-performance routine. Examples of such triggers used by athletes who have gone through IMT are gripping the club (golf) and bouncing the ball (tennis). The aim is to increase the conditioning between the trigger and concentration by using former experiences of being fully concentrated. Posthypnotic suggestion is involved in this part of IMT; the effect of a trigger will spontaneously manifest itself in competition without the athlete having to think about the trigger. Trigger 2 is for use only when normal induction of concentration fails. It could be a movement, a deep breath, a specific word or an image.

The third cassette is concerned with mental preparation for competition. It includes activation training and psyching up, mental rehearsal of competition, and programming of the 'ideal performing state' (the 'winning feeling'). Activation training makes a conditioning between activation (positive stimulation/tension increase) and two other triggers: inhalation (for quick and short-term effects) and the "energy machine" in the "inner mental room" (for a longer-lasting activation).

Mental rehearsal of competition is intended to replace anxiety with the 'ideal performing feeling' by reliving a 'model competition' in the past and the familiarising the body and mind with the future competition.

Programming the 'winning feeling' involves the use of posthypnotic suggestion – the suggestions are programmed during deep relaxation, but take effect during competition. This involves use of the inner mental room. Athletes can also give themselves suggestions in a wakeful state. In this case, the suggestions should be converted into a rhythmical formula before competition occurs without "thinking of or analysing the content". Unestahl advises that, at least initially, suggestions should be made through a recorded programme so then "all you have to do is relax and let the suggestions penetrate".

HYPNOSIS: POPULAR BELIEFS AND FEARS

Beliefs about hypnosis are ingrained in everyday psychology and popular psychology. Hypnosis captures the public imagination, and is often feared, because it is perceived to belong, at least partly, in the realm of the paranormal. Hypnosis has featured in both literature (e.g., in the novel *Trilby*) and in Hollywood movies (e.g., The *Manchurian Candidate*).

The 19th century novel *Trilby* by George du Maurier concerned a woman who became a famous singer after being hypnotised by Svengali – but Trilby's dependence on Svengali was such that when he became ill, her voice disappeared. Furthermore, when he died, she became hopelessly demented. Svengali is described as both a demon and a magician by his friend Gecko. [25, p. 352] He sought people to cheat, betray, exploit, borrow money from, make brutal fun of, or bully. Trilby's "singularly impressionable nature" made her readily susceptible to "Svengali's hypnotic influence" [25, p. 58]. Svengali literally mesmerised Trilby, making passes with his hands on her head and face, inducing eye catalepsy. [25, p. 54] Svengali would not allow Trilby to sing without him; nor even would he be parted from her for a minute or trust her out of his sight. [25, p. 298]

In movies *The Manchurian Candidate* [28, 29], based on the novel by Richard Condon [26], an American solider is returned to American society having been programmed by a communist hypnotist to respond to a post-hypnotic trigger, commit murder and not remember it later.

Hypnosis tends to be feared mainly because of stage hypnotists, who use it to make fools of volunteer subjects. [29] Common fears include:

> Hypnosis involves dabbling with the occult.
> Hypnosis turns you into a zombie.
> Hypnosis puts you under the control of the hypnotist.
> Hypnosis makes you dependent on the hypnotist.
> Hypnosis can make you do things you would never normally do.
> Hypnosis can trigger serious mental or physical illness.

Hypnotic phenomena are regularly reported in the national press. The work of Paul McKenna, the most well-known stage hypnotist/hypnotherapist in Britain, has featured strongly in British newspapers since the 1990s. As a consequence of a High Court case concerning one of his stage hypnosis shows, McKenna appeared to change his theoretical beliefs about hypnosis – from what he calls the 'Trance' theory (a traditional view) to the 'Social Compliance' theory (a challenge to the traditional view).

THEORIES OF HYPNOSIS
HYPNOSIS: THE TRADITIONAL VIEW
During the period from the end of the First World War to the end of the 1950s, the most commonly adopted conceptual and theoretical frameworks for hypnosis reflected late nineteenth-century thought. Psychotherapy was dominated by psychoanalysis, especially the work of Sigmund Freud, thus clinical hypnotism went into decline. In the early 1960s, the 'traditional view of hypnosis' (i.e., that reflecting late-nineteenth century thought) was challenged in what has been called the Barber Revolution. [30, p. 581]

Histories of hypnosis[4] have almost always taken each of the following notions to be axiomatic:

1. The term 'hypnosis' refers to a denotable state or condition of the person (c.g., 'trance state').
2. This state can be induced (at least in susceptible individuals) by certain identifiable rituals labelled 'hypnotic induction procedures'.
3. The hypnotic state induced by these rituals possesses at least some invariant or essential properties, which are independent of the means by which the trance is induced or the person's in when the state is induced. [31, p. 43]

---

[4]A historical overview of hypnosis, based on key individuals such as Mesmer, is shown in the Appendix. It shows that controversy has always been part-and-parcel of phenomena related to hypnosis.

Essential properties of the hypnotic state are: i) uncritical (or at least increased) acceptance of (or responsiveness to) suggestion; ii) the subject that he or she is hypnotised; and iii) being able to report hypnotic phenomena.

Hypnotic phenomena can be described as natural behavioural and experiential manifestations of the trance state, including subjectively experienced psychological events (such as remembering, forgetting, distortions in one's sense of time, and alterations in perception) as well as observable events (such as arm levitation). [32]

HYPNOSIS: CHALLENGE TO THE TRADITIONAL VIEW

The first modern theorist to explicitly reject the notion that hypnotic responding requires an explanation in terms of altered states of consciousness was Sarbin [33], who built upon White's [34] notion that hypnotic responding is goal directed. [35, p. 324]

White [34] has been regarded as a watershed in theorising about hypnosis in that he clearly recognised not only the goal-directed nature of hypnotic responding, but also the limitations of mechanistic notions such as ideo-motor action. [31, p. 64] Sarbin [33] used a dramaturgical (theatre) model to explain hypnosis, with the concept of 'role' being central:

> ...any role is enacted in a context, a narrative, involving another person. And because people have the power of imagination (i.e., silently acting as if) they can construct stories about themselves. [36, p. 304]

In the early 1960s, Theodore X. Barber began his important work on hypnosis. His early research was an attack on the 'traditional view of hypnosis'. Barber's [37] major criticisms of the 'state' (trance) concept have been summarised as follows:

1. Logical circularity – hypnotic responsiveness can both indicate the existence of a hypnotic state and be explained by it;
2. Hypnotic induction is not necessary for the production of a wide variety of phenomena associated with hypnosis. [38, p. 602]

With regard to the second point, a common trick of stage hypnotists is the 'human plank' in which a hypnotised subject is told she is a wooden plank and laid across two chairs, with her neck on one and her ankles on another. The audience is impressed because it assumes that the feat could not have been performed without the aid of hypnosis. [39] Actually, it can be done in the absence of hypnosis. Either way, while many people are capable of it, there have been anecdotal reports of spinal injuries. [14] Even if the behaviour that occurs in the hypnotic setting also occurs in non-hypnotic settings, however, there is still the question of why the behaviour occurs in the hypnotic setting. [40, p. 544]

Barber distinguished between 'Trance A' (various degrees of relaxation, calmness, passivity and unconcern or detachment from reality) and 'Trance B' (absorption, involvement in the ideas and words communicated by the hypnotist). [41, p. 53] Barber argues that Trance B is an essential part of hypnotic responding (as opposed to faking), but that Trance A is not. [41, p. 53]

Barber later developed a 'cognitive-behavioural' theory of hypnosis based on the premise that "subjects carry out so-called hypnotic behaviours when they have positive attitudes, motivations and expectations toward the test situation which lead to a willingness to think and imagine with the themes that are suggested" [42, p. 5].

Nicholas Spanos' socio-cognitive approach was built on a framework provided by Barber and also by Theodore R. Sarbin. Hypnosis is regarded as a "historically and culturally rooted social construction" as to how hypnotists and hypnotised subjects are supposed to act and feel while enacting their respective roles. [31, p. 44] Hypnotic subjects are regarded as agents who are "attuned to contextual demands and who guide their behaviour in terms of their understandings of situational contingencies and in terms of the goals they wish to achieve." [35, p. 324]

Other non-state theories include Response Expectancy theory, which follows Social Learning theory in proposing that hypnotic behaviour is predicted by the expectancy that it will lead to particular outcomes and by the value of these outcomes to the individual. Subjects may devise and implement various cognitive strategies in order to achieve the goal of experiencing hypnotic suggestions. [43, p. 439, cited by 38, p. 602]

A further criticism of the 'special-state' (trance) concept is the fact that unique physiological markers of the hypnotic state have not been identified. [38, p. 602] The finding that the brain shows electrical changes during hypnosis and that brain waves under hypnosis differ from 'normal' waking consciousness is irrelevant for establishing hypnosis as a 'special state':

> ...there seems to be a crucial difference between the proposal that a hypnotic subject is in an 'altered state of consciousness' because he or she is, for example, 'relaxed' or 'concentrating' and the idea that there is an altered state we can label 'hypnosis'. [44, p. 366]

Graham Wagstaff, quoted above, thus rejects the notion that there exists a particular brain state or an altered state of consciousness that can be labelled as 'hypnosis'. Furthermore, he argues there is no such state that is somehow important in accounting for phenomena we call 'hypnotic'. Wagstaff [44] rejects the use of terms such as hypnotic trance, and distinctions such as hypnotic vs. waking suggestibility, in favour of a vocabulary that includes terms such as conformity, compliance, belief, attitudes, expectations, attention, concentration, relaxation, distraction, role enactment, and imagination. A hypnotised person is thus one who responds in some way to the procedures designated as 'hypnotic' in a situation or context defined as 'hypnosis'. [44, p. 370]

Hypnotic susceptibility or trance capacity refers to the ability of a subject to achieve a given level of trance. [45, p. 21] Inventories such as the Stanford Hypnotic Susceptibility Scale are used to measure it. Special-state (trance) theorists have provided evidence that a person's hypnotic suggestibility remains stable over a long period of time, despite substantial changes in personal and social circumstances. [46, p. 573]

Non-state theorists argue that hypnotisability is not an unmodifiable trait or capacity. Rather, subjects exhibit dramatic changes in their responsiveness to suggestions as a function of the situation or context. [35, p. 335] Furthermore, there is evidence that hypnotisability can be improved following relevant skill training. Stability in hypnotic responding thus reflects stability in subjects' beliefs and expectations about hypnosis.

While most non-state theorists reject the notion that a unique or special state of consciousness (hypnotic trance) results from a hypnotic induction, they do not deny the subjective reality of the hypnotic experience and nor do they believe that hypnotic responses are necessarily faked or the product of mere compliance. [38, p. 602] From Spanos' non-state viewpoint, for example, subjects sometimes come to interpret their goal-directed, strategic responses as involuntary occurrences [35, p. 327]:

> People in our culture hold relatively well-developed schemas concerning what it means to be 'hypnotised'. Central to these schemas is the belief that the responses to suggestions made by 'hypnotised' subjects are involuntary occurrences. The procedures to which subjects are exposed in the hypnotic test situation usually reinforce the notion that hypnotic responses are involuntary rather than self-initiated action. The most important aspect of the hypnotic test situation is probably the wording of the test suggestions. Suggestions are worded in the passive voice to inform subjects that certain things are happening to them. [35, p. 327]

The experience of non-volition in the hypnotic situation can be understood as an attributional error; it is perceiving the locus of control as external instead of internal. [39, p. 165] It also reveals "an experienced separation between intent (to comply) and awareness of that intent" [38, p. 611]; subjects may not be conscious of the contextual determinants and cognitive processes that determine their hypnotic experiences. Shor [47] used the notion of 'generalised reality orientation' to argue that information can both exist and be influential either inside or outside a subject's awareness. Generalised reality orientation is "the structured frame of reference in the background of attention which supports, interprets and gives meaning to all experiences" [40, p. 545].

Martin Orne argued that the critical feature of hypnosis in need of explanation is the subject's interpretation and experience of events, rather than the objective features of the situation. [48, cited in 40] Kirsch [43] argued that hypnotic subjects are largely motivated by a desire to experience hypnotic phenomena, and their strategic behaviour is thus aimed primarily at generating those experiences.

Most people report that hypnotic induction produces a normal state of focused attention, rather than an 'altered state of consciousness'. [43, cited by 38] A sense of relaxation is also frequently reported. Consider two highly hypnotisable subjects who received the same suggestions from a hypnotist. One subjects reported *passive* concentration on the words of the hypnotist, and the other subject reported use of personally relevant strategies in an *active* manner in order to experience the suggested effect. [50, cited by 40] It is not the communications themselves that are important, but rather the subject's interpretation of the hypnotist's communications.

One of the longest-running debates in theorising about hypnosis has been that between Ernest Hilgard and Nicholas Spanos. Hilgard's Neodissociation theory postulates subordinate cognitive control structures that are organised hierarchically and controlled by an 'Executive Ego'. Hilgard argued that dissociations of cognitive functioning may occur during hypnotic responding even when the dissociations have not been directly suggested and when neither the hypnotist nor the subjects are aware of their presence. In other words, the subordinate cognitive systems may become somewhat isolated from each other. [51, p. 94-95] In several of Hilgard's experiments, subjects who reported little pain during hypnotic analgesia also reported feeling high levels of pain at the same time. These reports of high pain were supposedly obtained directly from a dissociated part of the hypnotic subject's cognitive system (the 'hidden observer'). In other words, during hypnotic analgesia, the hidden observer continues to feel high levels of pain. It should be noted that the hidden observer reports have been given only when the hypnotist has informed subjects they possess a hidden part that experiences events differently from does their 'normal' self:

> ...hidden observer reports, rather than reflecting unconscious dissociations, reflect role enactments carried out by the subjects who develop expectations concerning the characteristics of hidden-observer responding from the social demands inherent in their experimental test situation. Thus, rather than unambiguously reflecting unconscious dissociations, the findings of hidden observer studies can also be interpreted as providing more support for a view of hypnotic responding as context-supported, goal-directed action.
> [31, p. 70]

Thus notions of unconscious processing and misattribution are not regarded as being mutually exclusive. One critic of Spanos' socio-cognitive approach, Gauld [30], has distinguished between three categories of responding to suggestions: traditional passive responsiveness to suggestion, deliberate use of cognitive strategies, and absorption in or self-deceptive use of cognitive strategies ('gifted fantasy'). [30, p. 605] Some, but not all, 'gifted fantasisers', are good hypnotic subjects. Conversely, not all good hypnotic subjects are gifted fantasisers. Therefore, the sorts of cognitive strategies proposed by Spanos may account for all the behaviour of some, but not all, 'good hypnotic subjects'. The behaviour of other 'good hypnotic subjects' in some or all areas, however, may need other explanations. [30, p. 608] An essential point in Gauld's argument against Spanos' approach is that the 'cognitive strategy' aspect need not be tied to motives concerned with role-playing. [30, p. 604] Nevertheless, it can be seen that there has recently been a convergence in theories of hypnosis, with non-state theorists such as Spanos acknowledging the existence of cognitive strategies.

STAGE HYPNOSIS
A FORM OF ENTERTAINMENT
Hypnosis as a form of entertainment grew out of the popular mesmeric movement in America during the 1840s. By the early 1850s, it had spread into Europe. In the early 1950s, an American hypnotist working in England, Ralph Slater was involved in a court case that he won only on appeal. Not only did it receive considerable coverage

from the tabloid newspapers, but it also prompted attempts to pass a bill through Parliament that would have resulted in stage hypnotism being banned. Eventually, however, the Hypnotism Act (1952) was passed. It demands that all stage hypnotists must possess a license from the appropriate local authority. Paul McKenna has noted, with amusement, that only hypnotists and animal trainers need such licenses to perform! [52, p. 60] Under Home Office guidelines issued in 1989, hypnotists could be fined up to £400 for staging acts in a club or other places of entertainment without permission from the local authority. The statutory controls do not cover hypnotism for "medical, scientific research". In fact, there have been reports of stage hypnotism for 'research purposes' in pubs.

In December 1993, Sharon Tabarn died from a fit soon after she had been told to emerge from a trance at a stage hypnotist's show as if a 10,000 volt electric shock had passed through her chair. [53] Margaret Tabarn, Sharon's mother, has been quoted as saying:

> "Little did the hypnotist know that she had a morbid fear of electricity because she had a bad electric shock at 11. She knew exactly what it was like to have 10 000 volts go through you. I have always stated that it was the suggestion that triggered Sharon's death." [54]

The coroner had found her death to be due to natural causes unconnected with her having been hypnotised. Nevertheless, in January 1994 Margaret Tabarn founded the Campaign against Stage Hypnotism. Backing this campaign was Dr. Prem Misra, a consultant psychiatrist and chairman of the academic committee of the British Society of Medical and Dental Hypnotists. Misra was quoted as saying that stage hypnosis can do lasting emotional and physical damage, with symptoms including headaches, drowsiness, nausea, lack of energy, irritability, fits, the persistence of hypnotic suggestions, spontaneous trance, anxiety, depression, and in some cases full-blown psychosis. [53] One member of the public apparently became a compulsive onion eater after undergoing stage hypnosis and being told to eat onions rather than apples. Another man went into a trance every time someone clapped. Nevertheless, such symptoms cannot be directly linked to stage hypnotism.

In 1995, the Home Office produced a set of guidelines for stage hypnotists on the basis of an investigation into the alleged dangers of stage hypnotism shows. It was concluded that there is no evidence of serious risk to participants in stage hypnotism. [55] The main recommendation of the report was that procedures of the existing 1952 Hypnotism Act should be tightened to ensure that all performances of stage hypnotism are appropriately licensed.

STAGE HYPNOSIS AND PAUL MCKENNA

In 1996, a writ for damages was issued against Paul McKenna by a man who claimed that he suffered a serious mental breakdown after taking part in his stage show. The 28 year-old man, Christopher Gates, claimed that nine days after the show in March 1994 an acute attack of schizophrenia was directly triggered by the stage hypnotism. He was admitted to a psychiatric unit. McKenna was quoted as saying, "Schizophrenia is something people are born with. It can be triggered by absolutely anything, even queuing in the post office or going to the fair." [56] The writ alleged: "The act triggered an immediate post-hypnotic acute schizophrenic illness. This manifested itself in over-awareness and bizarre behaviour." [57] The "over-awareness" apparently included seeing monsters and hearing the voices of Jesus and Moses; "bizarre behaviour" included becoming an obsessive viewer of the television lottery show and the TV soap opera *Coronation Street* [58]. The stage hypnotism has been described as follows:

> In the course of the two and a quarter hour show, during which Mr Gates had been held in a trance for most of the time, including throughout the interval, Mr McKenna had instructed him to take on various personae and to act out different scenarios. As well as impersonating Mick Jagger and a schoolboy, he had been told to believe he was a ballet dancer and used a shoe as a telephone to receive the news that he had won £1 million. Next, Mr Gates had been told to imagine he was a contestant on the television show, Blind Date, conduct an orchestra and work as an interpreter for aliens. [58]

Mr Gates claimed that all McKenna did to bring him out of hypnosis was utter the words "wakey wakey". But McKenna said the 'de-hypnosis' process in all his shows took three minutes and involved music:

> "I ask them to go back in a trance, cast their minds back and remember some of the amusing and happy things we have done.
> "I ask them to realise that all the hypnotic suggestions that were part of the show are now cleared by hypnotic suggestion. I say once again they are masters of their destinies, their normal selves in every way." [59]

Before Christopher Gates volunteered to be hypnotised on stage by Paul McKenna, he had suffered a series of traumatic incidents in his life, including head injury at the age of five when he fell off his bike and being accused of sexually assaulting a 15 year-old girl when he himself was a 15 year-old. Any one of these incidents, claimed McKenna's defence team, could have been responsible for triggering the schizophrenic episodes he was to suffer after the stage hypnotism in 1994. Mr Gates had no family history of mental illness.

Mr Gates' expert witnesses included Professor John Gruzelier from Imperial College, who argued: "Hypnosis involves an uncommon alteration of brain activity." From research involving electroencephalography, Gruzelier concluded that susceptible subjects respond to hypnotism by relaxing some of the brain circuits in the frontal lobes, which usually monitor and plan thoughts and behaviours. After admitting there were everyday conditions where such frontal lobe activity could be found, the judge pointed out that the argument that hypnotism puts the brain in a 'special state' was undermined. The judge ruled that the absence of any recorded similar case made it unlikely that the stress during the stage hypnotism show triggered Mr Gates' disease:

> "Even if there were a connection, the strong probability must be that the

plaintiff was on the point of manifesting the illness in any event and the most the incident could have done was to affect its timing." [54]

EXPLAINING STAGE HYPNOTISM

It has been argued that stage hypnotism is a much more intense experience than medical hypnotism due to subject selection, audience expectation, and the influence of the group on stage. [53] With regard to the subject selection process, it is generally assumed that no more than 20% of the population is able to develop a trance suitable for the stage, but that shows tend to attract a greater proportion of these people. The complex selection process of stage hypnotism is designed to find from the audience the most obedient and compliant individuals who are likely to prove entertaining.

Paul McKenna has described a demonstration of hypnosis on television involving an audience of late-teenagers from which he was going to draw volunteers. These volunteers were initially "far too cool to let some guy get them doing silly things in front of their friends" [52, p. 43]:

> Just before we went on to the air the compère introduced me to the studio audience by saying, "This is Paul McKenna, and he's going to hypnotise some of you in a moment." Fifty people turned to look at me, as if to say, "Oh, yeah? Let's see you then, mate." [52, p. 43]

McKenna described how he had to make the situation less threatening to the audience. He did this by reframing the situation to provide a new, desirable context:

> "You know in our culture a lot of people drink alcohol and take drugs to change the way they feel. Hypnosis is amazing because it is a natural state-changer. You could say it's a natural high."
> Then as an added bonus, I said, "Some people even find it makes them better dancers as well." There was almost a stampeded as they all eagerly volunteered. [52, p. 43-44]

The stage hypnotist may use a suggestibility test such as the 'forward sway test' that involves the subjects standing a couple of feet from the hypnotist while looking into his or her eyes, and letting themselves fall forwards. This test informs the hypnotist of the subjects who are prepared to 'let themselves go'. [52, p. 74-75]

Once a subject has been carefully selected and has strong expectations about working for the hypnotist, the context of audience pressure and anxiety (or even stage fright), with lights and music, provides a helpful stage atmosphere. [42, p. 99] In order to get subjects to do 'silly things', a variety of tricks used by stage hypnotists have been reported. For example, the stage hypnotist can mislead the audience into believing that the subject is deluded (such as thinking he is a famous film star) when actually the subject is responding to a direct request to imitate the singer. [42, p. 101] The point is, the audience does not hear everything that the stage hypnotist says to the subject. Regarding hypnotic induction, a number of techniques are used. These include Braidism (the fixing of gaze on an object), visual distraction, mental confusion and misdirection, loss of bodily equilibrium, and surprise.

TRANCE VS. SOCIAL COMPLIANCE

Two of Britain's leading stage hypnotists, Paul McKenna and Andrew Newton, both had television shows in the autumn of 1994 [60], with viewing figures for *The Hypnotic World of Paul McKenna* reaching 12 million. In an interview with a journalist, Andrew Newton stated:

> "Hypnotism is the manipulation of the imagination using suggestion. That's all. It's something we can all do if we put our minds to it. You need to know a bit of basic psychology, but it's nothing to do with the subconscious. It's more to do with the social skills, with how you interact with people." [60]

The journalist noted that McKenna made "rather greater claims but is equally adamant that the process of creating a hypnotic state is no big deal" in that: "We've all been in that state at times when we day-dream or watch television" [60].

Andrew Newton's viewpoint has been termed (by Paul McKenna) the Social Compliance theory. McKenna's comments above allude to the traditional view of hypnosis; what he calls the Trance theory. In 1995, a television documentary entitled *Paul McKenna's Secrets of Hypnosis* was broadcast nationally in the UK. The script was written and narrated by McKenna himself. The two theoretical viewpoints of hypnosis were described, but there was little doubt as to which side of the fence McKenna sat.

The documentary started by showing one of his television stage-hypnotism acts. But, "stage hypnosis is only the tip of the iceberg" [61], McKenna said, invoking a metaphor of the unconscious mind. The use of hypnosis in areas such as forensics, surgery, psychotherapy and memory of text was discussed and McKenna spoke of "the enormous potential of the unconscious mind" and that "hypnosis is the best tool we have to realise that potential" [61].

The alleged use of hypnosis in areas such as religious cults, politics and the programming of assassins was described. Sensationalist commentary from McKenna included: "the secret language of hypnotists is similar to the rhetoric of politicians" and "take responsibility for programming yourself, otherwise someone else will do it" [61].

The documentary provided an insight into cult mind control. Two former high-ranking Scientologists demonstrated a hypnotic process in which a person learns to be controlled for two hours by totally focusing on another person who gives verbal commands in military-like fashion ("intention without reservation"). It is a hypnotic process in that it involves uncritical acceptance of suggestions, and can be likened to marching in military training. [52, p. 204]

With regard to the rhetoric of politicians, the documentary described some research on British politicians. It showed that John Major, unlike Tony Blair or Margaret Thatcher, was a logical rather than a persuasive speaker. He appeared not to use rhetorical devices such as the "3-point figure of speech", an example of which was given by Thatcher: "It's not because... it's not because... but because it's..." [61].

There was also discussion of the alleged hypnotic programming of Sirhan Sirhan, who assassinated Robert Kennedy. At his trial, psychiatrists testified that he was hypnotised at the time of the shooting and, as a consequence, reported no memory of the event.

McKenna appeals to the public's fascination with the paranormal, generates fear by making reference to religious cults and the use of hypnosis in crime, yet partially demystifies certain aspects of hypnosis such as the "secret language of hypnotists being similar to the rhetoric of politicians" [61] Overall, however, he lures the viewers into accepting Trance theory.

Remarkably, however, McKenna seemed to change his viewpoint during the Christopher Gates case in 1998:

> According to one expert [Graham Wagstaff] called in the case: "Hypnosis does not work...what matters is the subject's belief and willingness to act in accordance with his belief."
> McKenna said: "I would not have put it in those words. I think it works only if the person wants it to. I have always maintained that.
> "The point is, people can do interesting things. It has got nothing to do with hypnosis. You can achieve all of these things without the 'H' word."
> …
> He has changed his views over the years about what hypnosis does to the brain. He no longer believes it puts the brain into a "special state".
> "I have never claimed that is some magic power," he said. "Nobody is saying there isn't a change of consciousness with hypnosis, but then again, there is if you sing a song or operate a computer.
> This whole notion of it being some special weird state has been rubbished."
> …
> "I changed my position over a year ago. There should not be anything wrong with me changing my views. Science will be different in 30 years and so will my views on hypnosis." [62]

The judge in the case commented that perhaps McKenna had made "extravagant claims" for the power of hypnosis in his books, tapes and television programmes. When challenged by a journalist about the "extravagant claims," McKenna was reported as saying:

> "What am I supposed to do? Call it the Socially Compliant World of Paul McKenna? Or the Paul McKenna Communication Show? What is David Copperfield to do? Call his magic show The Mirror and Wires Show?" [62]

An American who was told under hypnosis by Paul McKenna that his penis had been removed wrote a letter claiming that he had enjoyed the experience. The judge hearing the case had earlier watched an hour-long video recording of the Howard Stern Show featuring the 'lost willy' routine. [63] McKenna has been quoted as saying:

> "The comedy is in the ludicrousness of his situation. He knows he hasn't really lost his willy, but at the same time he is behaving as though he has. He is merely acting a role." [63]

In other words, McKenna appeared to be subscribing to what he calls the Social Compliance theory. In his report for the high-court case, Wagstaff discussed social compliance:

> "Stage hypnosis, like a game-show, or many domestic situations, can be a powerful social situation in which *people feel a strong social obligation to do what they are told* (which increases the more things they actually consent to do). It has what psychologists term powerful "demand characteristics", thus, having volunteered, its subjects are then told to do something which they for some reason find embarrassing (such as do an impression of a pop star, at which they are very poor), they may feel socially obliged to do it, but also apprehensive about what they may be asked to do next, and annoyed to find themselves in this situation. Occasionally, therefore, some hypnotic subjects may report feeling "embarrassed", "out of control" and "annoyed", and, because they underestimate the influence of social or situational pressures, they may even express some surprise at their compliance, and attribute it to some feature of "hypnosis". [64, p. 29; italics added]

In his report, Mr. Justice Toulson, in discussing the theory and research on hypnosis of Graham Wagstaff ("an impressive witness") [64, p. 32], states that "what matters is the subject's belief and willingness to act in accordance with his belief" [64, p. 22]. Furthermore, in distinguishing between the traditional ("state") and non-traditional ("non-state") views of hypnosis, he writes that "hypnosis comes like Father Christmas only to those willing to believe in him and remains only for as long as they are willing to act out such belief" [64, p. 18-19]. In this regard, consider the following statement from the movie *The Exorcist* in which the Clinic Director says to Chris whose adolescent daughter, Regan, is possessed by a demon:

> "It's a stylized ritual in which rabbis or priests try to drive out the so-called invading spirit. It's pretty much discarded these days, except by the Catholics who keep it in the closet as a sort of embarrassment. It has worked, in fact, although not for the reason they think, of course. It was purely the force of suggestion. The victim's *belief* in possession helped cause it; and just in the same way this *belief* in the power of exorcism can make it disappear."
> [65; italics added]

NEUROLINGUISTIC PROGRAMMING (NLP)

A month or so after the High Court case, it was reported that McKenna would be announcing the launch of 'Perfect Night' which is:

> ...a machine that aims to give sleepers a restful night and fill them with vim for the next morning. The £80 machine will broadcast mood music and messages from McKenna, who aims to use his powers of suggestion to give people a good night's sleep. ... The machine claims to use something called neuro-linguistic programming, which uses the period of half-sleep just before people drop off or wake up to introduce positive messages into the listener's

subconscious. In this relaxed state, the makers believe, people are more susceptible to suggestion and therefore McKenna's messages will have a more powerful, mood-altering effect on them. The relaxing messages aim to produce a deeper, sounder sleep. The machines do not use any form of hypnosis say, Rio, the company that is launching Perfect Night with McKenna. [66]

Neurolinguistic programming (NLP) has been associated with the Human Potential Movement [67]. It was begun in the mid-1970s by Richard Bandler, a mathematician and computer scientist, and John Grinder, a linguist.

NLP emphasises a variety of communication and persuasion skills, but also self-hypnosis. With regard to hypnosis, NLP is strongly influenced by Ericksonian hypnosis. Milton Erickson is regarded as the father of an interpersonal communications approach to hypnosis and psychotherapy. [68] Erickson's approach to hypnotherapy has been described as 'indirect' rather than 'direct' or 'authoritarian'. For Erickson, hypnosis is an active process in that what develops from hypnosis does not derive from the presented suggestions *per se*, but from how the patient internally processes and idiosyncratically utilises these suggestions. Erickson used the patient's model of the world to guide the therapy. He would listen to the metaphors a patient used, to help him elicit their view of the world and then tell a story that helped to change their perspective. [52, p. 151] NLP modelled Erickson's techniques so that they could be taught to others.

NLP claims to help people change by teaching them to programme their brain. NLP promotional literature claims that "NLP offers you a user-manual to your brain". Indeed, the brain-manual seems to be a metaphor for NLP training, which is sometimes referred to as "software for the brain" [67]. Paul McKenna has used this metaphor in his work:

> The human mind has been likened to a computer...hypnosis is a way of reprogramming the computer. When the critical faculty is quietened during trance, new ideas may be put to a person which results in new patterns of behaviour. [52, p. 275]

McKenna has described how he helped a woman who was unable to play the piano in front of an audience: "So I trained her, within a few minutes, and re-programmed her. I overwrote the software of her mind and I taught her how to feel the confidence of when she plays alone." [69]

McKenna went into business with Richard Bandler in 1994 (for an insight into one of their seven-day courses on NLP which are delivered to groups of 500 to 700 delegates see [69, 70]).

Bandler also became McKenna's mentor, "helping him to reprogramme his mind" [71] and McKenna has been quoted as saying: "In the past I used to be quite controlling, almost robotic".[5] [71]

---

[5]A newspaper article has stated about Paul McKenna that:

> From 11 he attended a Catholic school in London run by Jesuit priests who, he claims, specialised in guilt. He was told he was worthless (a school report said: "If he carries on like this, he'll never amount to anything"). When he published his first book he sent a copy to his old English teacher, with "F*** off" written inside. ... "I spent years in a Catholic school so I understand from the kings of mind manipulation how human beings work," he says. [71]

CONCLUSION

NLP provided Paul McKenna with a means by which to perpetuate the myth of trance and the traditional or "state" theory of hypnosis. On the one hand, NLP, which is 'theoretically eclectic' in its approach [72, 73], emphasizes cognitive skills such as positive thinking and visualization; on the other hand, it appears to involve processes associated with mind control, especially when used in the context of 'mass therapy'. With regard to the latter, it could be argued that the approach to NLP used by McKenna and Bandler is closer to stage hypnosis than any concept of 'self-hypnosis'.

Paul McKenna is noted for his numerous celebrity clients, one of whom was the boxer Nigel Benn. After a fight in which he put his opponent into a coma, Benn said: "I want to thank Paul McKenna, who hypnotised me and made me believe in myself." [74]

Referring back to the Introduction of this article, if Tony Jacklin had received or engaged in hypnosis from Paul McKenna rather than from a doctor would it more likely have worked?

REFERENCES

1. Kahn, E., *Tony Jacklin: The Price of Success*, Hamlyn, London, 1979.

2. *The Independent*, 15 August, 1998.

3. Hassan, S., *Combatting Cult Mind Control*, Park Street Press, Rochester, VT, 1988.

4. Atack, J., "Never Believe a Hypnotist": An Investigation of L. Ron Hubbard's Statements about Hypnosis and its Relationship to his Dianetics, Http://home.snafu.de/tilman/j/hypnosis.html

5. Wikipedia, Scientology, Http://en.wikipedia.org/wiki/Scientology

6. Wikipedia/WikiProject Scientology/History Project Article, http://en.wikipedia.org/wiki/Wikipedia:WikiProject_Scientology/History_Article_Project

7. Carroll, R.T., Dianetics/Scientology, *The Skeptic's Dictionary*, Http://skepdic.com/dianetic.html

8. *The Daily Telegraph*, 18 June, 1999

9. Taylor, J., Horevitz, R. and Balague, G., The Use of Hypnosis in Applied Sport Psychology, *The Sport Psychologist*, 1993, 7, 58-78.

10. Centre for Sports Hypnosis™, http://www.sportshypnosis.org.uk/faqs.html, Accessed 25 March 2009

11. Grindstaff, J.S. and Fisher, L.A., Sport Psychology Consultants' Experience of Using Hypnosis in Their Practice: An Exploratory Investigation, *The Sport Psychologist*, 2006, 368-386.

12. Durbin, P.G., Hypnosis and Religious Faith, http://www.renewingyourmind.com/Articles/Durbin-Article2.htm

13. Nideffer, R.M., *Psyched to Win*, Leisure Press, Champaign, IL, 1992.

14. Zilbergeld, B. and Lazarus, A.A., *Mind Power: Getting What You Want Through Mental Training*, Little, Brown & Co., Boston, MA, 1987.

15. Liggett, D.L., *Sport Hypnosis, Human Kinetics*, Champaign, IL, 2000.

16. Ulett, G.A. and Peterson, D.B., *Applied Hypnosis and Positive Suggestion*, Mosby, St. Louis, MI, 1965.

17. Cox, R.H., *Sport Psychology: Concepts and Applications*, 3rd edn., WCB/McGraw-Hill, Boston, MA, 1998.

18. Unestahl, L-E., *Inner Mental Training*, Veje, Orebro, Sweden.

19.   Unestahl, L-E., The Ideal Performance State, in: Unestahl, L-E., ed., *Sport Psychology: In Theory and Practice*, Veje, Orebro, Sweden, 1986, 20-37.

20.   Jacobson, E., *Progressive Relaxation*, University of Chicago Press, Chicago, 1929.

21.   Vanek, M. and Cratty, B.J., *Psychology and the Superior Athlete*, MacMillan, NY, 1970.

22.   Schultz, J.H. and Luthe, W., *Autogenic Training: A Psychophysiological Approach to Psychotherapy*, Grune and Stratton, New York, 1959.

23.   Hoberman, J., *Mortal Engines: The Science of Performance and the Dehumanisation of Sport*, The Free Press, New York, 1992.

24.   Harris, D.V. and Williams, J.M., Relaxation and Energising Techniques for Regulation of Arousal, in: Williams, J.M., ed., *Applied Sport Psychology: Personal Growth to Peak Performance*, Mayfield Publishers, Mountain View, CA, 1993, 185-199.

25.   Du Maurier, G., *Trilby*, J.M. Dent & Sons, London, 1894.

26.   *The Manchurian Candidate*, Directed by: Frankenheimer, J., United Artists, USA 1962.

27.   *The Manchurian Candidate*, Directed by: Demme, J., Paramount Pictures, USA, 2004.

28.   Condon, R., *The Manchurian Candidate*, McGraw-Hill, NY, 1959.

29.   Inglis, B., *Trance: A Natural History of Altered States of Mind*, Grafton Books, London, 1989.

30.   Gauld, A., *A History of Hypnotism*, Cambridge University Press, Cambridge, 1992.

31.   Spanos, N.P. and Chaves, J.F., History and Historiography of Hypnosis, in: Lynn, S.J. and Rhue, J.W., eds., *Theories of Hypnosis: Current Models and Perspectives*, Guilford Press, New York, 1991, 43-78.

32.   Edgette, J.H. and Edgette, J.S., *The Handbook of Hypnotic Phenomena in Psychotherapy*, Brunner/Mazel, New York, 1995.

33.   Sarbin, T.R., Contributions to Role-Taking Theory: I. Hypnotic Behavior, *Psychological Review*, 1950, 57, 255-270.

34.   White, R.W., A Preface to the Theory of Hypnotism, *Journal of Abnormal and Social Psychology*, 1941, 36, 477-505.

35.   Spanos, N.P., A Sociocognitive Approach to Hypnosis, in: Lynn, S.J. and Rhue, J.W., eds., *Theories of Hypnosis: Current Models and Perspectives*, Guilford Press, New York, 1991, 324-361.

36.   Coe, W.C. and Sarbin, T.R., Role Theory: Hypnosis from a Dramaturgical and Narrational Perspective, in: Lynn, S.J. and Rhue, J.W., eds., *Theories of Hypnosis: Current Models and Perspectives*, Guilford Press, New York, 1991, 303-323.

37.   Barber, T.X., *Hypnosis: A Scientific Approach*, Van Nostrand Reinhold, New York, 1969.

38.   Lynn, S.J. and Rhue, J.W., Hypnosis Theories: Themes, Variations, and Research Directions, in: Lynn, S.J. and Rhue, J.W., eds., *Theories of Hypnosis: Current Models and Perspectives*, Guilford Press, New York, 1991, 601-626.

39.   Naish, P.L.N., ed., *What is Hypnosis? Current Theories and Research*, Open University Press, Philadelphia, 1986.

40.   McConkey, K.M., The Construction and Resolution of Experience and Behavior in Hypnosis, in: Lynn, S.J. and Rhue, J.W., eds., *Theories of Hypnosis: Current Models and Perspectives*, Guilford Press, New York, 1991, 542-563.

41.   Fellows, B.J., The Concept of Trance, in: Naish, P.L.N., ed., *What is Hypnosis?* Open University Press, Milton Keynes, UK, 1986, 37-58.

42.   Barber, T.X., Spanos, N.P. and Chaves, J.F., *Hypnosis, Imagination and Human Potentialities*, Pergamon Press, New York, 1974.

43. Kirsch, I., Mobayed, C., Council, J. and Kenny, L., Expert Judgements of Hypnosis from Subjective Reports: New Data on the Altered State Controversy, *Journal of Abnormal Psychology*, 1992, 101, 657-662.

44. Wagstaff, G.F., Compliance, Belief, and Semantics in Hypnosis: A Nonstate, Sociocognitive Perspective, in: Lynn, S.J. and Rhue, J.W., eds., *Theories of Hypnosis: Current Models and Perspectives*, Guilford Press, New York, 1991, 362-396.

45. Udolf, R., *Handbook of Hypnosis for Professionals*, 2nd edn., Jason Aronson, Northvale, NJ, 1995.

46. Banyai, E.I., Toward a Social Psychological Model of Hypnosis, in: Lynn, S.J. and Rhue, J.W., eds., *Theories of Hypnosis: Current Models and Perspectives*, Guilford Press, New York, 1991, 564-598.

47. Shor, R.E., Hypnosis and the Concept of the Generalized Reality Orientation, *American Journal of Psychotherapy*, 1959, 13, 582-602.

48. Orne, M.T., The Nature of Hypnosis: Artifact and Essence, *Journal of Abnormal and Social Psychology*, 1959, 58, 277-299.

49. McConkey, K.M., Opinions About Hypnosis and Self Hypnosis Before and After Hypnotic Testing, *International Journal of Clinical and Experimental Hypnosis*, 1986, 34, 311-319.

50. McConkey, K.M., Glisky, M.L. and Kihlstrom, J.F., Individual Differences Among Hypnotic Virtuosos: A Case Comparison, *Australian Journal of Clinical and Experimental Hypnosis*, 1989, 17, 131-140.

51. Hilgard, E.R., A Neodissociation Interpretation of Hypnosis, in: Lynn, S.J. and Rhue, J.W., eds., *Theories of Hypnosis: Current Models and Perspectives*, Guilford Press, New York, 1991, 83-104.

52. McKenna, P., *The Hypnotic World of Paul McKenna*, Faber and Faber, London, 1993.

53. *The Times*, 14 December 1994.

54. *The Daily Telegraph*, 15 August 1994.

55. Home Office, *Stage Hypnotism: Review of the Hypnotism Act 1952*, Home Office, London, UK, http://www.popan.org.uk/policy/documents/ReviewofHypnotismAct1952.pdf

56. *The Mirror*, 15 October 1996.

57. *The Sun*, 15 october 1996.

58. *The Times*, 14 July 1998.

59. *The Daily Telegraph*, 21 July 1998.

60. *The Observer*, 6 November 1994.

61. McKenna, P., *Paul McKenna's Secrets of Hypnosis*, Documentary for UK Independent Television Network, 1995.

62. *The Daily Telegraph*, 1 August 1998.

63. *The Times*, 23 July 1998.

64. *Mr Justice Toulson's Judgement, Christopher Gates vs. Paul McKenna*, August 14, 1998, http://www.ukhypnosis.com/gatesjudgement.pdf

65. *The Exorcist*, Directed by: Friedkin, W., Warner Brothers, Los Angeles, CA, USA, 1973.

66. *The Sunday Times*, 27 September 1998.

67. Hall, L.M., Was NLP Really a Child of the Human Potential Movement? *Resource Magazine*, 2006, 11, http://www.self-actualizing.org/articles/NLP_as_a_child_of_HPM.pdf

68. Zeig, J.K. and Rennick, P.J., Ericksonian Hypnotherapy: A Communications Approach to Hypnosis, in: Lynn, S.J. and Rhue, J.W., eds., *Theories of Hypnosis: Current Models and Perspectives*, Guilford Press, New York, 1991, 275-300.

69. Nielsen, T., Paul McKenna, *Director Magazine*, 2006, November, http://www.director.co.uk/MAGAZINE/2006/11%20Nov/mckenna_60_4.html

70. Ronson, Don't Worry, Get Therapy, *The Guardian*, 20 May, 2006, http://www.guardian.co.uk/lifeandstyle/2006/may/20/weekend.jonronson1

71.   Hoggard, L, Mind Games, 2008, *The Guardian*, 19 January,
       http://thescotsman.scotsman.com/features/Mind-games.3685401.jp

72.   Grimley, B., NLP Coaching, in: Palmer, S. and Whybrow, A., eds., *Handbook of Coaching
       Psychology: A Guide for Practitioners*, Routledge, London, 2007, 193-210.

73.   Jenkins, S., The Impact of the Inner Game and Sir John Whitmore on Coaching, *Annual Review of
       High Performance Coaching and Consulting*, 2009, 1, 1-22.

74.   Vernon, P., 'Look Into My Eyes', The Observer, 2004, 12 December,
       http://www.guardian.co.uk/theobserver/2004/dec/12/features.magazine67

75.   Gravitz, M.A., Early Theories of Hypnosis: A Clinical Perspective, in: Lynn, S.J. and Rhue, J.W., eds.,
       Theories of Hypnosis: Current Models and Perspectives, Guilford Press, New York, 1991, 19-42.

76.   Muses, C., *Consciousness and Reality*, Dutton, New York, 1972.

77.   Miller, J., Going Unconscious, *New York Review of Books*, 1995, April 20.

78.   Braid, J., *Neurypnology or the Rationale of Nervous Sleep...*, J. Churchill, London, 1843.

79.   Braid, J., *Braid on Hypnosis: Neurypnology or...* (Waite, A.E., ed.) George Redway, London, 1899.

80.   James, W., *The Principles of Psychology*, Henry Holt and Co., New York, 1890, 1893.

81.   Wundt, W., *Hypnotismus and Suggestion*, W. Engelmann, Leipzig, 1892.

82.   Coué, E., *Self Mastery Through Autosuggestion* (Van Orden, A.S., trans.), Malkan, New York, 1922.

83.   Hull, C.L., *Hypnosis and Suggestibility*, Appleton-Century-Crofts, New York, 1933.

84.   Arnold, M.B., On the Mechanism of Suggestion and Hypnosis, *Journal of Abnormal and Social
       Psychology*, 1946, 41, 107-128.

85.   Carpenter, W.B., *Mesmerism, Spiritualism, &c Historically & Scientifically Considered*, Longmans,
       Green and Co., London, 1877.

86.   *Ghost*, Directed by: Zucker, J., Paramount Pictures, Los Angeles, CA, USA, 1990.

87.   Janet, P., *Psychological Healing*, Crowell-Collier & MacMillan, New York, 1925.

APPENDIX – HYPNOSIS: HISTORICAL PERSPECTIVES
HYPNOSIS IN THE ANCIENT WORLD

More than 4,000 years ago, Wang Tai, the founder of Chinese medicine taught a therapeutic technique involving incantations and manual passes over the body of the patient. [75, p. 19] Other civilisations in the Ancient World, such as the Greeks and Romans, used the medium of induced trances for healing purposes. The Egyptians described healing methods similar to modern-day hypnosis. [76, cited in 75, p. 19]

MESMER

Friedrich (Franz) Anton Mesmer's name has passed into everyday language, with 'mesmerised' now being synonymous with 'hypnotised'. Mesmer was a medical student at the University of Vienna. In 1774 he learned of how a friend, Jesuit priest Father Maximilian Hell was successfully curing his patients with magnets applied to their bodies. Maximilian Hell was an astrologer to the Austrian court. This treatment was derived from the mystic medicine of Philippus Aureolus Theophrastus Bombastus von Hohenheim (known as Paracelsus) in the 17th Century. Paracelsus was a Swiss physician who believed in the astrological idea that the stars influence humans via their magnetic nature. He believed that all magnets influenced the human body via an invisible magnetic fluid.

Earlier in the 17th Century, Johann Van Helmont had introduced the notion of an 'animal magnetism' that emanated from the human body and had the potential to influence the minds and bodies of others.

Mesmer's doctoral dissertation from the University of Vienna in 1776 was entitled *The Influence of the Stars and Planets on Curative Powers*. Mesmer argued that the rotation of the heavenly bodies exerted gravitational influence on human physiology analogous to the tidal effect of the moon upon the ocean and that this accounted for the periodic incidence of various diseases. [77] Mesmer believed that a 'subtle fluid' permeated the universe and an imbalance of this fluid within the human body caused disease. In order to cure disease, it was necessary to redistribute and harmonise the flow of fluid by transmitting magnetic fluid from certain healthy individuals to the sick. These individuals were 'magnetisers' – usually men and were perceived as strong, powerful and intelligent.

Mesmer's treatment took place in a large, dimly lit hall that had reflecting mirrors and background music. There was a 'baquet', a large oak tub filled with water and other materials such as iron filings and ground glass. It had a wooden cover with holes through which projected moveable iron rods which the patients held in their hands or applied to afflicted areas of their body. So as to promote free circulation of the magnetic fluid, patients sat in a circle around the baquet, holding hands with the whole group being joined by a cord. In contrast to modern hypnosis, Mesmer's ritual was mainly non-verbal. He moved from one patient to another making passes with his hands and touching them with magnets. This ritual induced a convulsive (hysterical) reaction, a 'magnetic crisis', which was often accompanied by laughing or crying.

When Mesmer later discovered that it was not necessary to use magnets, he concluded that the curative effect was due to the animal magnetism contained in his own body. He would pass his hands up and down the length of the patient's body without actually touching the surface. [77]

Parisians were particularly receptive to Mesmer's ideas and methods of treatment. This was largely due to there being a large class of wealthy people who regarded it as a therapeutic novelty that was less unpleasant than orthodox medicine. Mysticism and the occult appealed to these same people, yet at the same time the application of science was prestigious and late eighteenth-century Paris had a degree of intellectual freedom that was not attainable in most other European capital cities. [30, p. 4]

It was science, however, that led to Mesmer's demise. In 1784, a Royal Commission was chosen from the Paris Faculty of Medicine and the Royal Academy of Sciences to investigate Mesmer and his methods. The Commission comprised of four medical men and five scientists. One of the four commissioners from the medical faculty was Joseph Ignace Guillotin. The five scientific commissioners included Benjamin Franklin and Antoine Laurent Lavoisier. (The latter met his death on the device named after their colleague Guillotin. [30, p. 26]) The primary question addressed by the Royal Commission was not whether animal magnetism works, but whether it exists. Sensitive scientific instruments were used to measure magnetism [39, p. 2], but no trace of 'magnetic fluid' was discovered. Later in the same year, the Royal Commission carried out a series of well-designed experiments. It was concluded that the curative power of magnetism was actually due to the patient's beliefs and imagination; no cures were produced unless the patients believed that they were being magnetised. [31, p. 4] It was also concluded that Mesmer's methods were potentially harmful, because of the convulsions produced. Furthermore, the methods were deemed immoral because of the sexual feelings stimulated by the close physical contact.

There was also a Royal Commission chosen from members of the Royal Society of Medicine. Their report was less influential than that of the Faculty/Academy. One of the five commissioners (Antoine-Laurent de Jussieu), however, did issue a separate and partially dissenting report stating that the positive effects of mesmerism had been overlooked by the investigation, and he raised the point that stimulation of the imagination might itself be a therapeutic force. [30, p. 26; 75, p. 26] Many copies of the report were quickly printed and distributed. Even though Mesmer fell into disrepute and had to leave Paris, the supporters of animal magnetism refused to be intimidated. [30, p. 29]

The name that stands second to Mesmer's in histories of animal magnetism is that of Armand-Mari-Jacques de Chastenet, Marquis de Puységur. [30, p. 39] A pupil of Mesmer, Puységur realised that the convulsive reactions were neither inevitable nor necessary. [31, p. 4] By making suggestions of relaxation, the patient would develop what was referred to as 'magnetic sleep', 'artificial somnambulism' or 'sleeping trance'. This was perceived to have an appealing paranormal dimension and by the end of 1784 Puységur's brand of animal magnetism had made significant progress throughout France. [30, p. 43]

Nevertheless, controversy followed animal magnetism into the nineteenth century and it was the subject of investigation by another Royal Commission in 1826. The report was not published until 1831 and some of the conclusions were actually a source of much satisfaction and encouragement to the 'magnetists', who frequently reprinted them. [30, p. 136]

A more mystical form of magnetism had started to spread across Europe in the late 1790s, but after 1850 this was largely absorbed by Spiritualism and related movements (see below). [30, p. 155]

Mesmerism did not make a significant impact in America and Britain until the mid-1830s. In America, Mesmerism was not only more important as a social and cultural movement than in Britain, but also more influential in determining the range of phenomena later classed under hypnotism. [30, p. 179] Oddly, however, summary accounts of the history of hypnosis have tended to place more influence on the mesmerism of Elliotson and Esdaile (see below). [30, p. 179] In contrast to Britain, America was far less institutionalised in terms of professional, intellectual, educational and religious matters. Between 1830 and 1850, the eastern United States was "a ferment of new ideas, new movements, and new cults, many of a reformist or utopian character, and was uplifted by an almost euphoric optimism as to the prospects for improving man's lot in the world or assuring his comfort in the next" [30, p. 179-180].

ELLIOTSON AND ESDAILE

In 1837, John Elliotson used mesmerism in order to control surgical pain in his patients. The following year he was denounced as a fraud by the medical journal *The Lancet* and was forced to leave his hospital post. [31, p. 4] Elliotson, a professor at University College in London, had become a convert following the arrival in Britain in 1837 of a noted French magnetist, Baron Jules Denis du Potet de Sennevoy. In

1843, Elliotson founded *The Zoist: A Journal of Cerebral Physiology and Mesmerism, and their Applications to Human Welfare*. It ran until 1856 and is the single most important source of information about mesmerism of the period. [30, p. 206]

A contemporary of Elliotson and James Braid (see below) was James Esdaile, a Scottish surgeon practicing in India. He read Elliotson's work and began using mesmerism with impressive results. Most medical journals, however, refused to publish his work. One of the reasons that mesmerism did not find widespread acceptance as an anaesthetic at the time, was the development of chemical anaesthetics. [45, p. 5]

BRAID

James Braid was a Scottish surgeon who set up a medical practice in Manchester. He was an accepted and conservative member of the medical community. [45, p. 5] In 1841, Braid attended a meeting in Manchester at which Swiss magnetiser Charles Fontaine gave a demonstration of mesmerism. After this demonstration, Braid was convinced it was a fraud and denounced it as such. At a second meeting, however, Braid was convinced by demonstrations of analgesia and eye catalepsy. Braid initially believed that the effects of animal magnetism were due to induced fatigue of the eye muscles, which in turn led to a sleep-like state. [75, p. 30] The term 'Braidism' is now used to refer to a method of hypnotic induction, devised by Braid, that involves having the subject stare at an object (such as a wine bottle) above their line of vision in order to produce fatigue of the extrinsic eye muscles. [45, p. 30] Braid described it as follows:

> ...I requested Mr Walker, a young gentleman present, to sit down, and maintain a fixed stare at the top of a wine bottle placed so much above him as to produce considerable strain on the eyes and eyelids, to enable him to maintain a steady view of the object. In three minutes his eyelids closed, a gush of tears ran down his cheeks, his head drooped, his face was slightly convulsed, he gave a groan, and instantly fell into a profound sleep, the respiration becoming slow, deep and sibilant... [78, p. 99-100]

In 1843, Braid published a book entitled, *Neurypnology, or the Rationale of Nervous Sleep*. This was at a time when the scientific zeitgeist had shifted to seeking explanations of physiological functioning and behaviour in terms of neurological functioning rather than spiritualist or 'fluidist' processes. [31, p. 58] The word 'hypnosis' is derived from Hypnos, the Greek god of sleep. Apaprently, the word 'hypnosis' was first used in 1820 by Etienne Felix d'Henin de Cuvillers, a French mesmerist. Braid reported several minor operations performed upon patients who had been subjected to Braidism. The patients were apparently rendered cataleptic and analgesic in the absence, from Braid, of any verbal suggestions of the absence of pain. [30, p. 489]

In 1847, Braid issued a revised version of his theory, abandoning the term 'hypnosis' in favour of 'monodeism', which he defined as the "condition resulting from the mind being possessed by dominant ideas" [79]. Monodeism was based on the idea of 'ideo-motor action,' i.e., ideas that remain contradicted by other ideas lead automatically to the corresponding action. [80]

The Nancy School (see below) made ideo-motor action the central tenet of its theory of hypnosis as suggestion. In turn, it was central to theories of hypnosis and/or suggestion postulated by subsequent theorists such as Wundt [81], Coué [82], Hull [83], and Arnold [84]. [31, p. 62]

Braid's work captured the interest of William Benjamin Carpenter, one of the most distinguished physiologists of the 19th Century and a professor at University College, London. Carpenter argued that hypnotism induced a temporary suspension of the will:

> In those states in which the directing power of the will is suspended, hypnosis being one of them, the course of action is determined by some dominant idea which, for the moment, has full possession of the mind. [85]

Most doctors and scientists, however, were not convinced by the work of Braid and Carpenter. If it had not been for publications by Carpenter such as *Mesmerism, Spiritualism, &c. Historically and Scientifically Considered* and his frequently reprinted *Principles of Mental Physiology*, hypnotism may have been forgotten entirely. [30, p. 348] In fact, the ideas and practices of mesmerism did not actually disappear in the late 19th Century – the magnetists held a conference in Paris (in 1889) at the same time as the first International Congress of Hypnotism. Beyond the early 1850s, however, mesmerism survived only in so much as it was associated with Spiritualism or as part of the opposition to Spiritualism. [30, p. 193] This did not prevent stage performers and charlatans from using the term mesmerism to promote their work, which combined animal magnetism with astrology, fortune-telling and phrenology (reading a person's character from protrusions in their head).

SPIRITUALISM

Spiritualism in America can be traced back to the Fox sisters, who lived in New York State. In 1847, they claimed to be able to communicate with the deceased through the medium of raps and bangs. They were later exposed as a fraud – the raps were actually derived from the clicking of certain joints in their feet! The 'Hollywood sèance' (as in the movie *Ghost* [86] that starred Demi Moore, Patrick Swayze and Whoopie Goldberg) is actually typical and shows how Spiritualism is related to mesmerism in that people sit around a table, in a darkened room, holding hands and a medium then fakes a trance and articulates messages from spirits.

In 1882, the Society for Psychical Research was founded in Britain, with the stated purpose being "to investigate that large group of debatable phenomena designated such terms as mesmeric, psychical, and Spiritualistic" and to do so "without prejudice or prepossession of any kind, and in the same spirit of exact and unimpassioned inquiry which has enabled Science to solve so many problems, once not less obscure or less hotly debated" [30, p. 390]. A similar society was founded in America in 1884.

NANCY SCHOOL

Étienne-Eugene Azam, deputy professor at the School of Medicine in Bordeaux, was a disciple of Braid's work. [30, p. 287] He experimented with hypnotism and suggestion in the context of anaesthesia and psychotherapy. Azam's work eventually led to the establishment of the Nancy School of Hypnosis. Ambrose-Auguste Liébeault is regarded as the 'father' of the Nancy School. [30, p. 288] After qualifying in medicine at Strasbourg in 1850, Liébeault spent most of his remaining life around Nancy. [30, p. 319] It was through the publication in 1884 of Hippolyte Bernheim's *De la Suggestion Dans L'Etat Hypnotique et Dans L'Etat de Veille*, however, that the views of the Nancy School were widely disseminated. [30, p. 324] At this time, Bernheim was President of the Nancy Medical Society.

NANCY SCHOOL VS. PARIS SCHOOL

The Nancy School became involved in an intellectual struggle with the Paris School which was championed by Jean-Martin Charcot. The most noted neurologist of his time, Charcot was also a mesmerist who believed that magnets, auditory stimulation, tactile pressure and certain metals could induce a trance state. [75, p. 33] He believed that hypnosis was a brain disorder mimicking hysteria. Furthermore, he also drew attention to the similarities between symptoms of hysterics and the behaviour of 'demonically possessed' people of previous centuries as evidence that such people were actually suffering from hysteria. [31, p. 58] Charcot and his pupils began serious investigation of hypnotism in 1878. [30, p. 311] Three distinct stages of hypnosis were distinguished: a lethargic state of relaxation, a cataleptic state in which the subject held a fixed position, and the deep somnambulistic state of complete hypnosis.

In 1884, the theories of Charcot were decisively challenged by Bernheim, who explained all hypnosis in terms of suggestibility and viewed it as a nonpathological state of mind. Charcot eventually converted from the views of the Paris School to those of the Nancy School and Bernheim was to become the most prominent turn-of-the-century theorist who tackled hypnosis from a psychological perspective. [30, p. 537] Central to Bernheim's later theorising, was his rejection of the view that hypnosis is a 'special state' of heightened responsiveness to suggestion. Bernheim claimed that suggestions made to subjects who were not, and have never been, hypnotised can be as effective as suggestions made to subjects who had been hypnotised. [30, p. 548] One of the most prominent hypnotists at the turn of the century was the German Oskar Vogt, whose theory of hypnosis was physiological in that hypnosis was viewed as a sleep-like state. Contrary to Bernheim's later views, Vogt asserted that suggestibility is heightened in hypnosis, and heightened in proportion to the depth of hypnosis. [30, p. 548]

Although Charcot converted to the views of the Nancy School, his notion of hypnosis as a neuropathological state that could be fully produced only in hysterics was later modified and expanded upon in Janet's [87] concept of 'dissociation'. [31, p. 63] By dissociation is meant that ideas or behavioural patterns that normally occurred together or in sequence could become separated from one another. Dissociation theory initially received significant support, but eventually had a similar fate to Charcot's original notions. In the mid-1970s, Ernest Hilgard reintroduced notions of dissociation into theories of hypnosis.

FREUD

Sigmund Freud, a Viennese physician, was exposed to Charcot's influential views on hypnosis while studying under him in 1884-5. [74, p. 34] Hypnosis was instrumental in the development of psychoanalysis. Under hypnosis, Freud's patients were able to remember the repressed memories that he diagnosed as causing their neuroses. In 1896, Freud abandoned the use of hypnosis for a number of reasons including the alarming results of hypnotic transference, whereby the patients substituted him (the analyst) for someone close to himself. In 1889, Freud converted to the Nancy School ideas on suggestion.

COUE

The work of Emile Coué was a by-product of the Nancy School:

> The story goes that Coué, a chemist in Troyes, one day substituted coloured water for a drug which a patient demanded but which he was not permitted to prescribe. The patient's symptoms duly disappeared. Could it be, Coué wondered, that the imagination within certain limits can perform the same function as a drug? He made a pilgrimage to Nancy in 1885, and came back to Troyes convinced that suggestion under hypnosis was very effective; but he had not hypnotised the patient to whom he gave the placebo – the coloured water. The patient's own imagination must have supplied the cure. Surely, then psychotherapy's objective should be the training of patients to heal themselves, through autosuggestion? [29, p. 142]

For Coué, "autosuggestion was nothing but hypnosis" [82, p. 15]. He had patients repeat the formula, "Every day, in every way, I get better and better". Having originally used it with patients in a light trance, he then told patients to use it themselves when in a relaxed mood. On the title page of *Self Mastery Through Conscious Autosuggestion*, it is stated, "Our actions spring not from our Will but from our imagination". This is how Coué distinguished between the conscious and unconscious minds, and he described the power of the unconscious mind ("imagination") with examples such as the difficulty of walking along a plank at the height of a cathedral.

Sport Psychology, Hypnosis and Golf:

A Commentary

Stephen Simpson
Cherry Tree House, Straight Road,
Polstead Heath, Colchester, CO6 5BB, UK
E-mail: stephensimpson@msn.com

INTRODUCTION

Golf coaching forms only part of my practice. I have worked with clients in groups, individually, and also remotely. This last group are the clients who have purchased one of my golf instruction audio CDs. Like Robert Nideffer, I too recognize the benefits of self hypnosis. During the last year I have coached more than 100 clients, either personally or via my audio CD. In each case, I teach meditation and relaxation techniques. I also teach a little about how our brains work, and the importance of internal dialogue, self-confidence, and visualisation skills. Then the client develops their own techniques and finds out what works for them. That is when the real breakthroughs occur. The results are usually excellent and immediate. Almost all of my clients cut their handicaps, and go on to win competitions. More importantly, they are happier golfers. A client described, "*When I stand up to a shot I am thinking I know this shot and I can do it! Before this I would sometimes shake with fright.*"

I previously thought that a physical connection between therapist and client was important. Historically, some hypnotists have referred to magnetism or some other ill-defined energy as important to their work. To my surprise, I found that clients who had bought and used my CD achieved at least as much success as the clients that consult me personally. This is great news for those who cannot travel to see their practitioner, and certainly more time and cost-effective.

INNOCENT SELF-BELIEF

I do not have any knowledge of Scientology, but Tony Jacklin's statement that "sportsmen need to be more childlike" resonates strongly. Many of my clients make similar statements, and believe that hypnosis has helped them reach this state. An example is a professional golfer who wrote to me recently. He was struggling with his game and had bought one of my audio hypnosis and meditation CDs after realising that the mental side of his game was holding him back. He wrote a long and moving note, and was on the verge of giving up golf, with words that included: "*I am sure your CD has helped immensely...I am slowly remembering how I played as a kid and enjoying my golf more than ever.*"

I enjoy watching young children play sport. They are full of enthusiasm and have great imaginations. When kicking a football with friends, there is usually a running commentary. They adopt the name of their hero as part of their visualisation. When something doesn't work out as they intended, they look genuinely surprised. Wouldn't it be wonderful if they could preserve this innocent self-belief through their adult years?

Another of my clients is a 15 year-old cricketer who has just been selected for the England squad. He told me that what he likes most about cricket are the practice sessions, when he can fool around and try different things, i.e. behave like a normal child. During matches he feels under pressure to adhere to coaching instructions, and not let the side down. My work with him focuses on taking the confidence gained from the wonder and excitement of practice sessions to the match itself.

Negative thinking and fear of failure are acquired thought patterns. The lengthening list of missed putts for a golfer, or missed penalties for a footballer, can exert a stronger negative mental impression than the many successes in a player's career. This may be an important contributing factor that limits an athlete's length of career other than increasing age.

Much of my work with athletes from any discipline is to focus on having fun, to feel like a child again, and then the results usually take care of themselves.

HYPNOSIS, CULTURE AND HISTORY

I do not believe that under normal circumstances hypnotic processes could be used for mind control. I do know from first-hand experience some of the benefits of using hypnotic processes.

It is worth noting that hypnotic processes are ubiquitous in our society, and in history. We are surrounded by hypnotic language in music, poetry, literature (Shakespeare and Dylan Thomas are great examples), and in most circumstances they enrich our culture.

When a mother reads a fairy story to her child in bed she is using hypnotic language, hypnotic imagery, and hypnotic tones. Whether she recognizes this or not she knows that this is the best way to relax her child and encourage him or her to fall asleep.

Speech is a relatively recent human evolution. Before its development, other sound-based methods of communication would have been an important tool for social cohesion. When a mother makes soothing noises to her crying child she knows instinctively it will calm her child, and perhaps herself too. Hypnosis might be a relatively simple atavistic evolutionary trait that preceded the development of more complex language skills, and remains more developed (or less latent) in some individuals than others.

To my mind, Sir David Attenborough is the best exponent of using hypnotic processes on TV. His language, tonality, and imagery are truly wonderful. These are gifts that he may consider entirely natural, and he is probably unaware of their hypnotic nature. In medieval times, jongleurs similarly mesmerised their audiences with their spell-binding stories.

While I might suggest different ideas and scenarios, I always stress that the client will use their imagination to generate their own ideas, and choose or reject those thoughts that are most appropriate for them. I do not believe that an individual would adopt alien beliefs just as a consequence of undergoing simple hypnosis.

In my work with clients, hypnosis is used as an aid to relaxation to facilitate deep thought and reflection, an experience that is always described as pleasurable. So much so that clients are often reluctant to return from trance.

PROFESSIONAL QUALIFICATIONS

Referring back to the Introduction of this article, if Tony Jacklin had received or engaged in hypnosis from Paul McKenna rather than from a doctor would it more likely have worked?

We will never know the answer to this rhetorical question, but my guess is that Paul McKenna and his methods would have been more successful. The 'best predictor of grades is grades!' The following example sheds further light on the imprecise correlation between performance and professional qualifications.

In a previous career position, I managed a multi-national company's Employee Assistance Programme (EAP). In essence, an EAP is a confidential counselling service for employees who are struggling with psychological issues. The Contractor who provided the EAP service kept detailed records of client interactions and outcomes using the CORE (Clinical Outcome in Routine Evaluation) methodology. The Contractor used a network of about 60 counsellors. It soon became clear to their managers that a very small number of counsellors consistently produced superior outcomes in their clients compared to their peers. It was similarly clear that these outcomes had no relationship to the qualifications of such counsellors. In this example at least, other factors – possibly their skill in building rapport with their clients – were of greater therapeutic value than their individual qualifications. Therefore, whether a practitioner is medically qualified or not is less important than the other skills that they bring to their work.

No-one would argue that practitioners should have the necessary skills, experience, and supervision to work safely in this field. However, such standards should be evidence-based, and not used as an arbitrary barrier to entry. Hypnosis, at least in its present form, is far more of an art than a science.

MUTUAL RAPPORT

I do use the word 'hypnosis' openly, and use its consequent explanation as an introduction to how our minds work. If some practitioners are avoiding using the word 'hypnosis' because *"I had to spend a whole session on misconceptions and stuff"* they are missing a great coaching opportunity. I have reservations about the word 'hypnosis', mainly due to lack of a satisfactory definition. I sometimes use 'meditation' as a synonym. For example, athletes such as Justin Rose talk openly of the benefits that meditation has brought them. The following quotation from Justin appeared in *The Times*:

> "I know Tiger meditates a lot. For me, this has helped. The brain's a muscle, too, and it's something you've got to invest time in. It's as simple as relaxing, breathing, getting myself into a subconscious state where a lot of positive thoughts can sink in." [1]

Hypnosis can be as simple as two people conversing with each other, either or both may be totally unaware they are using hypnotic techniques. Another misconception is that hypnosis involves watching a swinging watch until the eyes become tired, or that it is necessary to fall into deep trance.

A definition I use is that hypnosis is 'a state of mind of inward focus with few external stimuli, shared by both client and therapist'. Therapists often talk about the importance of *'going there first.'* It can occur with 'eyes open' and during apparently normal conversation. The most important factor is that both client and therapist feel relaxed and have established mutual rapport.

REMEMBERING PAST EVENTS

Practitioners appeared to vary in the extent to which they might regard hypnosis as being contraindicated in particular cases. For example, one practitioner stated trauma during childhood such as physical abuse would be a contraindication for use of hypnosis.

This is a very important point. It is relatively common for clients to remember past events that they thought were long forgotten. When people are deeply relaxed they are capable of performing at a higher level. We all remember favourite teachers from our school days who created an environment of trust and relaxation in their classrooms. The subjects they taught were the subjects that we most enjoyed, and were likely the ones where we scored the highest marks. So too can the memory perform at a higher level when relaxed with few external distractions.

Therefore considerable caution should be used in any client who has experienced severe physical or mental trauma. Such clients should only work with suitably qualified health professionals who have experience of dealing with such individuals, and the reactions that might ensue. Abreaction is a distinct possibility in such clients, and requires skilful intervention.

CONCLUSION

In the medical context, no service or a treatment should be offered to an individual without their informed consent. Even if this involves spending time dispelling myths and misconceptions, it should still be pursued. I have already mentioned the difficulty of defining hypnosis, and where a hypnotic process might start or end. I also mentioned that hypnotic processes are ubiquitous in our society. Furthermore, I believe that most if not all individuals have the latent ability to use such hypnotic processes on themselves or others, either consciously or unconsciously.

Using simple hypnosis and meditation techniques enables many of my clients to immediately knock shots off their scores, win competitions, and they are also a lot happier both on and off the golf course. I know this to be true from their verbal and written feedback. So the question is not *'Does hypnosis work in golf?'* but *'How does hypnosis work in golf?'*

Practitioners, clients, and the relevant sporting authorities have a responsibility to address this objectivity gap. This will help to remove the many misconceptions that surround hypnosis, which currently limit both its acceptability and accessibility. Examples of such misconceptions have been elegantly described in Jenkins' article. Furthermore, the results of research will pinpoint the techniques that are most useful, and those that are not. Some practitioners will have doubts about or even resist such external scrutiny. Others will positively welcome and embrace such scrutiny. In the long term, such audit can only help athletes excel at their sport, and enrich the credibility of the professionals that work with them.

REFERENCE

1.   Slot, O., Meditation is Driving Force as Pro-Golfer Rose Starts to Stand Tall, *The Times*, July 19, 2007, reproduced in: The Buddhist Channel, http://www.buddhistchannel.tv/index.php?id=9,4504,0,0,1,0, Accessed June 2009.

Editor's Note: Dr. Stephen Simpson is a Personal Development Coach who works as a Trainer with Paul McKenna. He is a General Medical Council (GMC) Registered Medical Specialist and Fellow of the Royal Society of Medicine. (Http://www.secretstozengolf.com)

Sport Psychology, Hypnosis and Golf:

A Commentary

John Morgan

108 Tomahawk Trail, Cranston, RI 02921, USA

E-mail: john-morgan@cox.net

INTRODUCTION

Hypnosis is highly misunderstood and overly mystified. The question I find interesting to ask is, "What did they call it before they called it hypnosis?" The term hypnosis has only been with us since the 1800s, yet the phenomenon has a recorded history back to the ancient Egyptian sleep temples over 4000 years ago. People came to these temples with the intention of healing themselves from certain maladies. One of the remedies offered was to just sit in quiet contemplation. Enough people left without any evidence of the symptoms they entered with, keeping this practice alive and well over many millennia.

ALL HYPNOSIS IS SELF-HYPNOSIS

What many people don't realize, and this includes many hypnotists, is that all hypnosis is self-hypnosis. Hypnosis is nothing you do to anybody, although stage hypnosis would have it appear that way. Stage hypnotists qualify their stage candidates by paying attention to who is paying attention to them. They do this during their warm-up speech by offering subtle suggestions and observing who is following those suggestions the most. These are the people they invite on stage to perform. Just as some people are highly intelligent or highly irritable, some people are highly suggestible. These are the people who have no qualms about quacking like a duck or worse. This suggestibility makes it appear like the hypnotist has power over them. Nothing could be further from the truth. They have just tipped their hand that they are willing to perform. Everyone is suggestible to what they want to be suggested to about. Not everyone wants to quack. Someone called a hypnotist is really a guide – guiding you into a frame of mind where change happens faster and easier.

We are caught up in the illusion that a teacher puts something inside a student's head.

EDUCATION

No teacher has ever taught anything to a student. The word "education" comes from the Latin root "educare" which means to lead. You remember the old axiom, "You can lead a horse to water, but . . ." A gifted teacher/parent/hypnotist will lead a person to a frame of mind where it's easier to learn. This means the student's critical consciousness gets out of the way and the part of their mind that does the learning, learns easily. That's how we learned to walk and talk, and it's how we learned many of our belief systems. There was no conscious effort. There were no internal pep talks. We just learned. Then when a child turns two years of age, their capacity to learn begins to taper off as critical consciousness forms. Validate this in your own experience by envisioning a resistant two year-old saying "No."

The intellect, once formed, wants to run our lives and often gets in the way of the learning process, which is done at a non-conscious level. What the learning part of our mind learns are patterns – patterns of walking, patterns of speech, patterns of behavior, patterns of belief, patterns of thinking, etc.

To see how much more powerful patterns are than the intellect, try intellectually talking yourself out of one of your strongly-held, patterned beliefs. There may be enough factual data present to change your belief, but your patterned mind won't let you. As an example, what smoker doesn't intellectually have enough information to ascertain that smoking is suicide on the installment plan? Yet, their smoking pattern continues to run. What dieter doesn't want to lose weight? They approach the difficulty intellectually and go on the latest diet. By and large, they lose weight and gain it back. They never outgrow the underlying pattern which keeps their weight coming back.

Hypnosis is a way to update old patterns so they can be useful to us today. You may have formed a pattern of being a "dutiful, obedient child" by eating everything on your plate as instructed. Now that you're an adult, that pattern is no longer working for your weight-loss goals, but it's still working in the background.

TRANCE AND SUGGESTIBILITY

Many will never consider hypnosis for help in learning something new due to fear and misconception. That's because they don't have a full appreciation for hypnosis. So let me demystify it for you. Hypnosis, pure and simple, is "accelerated learning." You learn much more quickly when your critical consciousness calms down and you enter a "trance."

We live our lives in trances, but we don't call them that. When you day dream, you're in a trance. When you talk to yourself inside your head, you're in a trance. When you drive from Point "A" to Point "B" and you forgot how you got there, that's called highway hypnosis.

We go in and out of trances all day long, hundreds of times a day. What people don't realize is that when they are in this frame of mind called a trance, they are a bit more suggestible than they normally are.

The hypnotist's job is to guide you into a frame of mind that you get into everyday, but with their help. They just help you stay in this natural trance state longer, so you are more open to the suggestions you want to impress upon the part of your mind that learns rapidly. When your intellectual-mind noise calms down, there is an opening for a suggestion to take hold.

IMAGINATION AND FEELING

When working with sportsmen of all stripes, especially golfers, I find it valuable to have them use their visual and feeling senses more than they normally do. This focus on their imagination and feeling naturally bypasses their critical consciousness, allowing learning to take place without step-by-step, technical instruction.

If you've ever hit one great shot, you have the ability to replicate that event many times over. There is a part of you that knows what a great shot looks like, feels like and sounds like for you. You just need to practice the mental game by engaging your senses rather than your intellect.

Here's an exercise you can do in less than a minute. Imagine your favorite golfer about to hit a stellar shot. Notice how they position themselves over the ball. Next, imagine what it must feel like to have that confident feeling in your body to flawlessly execute that shot. Then watch them swing the club and strike the ball with perfection.

Then imagine yourself stepping into their body, seeing what they see and feeling what they feel. When you can feel that imagined energy within you, step over the ball and make your swing. Practice this hypnotic technique over and over on the range and watch your shots improve without one piece of conscious criticism or direction from your intellect.

You could also remember and mentally and physically rehearse an exquisite shot that you once made. It could have been one hole ago or 25 years ago. The only necessary ingredient is to engage your imagination and feeling sense. You can add to the depth of this rehearsal by hearing the unmistakable sound of a finely struck ball. This reminds me of a story. I was asked by a well respected Rhode Island teaching pro to help him with his 60-yard pitch shot. He used to knock it stiff, but was now missing it more often than not. I didn't have the credentials to offer any technical advice, but simply the ability to lead him through a mental rehearsal. After a few mental/physical, eyes closed rehearsals, here is what I suggested: Every time you see or hear a well-struck ball, either by a person you are coaching or one that you hit yourself, it will reinforce in your mind how confident, committed and concentrated you are when faced with a 60-yard pitch. There was good news all around. He offered me high-priced technical instruction for free, recommended my services to numerous clients, and his consistent 60-yard pitch shot came out of retirement.

CONCLUSION

By all means, get some technical instruction from a respected teacher, make time for physical practice, and groove your mechanics so they become second nature. However, my golf coaching experience is that not one more conscious tip from a teaching pro, *The Golf Channel* or *Golf Digest* will turn your game around. What does work is some mental and physical sensing of your ideal swing. If you are uncomfortable with the term "Hypnosis," think of these practice sessions as "Fantasy Golf."

None of this is true because I declare it to be so. It only becomes true for you when you can validate this practice in your own game. Make some quiet time and rehearse yourself in the mental game and watch your scores come down and your position on the leaderboard go up. More importantly, witness your improved demeanor on the golf course and feel your enjoyment of the game return. Who knows, you may want to celebrate the next time you hit a successful shot over a water hazard. Instead of hitting a duck hook, you may start quacking like a happy duck!

Editor's Note: John Morgan is a Certified Practitioner of Neuro-Linguistic Programming (NLP) and a Certified Hypnotist with the National Guild of Hypnotists. (http://johnmorganseminars.com/golf-mastery.html)

Sport Psychology, Hypnosis and Golf:

A Commentary

Craig Sigl

9 Lake Bellevue Dr, Suite #214, Bellevue, WA 98005, USA

E-mail: craig@hypnosiswest.com

INTRODUCTION

I am a full-time hypnotherapist specializing in Sports Hypnosis and practicing in the Seattle area. Getting new clients is a huge barrier to entry in this field and part of that requires correctly explaining what hypnotherapy is and dispelling all of the many myths. There are so many false beliefs floating around in the public consciousness about what hypnosis is and how it is applied. A recent story on sports hypnosis was picked up by *USA Today* and illustrates this perfectly. In the story, a sports psychologist actually was quoted as saying: "hypnosis isn't believed to be very effective in sports...It's not used in sports with the leading athletes" [1]. I guess he wouldn't consider Tiger Woods, Rod Carew, Mary Lou Retton, Jimmy Connors, Kobe Bryant, Muhammad Ali, Nolan Ryan and the like as "leading athletes."

Actually, I am thankful that the mainstream sports psychology community is teaching this view as it keeps folks coming to see me.

OVERCOMING FEARS AND DOUBTS ABOUT HYPNOSIS

When I meet folks who are skeptical or fearful of hypnosis, I have no problem at all in overcoming objections. It's simply a matter of explaining to them a few things and putting them in charge of the process. I guess some practitioners have too much ego for that. I only care about getting my clients what they come to me for and will flex to do whatever it takes. Here is where I stand:

1. There is no mind control. The hypnotist has no power over the client. The client is completely under his own control, will hear everything and can reject anything the hypnotist suggests.
2. Everyone can by hypnotized, has been hypnotized, and everyone already does hypnosis normally and naturally. It is not magic. I don't "hypnotize" people. I help them "achieve hypnosis" to make changes. Much of the work happens before I ever do official hypnosis in setting the client up for success.
3. Hypnosis is nothing more than learning at the unconscious level and it happens everywhere. I tell my clients that the only difference between the hypnosis you've already experienced and what we do in my office is that in my office, we use it as a tool, on purpose, and for what you want.

4.   I ask my clients what their problem is and listen for the "feeling" or "emotion" words. I then explain that they have a conscious and an unconscious mind and that their unconscious mind regulates those emotions.

5.   I sell the benefits of changing their emotional response to situations and they are ready to go.

6.   You may have to explain how a stage hypnosis show works to some who have seen one and is their only exposure to hypnosis.

CONCLUSION

Honestly, this is such a simple thing to do that if any practitioner is not easily able to overcome the pre-conceived notions that folks have and get them excited about their successful outcomes, then they don't know enough about hypnosis to practice it. I do public speeches and presentations everywhere, including teaching other hypnotists and I can't remember not being successful in changing these silly beliefs that people bring to me.

REFERENCE

1.   Associated Press, High School Hoops Coach Told to Stop Hypnotizing Team, 4 February 2009, http://www.usatoday.com/sports/preps/basketball/2009-02-04-coach-hypnosis_N.htm

Editor's Note: Craig Sigl is a Certified Hypnotherapist with the National Guild of Hypnotherapy and Vice President of the Washington Chapter. (Http://www.SportsHypnosisWest.com)

Sport Psychology, Hypnosis and Golf:

A Commentary

Jay Granat
StayInTheZone.com, 1060 Main St., Suite 307,
River Edge, NJ 07661, USA
E-mail: info@stayinthezone.com

INTRODUCTION

Simon Jenkins has written a thorough and comprehensive review on the use of hypnosis with golfers outlining many of the key historical, ethical and clinical issues. He also does a fine job of addressing some of the fears and misconceptions associated with hypnosis and self-hypnosis.

I would like to add a few additional comments about the use of hypnosis with golfers. Specifically, I would like to outline a few case examples as a way of showing how hypnosis is employed clinically and how it can be used to help golfers to perform well during competition. I have counseled thousands of golfers and there are many cases I could present in this article. I am selecting just a handful which illustrate how hypnosis and hypnotic techniques are incorporated into the counseling process and the coaching relationship.

I believe it is important to understand that effective hypnosis and hypnotherapy do not take place in a vacuum. That is, when used wisely, these tools are frequently combined with other aspects of psychotherapy and the counseling process.

ANXIETY AND SIBLING RIVALRY

I utilize hypnosis with golfers and with athletes from virtually every sport imaginable. Hypnosis can be used to build confidence, manage stress, improve focus, clarify goals, better relationships, obtain insight, improve motivation, and manage pain.

These are very important matters for the golfer-athlete. For example, recently a golfer who came to see me, because he found himself becoming quite tense when he played golf.

Some therapists or hypnotists might have simple taught this man a self-hypnotic technique which could promote increased relaxation. While there is nothing wrong with this idea, I believe it is important to learn as much as possible about the etiology of a person's anxiety. While taking a history from this man, he explained to me that he is most tense when he competes against his regular playing partner who happens to be his older brother. We discussed the nature and history of their competitiveness and their sibling rivalry. Apparently, my client felt that he could never beat his "big brother" at golf or for that matter at anything. I explained how hypnosis might be helpful to this man. He agreed to try a hypnotic exercise. I helped him into a comfortable trance and suggested that imagine that he was the older brother. He enjoyed being in this powerful role very much. He loved the hypnotic experience very much and he went on to beat his brother by five strokes the next time they played with one another. He called me on Monday morning to share the big news about his victory with me.

HYPNOSIS IN CONJUNCTION WITH GESTALT THERAPY AND PSYCHODRAMA

Hypnosis can also be easily integrated with supportive counseling, insight oriented therapy, behavioral therapy, gestalt therapy, psychoanalysis, dream work, psychodrama and cognitive-behavioral therapy. The literature contains many examples and illustrations of how hypnosis is used by therapists with a wide range of orientations.

I frequently develop hypnotic trances in which golfers can mentally recreate good rounds and bad rounds in my office. I use hypnosis to help them to become deeply aware of what playing well feels like and what playing poorly feels like for them. I sometimes combine this hypnotic experience with a technique from Gestalt therapy and psychodrama known as the "double chair." This two-chair method is a way of helping people to get in touch with two sides of themselves. For example, it can help a golfer to learn about his psychological strengths and his weaknesses.

It can also be used to help a person resolve conflicts or ambivalent feelings. For instance, it could be helpful in treating a golfer who wants to be successful, but has some underlying fear of being successful. While in a hypnotic trance, I frequently have golfers move from the positive chair to the negative chair. Again, this helps the athlete to learn more about what drives each kind of performance on the course. Frequently, this method helps the client to learn an important but subtle difference between feeling good and performing well and feeling poorly and performing poorly. As one golfer noted after trying the double-chair exercise: *"I never realized that a smile helps me to feel more comfortable and play better. Prior to this hypnosis, I mistakenly believed that I had to be serious to be in control and play my best. I will bring a little levity with me the next time I compete."*

USING HYPNOSIS WITH THE GOLFER'S SUPPORT SYSTEM

In addition to working with the golfer by himself or herself, I frequently include parents, coaches, agents, caddies, managers, spouses and significant others in the process. They are the athlete's support system. And sometimes, I lead this support system through a group exercise which is a combination of hypnosis, and guided imagery. This can be quite powerful since it can help everyone to discover interesting ideas and it can help all the key people to get on the same page as the golfer.

In some instances, I have hypnotized both the golfer and his or her caddie in order to prepare them for an upcoming event. Recently, after a placing a golfer and his caddie into a trance, the caddie and the golfer told me in great detail a lot about their goals, and their dreams and how they felt their lives might change if they were successful in their sport. This conversation gave us all some insight into what was motivating this duo.

In my view, when a caddie and golfer are functioning as a team, they enter a rather special shared mental space. Some therapists would say they move into a shared trance state or a joint hypnotic state. Knowing how to get into this kind of state of mind can help the duo to improve the synergy between them and to learn how to perform to their full potential more often.

CONCLUSION

While some golfers can benefit from being hypnotized or learning self-hypnosis, many golfers will find it exceedingly helpful to work with a therapist who can, when necessary, integrate hypnosis into the counseling and coaching processes.

Editor's Note: Jay P. Granat, Ph.D. is a Psychotherapist and is the Founder of StayInTheZone.com. *Golf Digest* named him one of America's Top Ten Mental Gurus. He is the author of *How to Lower Your Golf Score with Sport Psychology and Self-Hypnosis*.
(Http://stayinthezone.com)

Sport Psychology, Hypnosis and Golf:

A Commentary

Bee Epstein-Shepherd

P.O. Box 221383, Carmel, CA, 93923, U.S.A

E-mail: DrBee@aol.com

INTRODUCTION

I found this article to be a quick review of the early history of hypnosis and a discussion of a few applications and issues such as stage hypnosis and NLP. I do agree that it is important for anyone utilizing hypnosis as a golf improvement technique to have some knowledge of the science or research behind the technique.

However, I am devoted to the practical application of hypnosis as a tool that can be utilized to achieve various goals. For the stage hypnotist, hypnosis is a vehicle for entertainment, which by the way, I believe dilutes the power of the technique and only serves to perpetuate the myths that the subject loses control as he gives over his volition to the powerful hypnotist. This is a disservice to the profession of hypnotherapy.

BELIEF AND TRUST

Even though I have formally studied hypnotic phenomena for 30 years (after a life-long interest in the mind-body connection), I am less interested in the science behind hypnosis than I am in its application. I know hypnosis works with subjects who have developed a belief that there is power in the hypnotic state, and who have trust in the hypnotist. Belief is far more important than understanding. I have given my own clients only the information that initiates belief in the process. I focus on the difference between conscious thought and the power of the subconscious to regulate behavior. Examples I might use include driving, playing basketball or the most dramatic, a concert musician.

When I decided to work with golfers, I took lessons from professionals, subscribed to golf magazines, read numerous biographies of well-known golfers, learned the rules of golf, and conscientiously followed the tours in the newspapers and television. I even kept up to date on weekly golf statistics. Thus when I talked to my golfing clients, they were assured of my knowledge and were ready to follow all my suggestions. In order for hypnosis to work for the client, trust in the hypnotist is essential.

I have hypnotized many professional golfers on all major tours, including members of the Ryder Cup and Presidents Cup teams.

HYPNOSIS FOR GOLF

I have heard many audio recordings of hypnotist golf improvement programs. All of them start with a standard induction. Hypnotic suggestions for relaxation and for the proper execution of the swing follow. Most include suggestions for confidence and focus. The relaxation of an induced hypnotic state and the positive suggestions generally have a positive impact on the golfer, who will notice some improvement in performance. This type of hypnotic intervention is simple and it does not take a highly qualified or trained person to get some sort of result. The results are generally short-lived, because the generic posthypnotic suggestions are not customized. In addition, the golfer goes back to focus on mechanics with his swing coach. We know that conscious processing does create tension in the body – sometimes a great deal and sometimes tension that is barely perceptible. But all tension causes poor shots in golf. In my work, I rarely if ever use generic improvement suggestions.

Golf psychology is more than teaching relaxation, confidence and making suggestions for a positive mental attitude. I believe it also involves discovering underlying issues, which hold the golfer back from performing to potential consistently. To this end, I practice analytical hypnotherapy. Analytic hypnotherapy is far more than reprogramming through posthypnotic suggestions. It involves fairly extensive exploration both consciously and subconsciously through hypnosis of the origins of performance blocks. This should not be attempted by someone who does not have a strong psychology background.

One talented young competitor, who had a beautiful swing, came to work with me after her game deteriorated. She had started working with a well-known golf professional to take her game to the next level. This instructor convinced the young woman that she must change her swing in order to improve. Instead of improving, her game deteriorated and she was unable to compete at the high level she had previously attained. No amount of practice improved her game. Since the original swing was in her memory, I used analytical hypnotherapy to regress her to the time that she was playing her best, and her beautiful swing returned after one hour of hypnotic intervention.

I also work with yips, those involuntary spasms that occur when a golfer is under pressure to make a short putt. Tom Watson suffered from yips for years, as did Bernard Langer and others. The conclusion of most "experts" is that yips are a neurological problem. I maintain that this condition is psychological since it does not show up in practice. I confirmed this by getting rid of the problem in a prominent female tour professional. Once again, analytical hypnotherapy provided a "cure" in as little as two hours. In every case, the problem had an origin in an event that the conscious mind had forgotten, but was recalled in hypnosis. Reprogramming effectively "cured" the problem.

An amateur golfer client was extremely sensitive to any sort of noise or movement when she was preparing to hit the ball. A few hours of hypnotic treatment solved this problem for her. She was able to imagine herself encased in a large semi-permeable bubble in order to block out all distractions.

CONCLUSION

I believe that when properly utilized, hypnosis can have a tremendously positive and lasting impact on performance. But the proper utilization comes only when the hypnotist is well versed in a variety of techniques and is experienced enough to know which is appropriate for the presenting problem. I also believe that the hypnotist must have a thorough knowledge of golf so that the golfer's subconscious can trust and accept the reprogramming.

Editors Note: Dr. Bee Epstein-Shepherd is a Certified Hypnotist with the National Guild of Hypnotists and is author of *Mental Management for Great Golf: How to Control Your Thoughts and Play Out of Your Mind*.
(Http://drbee.com)

Sport Psychology, Hypnosis and Golf:

A Commentary

Michael Lardon

University of California, San Diego, School of Medicine,
Department of Psychiatry, 9500 Gilman Drive, MC 0602,
La Jolla, CA 92093-0602, USA
E-mail: mtl@drlardon.com

INTRODUCTION

In the last fifteen years, helping players on the PGA Tour as a sports psychiatrist, I have rarely heard the term hypnosis used. However, hypnosis is often defined by a state of attentive and receptive concentration, with a relative suspension of peripheral awareness that is common when players are playing their best. This timely article by Dr. Simon Jenkins presents a historic overview of hypnosis theory and practical application. Dr. Jenkins' presentation makes it easily understandable why the term hypnosis is so often associated with the occult and is not well understood and often misunderstood.

Hypnotizability is a stable and measurable trait. Research has demonstrated that highly hypnotizable subjects can alter the how their own brain-process stimuli. By extrapolation, these research studies can lead one to hypothesize that a baseball player in deep trance, while at bat, may in fact perceive the moving baseball with greater speed and efficiency.

Some individuals are more hypnotizable than others, and hypnotizability in the general population is thought to reflect a statistically normal distribution. Hypnotizability is not a sign of weak-mindedness, nor is it intrinsically dangerous. Hypnosis is not something you do with a client or to a client. At some level, all hypnosis seems to be a form of self-hypnosis. If clients can be helped to understand that they have the ability to influence their own mental processes, they will have developed a powerful and practical tool. Indeed, as Dr. Jenkins asserts, hypnosis is best utilized when it is well understood by the practitioner.

Dr. David Spiegel and Dr. Ernest Hillgard from Stanford University developed the Hypnotic Induction Profile and Stanford Hypnotic Clinical scale, respectively. Dr. Spiegel has suggested that hypnosis is best conceptualized by understanding its three componets: absorption, dissociation, and suggestibility. Absorption refers to an individual's ability to mentally focus with complete immersion in a central theme, such as completely falling into the experience of watching a good film and transiently losing track of the surrounding world. Dissociation is complementary to absorption, such that an individual can remove certain perceptual experiences out of conscious awareness. This phenomenon may be an evolutionary adaptation that allows an individual to endure horrific traumas involving the experience of pain, such that the pain is dissociated from conscious awareness thereby facilitating attention to critical survival tasks. Suggestibility is conceptualized as a heightened responsiveness to social cues involving the suspension of conscious curiosity. It is a way that allows one to believe whatever they are being told. These three components imply that hypnotic trance may alter normal perceptual processing in productive ways.

AVOIDING THE TERM 'HYPNOSIS'

In the world of sport, the application of hypnosis is insidiously present but rarely discussed. In my clinical experience, most elite athletes engage in some form of self-hypnotic techniques whether it is termed progressive relaxation, positive self-talk, "getting into their game face," or visualization. As sport psychologists and psychiatrists, therefore, we have an opportunity to help athletes benefit from their own natural ability to be hypnotized.

Like many clinicians, I often avoid the term 'hypnosis' when working with clients because of the negative associations involved. However, before utilizing hypnotic trance, I evaluate its likelihood, value and appropriateness. The client's ability to enter a trance-like state can be assessed by administering the Hypnotic Induction Profile; a high score indicates that hypnosis is likely if resistance can be overcome. Because psychiatric illnesses such as post-traumatic stress, anxiety and conversion disorders all have a strong association with hypnotizability, a comprehensive clinical psychological assessment is a prerequisite. If an individual has a history of psychopathology, past hypnotic induction carries a greater risk of unmasking repressed memories and accessing painful experiences that can lead to the de-stabilizing of the client. Thus, use of hypnosis as a tool to enhance sport performance may require considerable clinical experience and judgment.

Most PGA Tour golfers do not have psychiatric illness, but the possibility nevertheless remains an important consideration that mandates solid clinical training before getting involved with a client's unconscious mind. In addition, highly hypnotizable individuals may be given a variety of post-hypnotic suggestions that may not be appropriate; e.g., "bark like a dog" or "kiss your friend's wife", when you are awoken. The impressive phenomenon of post-hypnotic suggestion mandates that the practitioner should not only be clinically trained, but also consistently practice with the highest ethical standards.

If the clinician does not possess the necessary clinical training to navigate ethically and therapeutically through the unconscious mind of the athlete, teaching self-hypnotic techniques are preferable. Although self-hypnotic techniques often result in lighter trance states, they can still be very effective. Self-hypnosis also involves the three basic components of hypnosis, but because the trance is self-induced inappropriate post-hypnotic suggestions are avoided and the phenomena of unmasking repressed memories are rare.

CONCLUSION

Dr. Jenkins' article provides clinicians, coaches and teachers with the necessary overview if they want to take advantage of an athlete's own gift for trance. When an athlete is in trance they often perform their best. Whether the clinician actively hypnotizes the client or teaches the client self-hypnotic techniques, the resulting trance state often enhances the athlete's sense of mastery, independence, and confidence – all of which are fundamental goals of the practicing sports psychologist or psychiatrist.

Editor's Note: Dr. Michael Lardon is an Associate Clinical Professor in the Department of Psychiatry at the University of California, San Diego. He also provides general psychiatry, psychopharmacology and performance enhancement for members of the PGA, LPGA and Nationwide Tours. He is author of *Finding Your Zone: Ten Core Lessons for Achieving Peak Performance in Sports and Life*. (Http://www.drlardon.com)

Sport Psychology, Hypnosis and Golf:

A Commentary

Gio Valiante
Department of Education, Rollins College,
1000 Holt Avenue, 2726 Winter Park, FL 32789, USA
E-mail: gvaliante@rollins.edu

INTRODUCTION

The purpose of the Simon Jenkins' article is to "encourage practitioners … to reflect on how they use the term 'hypnosis' and how they inform their clients about their use of hypnosis" (p. 149). As such, the article presents an overview of differing theoretical orientations and underpinnings regarding mental training, specifically as mental training relates to hypnosis and hypnotic techniques. A clear strength of the article lies in its broad review of relevant literature and techniques as they apply to performance enhancement in the game of golf. Additionally, the author does a nice job of integrating the scholastic with the practical, specifically with the use of anecdotes from professional golfer Tony Jacklin.

With the field of sport psychology growing rapidly, and the research growing in a correspondent manner, the number of issues covered by "the mental game" continues to increase. Previous research and practice show that there is no single magic bullet to effective functioning. Great psychological functioning requires an effective integration of emotional, cognitive, and physiological processes that operate at both conscious and non-conscious levels. Certainly hypnotism can make a valuable contribution to both research and practice in the area of golf as it been shown to be effective in treatment of pain, depression, anxiety and phobias, stress and many other conditions [1].

HYPNOTHERAPISTS LABELING THEMSELVES AS SPORT PSYCHOLOGISTS

As the author pointed out, there is a good deal of debate surrounding the use of hypnosis in general, and within the game of golf in particular. The primary reason for the debate, as the author pointed out, has to do with lack of clarity regarding the definition of hypnosis, lack of definitiveness regarding proper circumstances for which hypnosis might be the ideal application, and lack of credentialing for those practitioners who are hypnotizing their clients. For example, a disturbing trend is for hypnotherapists to label themselves as "sport psychologists." The problem with this comes when clients arrive with problems that do not lend themselves to hypnotherapy, and the hypnotherapist – with no training or credentialing in psychology – does not have the requisite skill set to refer clients to appropriate counseling. Worse still is when they try to apply hypnotherapy in situations where it is powerless or worse, damaging. According to the *American Psychological Association (APA)'s Division of Psychological Hypnosis*:

> Hypnosis is not a type of psychotherapy. It also is not a treatment in and of itself; rather, it is a procedure that can be used to facilitate other types of therapies and treatments. Clinical hypnosis should be conducted only by properly trained and credentialed health care professionals (e.g. psychologists) who also have been trained in the use of hypnosis and who are working within the limits of their professional expertise. [2]

ISSUES IN HYPNOSIS

Even within the field of hypnosis, there remain profound controversies. For example, inside experts cannot say decisively whether or not hypnosis actuates an actual *state change*. Depending on which theoretical orientation (e.g., psychoanalytic, sociocognitive, neodissociative) one approaches hypnotism from, one will end up with different uses and explanations for the use of the technique. At the crux of the issue is the degree to which consciousness is unified or divided; an issue that remains hotly debated across psychological domains [1].

Another major issue in the realm of hypnosis is whether or not certain people have traits that make them more available to hypnosis [3]. Research and practice strongly indicate that there is a trait that explains how much people can respond to hypnosis, but there remains no theoretically grounded or widely accepted explanation as to why that may be the case. If, indeed, hypnosis works for only some individuals, the question of how to screen those individuals remains at large. In my own work, I have come across golfers who are highly suggestible during hypnosis and thus have had excellent results, as well as others for whom hypnosis was ineffective.

REGULATION VERSUS FREE THINKING

This use of trained experts is often not the case, and the use of hypnotism by those unschooled in its proper use is largely responsible for weakening its reputation. With that said, it is easy to think that the correct answer – much as Western governments are implementing – might be greater regulation and control over the field. However, overregulation can often stifle effective therapies that emerge outside of traditional practice. Many of psychology's greatest minds – Erickson, Maslow, Freud – developed their ideas to address the limitations of traditional psychology. Much as is the case with modern day hypnotherapy, to have overlooked their theories because they were developed outside of traditional lines would have been to throw the baby out with the proverbial bathwater. Much as breakthroughs in "nontraditional" medicine are yielding powerful healing techniques, nontraditional healing of the mental and emotional functioning of athletes has a place in the field, albeit when carefully and cautiously applied.

While there exist a number of organizations which work under the umbrella of the American Psychological Association (e.g., American Board of Psychological Hypnosis, American Board of Medical Hypnosis) those practicing hypnosis in golf are not required to participate in, or be certified by, these groups. The question remains, what – if anything – ought to be done for those selling snake oil? Unfortunately, innovation in science and medicine requires the type of free inquiry that is enabled by free thinking. This process will invariably lead to as many ineffective practices and practitioners as breakthroughs and competent nontraditional healers. It is under such conditions that the admonition *caveat emptor* – buyer beware – has to be heeded. Just as it is incumbent on patients to take responsibility for their own health by scrutinizing their doctors and subsequently working with their doctors to jointly work toward health, it is incumbent on golfers to take responsibility for their own mental health by scrutinizing the methods and techniques of their mental health practitioners. It is also incumbent on those practitioners who make up the field to police themselves and others, and ensure that those using hypnosis are fully qualified. Such personal responsibility for themselves and their field filters out ineffective methods, and allows for effective practices – regardless of whether they are hypnosis, behavioral conditioning, social cognitive, or other – to flourish and provide the most fertile ground to help golfers achieve optimal mental functioning.

CONCLUSION

To come full circle, when applied properly and by competent practitioners, hypnotherapy can be a powerful vehicle for psychological change in golfers. The improvements in focus, relaxation and confidence that can result from hypnotherapy are exactly what many golfers need. While those who apply hypnosis for entertainment certainly devalue the method, it would be imprudent to categorically dismiss the value of hypnosis. Those coaches and athletes looking for help with their minds should take it upon themselves to research various practices and methodologies, and make discriminating choices for their own self-improvement.

REFERENCES

1.   Lynn, S.J. and Kirsch, I., *Essentials of Clinical Hypnosis: An Evidence-Based Approach*, American Psychological Association, Washington, DC, 2006.

2.   American Psychological Association, Media Information, 2009,
     Http://www.apa.org/releases/hypnosis

3.   Society of Psychological Hypnosis, Division 30 – American Psychological Association, PowerPoint Presentation, Http://www.apa.org/divisions/div30/powerpoint.html

Editor' Note: Gio Valiante, Ph.D., is mental game consultant to the Golf Channel, *Golf Digest*, the University of Florida, and many of the game's top players. (Http://drgiovaliante.com)

Sport Psychology, Hypnosis and Golf:

A Commentary

Robin Vealey
Department of Kinesiology and Health,
Miami University, Oxford, OH 45056 USA
E-mail: vealeyrs@muohio.edu

INTRODUCTION

"O, be some other name! What's in a name? That which we call a rose by any other name would smell as sweet." This famous Shakespearean line uttered by Juliet Capulet about Romeo Montague means that what matters is what something truly is, as opposed to what it is named or called. The term "hypnosis" is an example of a widely misunderstood name, in that the name itself conjures up many misconceptions and biases. In Simon Jenkins' article on hypnosis and golf, he provides an extensive and useful review about the phenomenon of hypnosis in an attempt to clarify these misconceptions and biases. My intent in this commentary is to: a) suggest that the term "hypnosis" has hampered mental training in golf and perceptions of sport psychology overall; and yet b) that golfers and mental training consultants actually use all of the techniques and strategies that are part of the realm of "hypnosis."

TRANCE

High-level golf performance requires strong mental skills, and therefore "hypnosis" is intriguing to many in the golf community because the term suggests a trance-like outcome where the golfer is completed zoned into an unshakable focus. However, as Jenkins describes in his article, stage hypnotism shows and Hollywood imaginations have created misperceptions about not just hypnosis, but any form of mental training engaged in by golfers and mental training/sport psychology consultants.

First, the term hypnosis fuels the dependency myth of working with a mental trainer. That is, popular opinion is that you have to be "hypnotized" by another person – someone has to do something *to* you – to gain the focus and energy that you need to perform well. Dictionary.com defines hypnosis as "an artificially induced trance state resembling sleep, characterized by heightened susceptibility to suggestion." The word "artificial" is interesting to me, indicating that it is not natural, but rather forced or contrived or induced by another person. Another term associated with hypnosis is *trance*, defined as "a half-conscious state or state of complete mental absorption."

The key point to me is that we all have the trainable ability to induce in ourselves a natural state of focused attention for a round of golf. As a 12-handicapper, there are a few times each year when I play a "pure" round of golf where my focus and energy and performance are in tune so as to produce effortless excellence. This is clearly a "trance-like" state of complete mental absorption, defined in the sport psychology literature as flow [1] or peak experience. But this is natural, and certainly not artificial. I *allow and enable myself* to *naturally* flow with the game by completely blocking out all internal and external distractions. I guess you could call it a trance if you wanted to, but I prefer to call it flow or better yet call it nothing and just enjoy it! Whatever we call it, a state of complete mental absorption when you engage completely in the moment is the essence of any activity, particularly a sport like golf. It's the most natural state we all have, and we all have the ability not only to get there, but to get there by ourselves or by working with a partner.

The use of a mental training consultant becomes a "partner" arrangement, where someone works with golfers to help them learn about themselves and then devise strategies or approaches that lead to productive mental focus and energy. A plethora of mental training programs and consultants are available and very useful to help golfers identify and induce their natural state of focused attention to perform, especially under pressure. Jenkins mentions two (Unestahl's [2] Inner Mental Training and Nideffer's [3] self-hypnosis approach) that are often described using the term "hypnosis." But neither of these programs focus on a trainer doing something *to* an athlete. Rather, they focus on teaching athletes skills that they can utilize themselves. Both Unestahl [2] and Nideffer [3] use the term "self-hypnosis" that emphasizes a self-induced state of focused attention and relaxation that allows you to become immersed in the activity.

The second problem in the popular perception of "hypnosis" – and thus all mental training – is that "you either have it or you don't." This refers to the ability to be "hypnotized" or simply mental skills, such as confidence or the ability to handle pressure. As Jenkins explains, there are measures of "hypnotic susceptibility," and there is evidence that hypnotizability can be improved through training. A basic premise of mental training is that it's just like physical training in terms of the need for deliberate practice. Mental skills, like physical skills, can be developed and enhanced, but only through continuous, systematic deliberate practice. This is the basic theme of Bob Rotella's *Your 15th Club* [4], in which he states that golfers' mental games slide back to softness and weakness if they fail to continue to work at it.

The seemingly magical transformation of people's behavior on stage during a hypnosis show translates to the popular perception that hypnosis is a form of "magic," not systematic skill training. Unfortunately, this influences popular perceptions of sport psychology and mental training, particularly the expectations for, personal commitment to, and responsibility for mental training outcomes. I once had a college golfer phone me and ask to come to my office and talk about mental skills and golf. He was very excited to talk to a sport psychologist, with his stated goal to gain more self-confidence in his abilities. After we chatted for about an hour, I gave him some material to read over and attempted to set up our next meeting. He was astounded and became angry that I could not do anything to him to make him confident that day! I apologized for not being able to magically conduct the Vulcan mind meld made famous by Mr. Spock on "Star Trek", but being from the planet Earth I was a bit limited and required him to actually work to build his own confidence. He sheepishly explained that he just thought I could "hypnotize him or something" based on what he thought sport psychology was all about. Once he realized the importance of, and committed to, putting in the work to become more confident, we went on to have a productive partnership.

There are many strategies in the sport psychology literature that golfers and sport psychology consultants can use to build mental skills. These strategies are common to descriptions of hypnosis as repetition of words/behavior and focused attention. Unesthal's Inner Mental Training [2] is a prototypical example of a systematic progression of mental training using relaxation training, imagery, self-talk and affirmations, goal programming, cognitive restructuring, and concentration training. I'm a big fan of sport psychologist Bob Rotella, who I believe would be the last person on Earth to say he practices hypnosis with golfers. But all of his writings are "hypnotic" to me (and to other golfers based on his success), because his words induce you to examine your own ways of thinking and almost shame you into taking a more rational and logical approach to how you think about competition and the game of golf. The sample affirmations he provides in the appendix of *Your 15th Club* [4] are clearly the type of powerful self-suggestions that are part of "hypnosis."

A final point relevant to golf performance is to clarify that applying strategies of "self-hypnosis" or mental training does not always lead to flow or the "trance-like" state of complete absorption in the moment. In fact, golfers spend much more time grinding than flowing, meaning that they must doggedly work their mental plan and focus to play as well as possible on the days when they're struggling with their game. It's important to clarify the misconception that golfers can only go low in their scores when they are in flow. The real test of any athlete, particularly a golfer, is their ability to perform at a reasonably high level when their physical execution of key skills is not occurring easily and flawlessly. Any mental training program designed to build "self-hypnosis" skills in golfers must include focus plans, self-suggestions, energy management, and relaxation strategies for grinding through competitive rounds when they are not at their best. To "hypnotize" oneself to productively respond no matter what occurs in competition is perhaps the most important mental skill.

CONCLUSION

What's in a name? In the case of hypnosis, the answer is a wide range of perceptions, including misperceptions that need to be clarified for effective mental training in golf. Various forms of "hypnosis" may be used effectively by sport psychology practitioners, but I believe it is important to clarify to athletes that they are ultimately responsible for, and able to build, their own mental skills. That is, we all have the ability to "alter" our own state of consciousness in mentally productive ways to respond effectively.

REFERENCES

1.   Csikszentmihalyi, M., *Flow: The Psychology of Optimal Experience*, Harper & Row, New York, 1990.

2.   Unestahl, L., *Inner Mental Training: A Systematic Self-Instructional Program for Self-Hypnosis*. Orebro, Sweden: Veje, Orebro, Sweden, 1983.

3.   Nideffer, R.M., *Psyched to Win*, Leisure Press, Champaign, IL, 1993.

4.   Rotella, B., *Your 15th Club*, Free Press, New York, 2008.

Editor's Note: Robin Vealey, Ph.D., is a professor of Kinesiology and Health who specialises in mental skills training for athletes. She is author of *Coaching for the Inner Edge*.

Sport Psychology, Hypnosis and Golf:

A Commentary

Patricia Donnelly
Mental Edge, 48 Wells Hill Road, Weston, Connecticut 06883, USA
E-mail: pdonnellyphd@optonline.net

INTRODUCTION

Simon Jenkins bravely and astutely wrestles the concept of hypnosis and how it applies to sport psychology and golf. His well-researched article provides a useful and comprehensive context to evaluate the role of hypnosis in sport psychology and specifically golf. Jenkins' treatise gives pause to define exactly what this notion of hypnotism is and how best it is used as part of one's practice. Before embarking on using hypnotherapy in one's practice, it is essential to have a clear definition of hypnosis and a roadmap for its use. The following commentary attempts to provide a clear recommendation to untangle the quagmire that revolves around hypnosis.

NOMENCLATURE, DENOTATION AND CONNOTATION

What surfaces from Jenkins' article is that there is much confusion as to what exactly is meant by hypnosis not only to the layperson, but to many practitioners as well. Although today most practitioners accept hypnosis as a legitimate form of therapy, it still suffers from "an embarrassing historical heritage" [1].

Its history has gone through three varied phases. The first phase focused on religion and occurred during the time of ancient Egyptian and Greek civilizations, and medieval Christianity. Mesmer and his emphasis on physics and nature led the second stage. The third and final phase was based on psychology and "suggestionism." [1] Unfortunately, many people possess attitudes and beliefs that are often a composite of these three phases. As a result, the denotation of the word hypnosis is confused by its long and varied history.

The important work of Anton Mesmer in 1785 was followed by a period of authoritarianism that lasted until after World War II. Even Freud was party to this authoritarian treatment. After World War II, however, an important shift occurred and a liberalization of hypnosis was begun. This new liberalization was characterized by hypnotherapists realizing not only that they did not know what best served their patients, but also they should not become a parent figure. Instead, they realized they should empower their patients to find their own solutions. [2]

Although clear in any historical account of hypnosis, this shift is not clear in the minds of most lay people. The popularity of stage hypnosis and the cliché of the person being hypnotized clucking like a chicken works against the notion that hypnotherapy empowers the subject. As a result, hypnosis is a misleading term. Often the meaning is charged with associations and emotion. When information, which is activated in one's memory, involves emotional associations, it is difficult to shift attention away from an emotional cue.

Thus, the connotation of the word hypnosis has immense power over the attitude it will create by the person perceiving the connotation. Jenkins makes this point in his description of Jason Grindstaff and Leslee Fishers's work. They asked whether or not the word hypnosis should be used. Before that can be answered, it is important to have a "standardized" definition of hypnosis. The American Psychological Association, Division 30 has defined hypnosis as follows:

> Hypnosis typically involves an introduction to the procedure during which the subject is told that suggestions for imaginative experiences will be presented. The hypnotic induction is an extended initial suggestion for using one's imagination, and may contain further elaborations of the introduction. A hypnotic procedure is used to encourage and evaluate responses to suggestions. When using hypnosis, one person (the subject) is guided by another (the hypnotist) to respond to suggestions for changes in subjective experience, alterations in perception, sensation, emotion, thought or behavior. Persons can also learn self-hypnosis, which is the act of administering hypnotic procedures on one's own. If the subject responds to hypnotic suggestions, it is generally inferred that hypnosis has been induced. Many believe that hypnotic responses and experiences are characteristic of a hypnotic state. While some think that it is not necessary to use the word "hypnosis" as part of the hypnotic induction, others view it as essential. Details of hypnotic procedures and suggestions will differ depending on the goals of the practitioner and the purposes of the clinical or research endeavor. Procedures traditionally involve suggestions to relax, though relaxation is not necessary for hypnosis and a wide variety of suggestions can be used including those to become more alert. Suggestions that permit the extent of hypnosis to be assessed by comparing responses to standardized scales can be used in both clinical and research settings. While the majority of individuals are responsive to at least some suggestions, scores on standardized scales range from high to negligible. Traditionally, scores are grouped into low, medium, and high categories. As is the case with other positively scaled measures of psychological constructs such as attention and awareness, the salience of evidence for having achieved hypnosis increases with the individual's score. [3]

Jenkins's summary of the Grindstaff and Fisher interviews highlighted one practitioner who avoided using the term hypnosis to avoid taking the time to properly define it and clear up misconceptions concerning hypnosis. This attitude is antithetical to what is needed to clear up the mistaken ideas surrounding hypnosis.

I think it is equally important, however, to not only use and explain the term hypnosis, but to use other words in conjunction with hypnosis as well. It is useful to employ the concepts of focused attention, heightened suggestibility and vivid fantasies, all of which are characteristic of hypnosis. This will help to neutralize any mistaken negative connotation that the subject possesses.

A ROADMAP FOR THE PRACTICE OF HYPNOTISM

Hypnotherapy has been shown to work more quickly than many other interventions. Practitioners using hypnotherapy must be mindful of their moral responsibility. It is important that they acutely guard their patients' well-being. Likewise, they must be careful not to exploit their patients' proclivity toward obedience. Basically all caveats and guidelines that apply to a therapist must be followed in hypnotherapy, but more so. [1]

It is important for the practitioner to explain the following before using hypnosis [1]:

- All ethical guidelines that apply to a counseling session still apply.
- Hypnosis is considered to be a psychological condition in which changes in behavior and thought may occur. Although some people experience an increase in suggestibility and what is described as an 'altered state of consciousness,' this is not true for everyone.
- The hypnotist does not hypnotize the individual. The hypnotherapist facilitates the person to achieve goals previously discussed and agreed upon.
- Hypnosis can vary dramatically from one person to another. Often hypnosis is described as a sense of detachment or extreme relaxation. Others have described it as being outside of their consciousness. On the other hand, there are those who remain fully aware and can even engage in conversations while under hypnosis.

It is equally important to be mindful of abuses that must be avoided. These include:

- Creating a situation in which the patient acts in a way that violates his/her moral standards.
- Coercing a hypnotized person to act dangerously.
- Age-regressing a patient to a previous lifetime.
- Imposing one's will onto his/her patients.

Although frequently used as a parlor game, or more recently as a cruise-ship entertainment, hypnotism is nonetheless a legitimate intervention. Its successful use as a treatment for traumatic care, specifically shell shock, points to its strength. It is reported as sometimes being not only more effective, but also safer than other interventions such as medicine. It appears to be especially robust to lower incidences of anxiety and pain.

In the teaching of golf, hypnosis is an important component of anyone's mental arsenal. It is useful in one's pre-competition routine, especially if one is combating anxiety. In order to rid oneself of fear, it is necessary to change the aforementioned "subjective experience". One way this can be accomplished is through the routinization of the pre-shot preparation before one begins the competition. Although this routine varies from person to person, depending on their optimum level of arousal, it is critical to be consistent. By having the same routine each time, it allows the golfer to have a clear mind and to be ready to focus intently and relax as completely as necessary.

Similarly, hypnosis is a formidable addition to one's post-competitive routine. A consistent routine is also necessary after one's round of golf. After evaluating one's personal goals, it is essential to return to an optimal frame of mind. This is done through a previously planned mental routine. This is where it is sometimes necessary to alter one's previous perceptions (as in the case of a difficult loss) and to likewise change one's emotional response.

CONCLUSION

Hypnosis must be administered by a responsible practitioner who is willing to explain, define and educate the subject as to the history and popular psychology concerning hypnotism. Jenkins's article will serve as a template to do this. After demystifying the notion of hypnosis, the empowerment of the client can begin.

REFERENCES

1.   Gezundhajt, H., An Evolution of the Historical Origins of Hypnotism Prior to the Twentieth Century: Between Spirituality and Subconscious, *Contemporary Hypnosis*, 2009, 24(3), 178-194.

2.   Fromm, E., Values in Hypnotherapy, *Psychotherapy: Theory, Research and Practice*, 1980, 17, 1-4.

3.   Society of Psychological Hypnosis, Division 30 – American Psychological Association, New Definition of Hypnosis, http://www.apa.org/divisions/div30/define_hypnosis.html.

Editor's Note: Patricia Donnelly, Ph.D., is a mental-game consultant who works with elite and recreational athletes in her private practice.

Sport Psychology, Hypnosis and Golf:

A Commentary

Tom Ferraro
2 Hillside Avenue, Suite E, Williston Park, NY 11596, USA
E-mail: dtferraro@aol.com

INTRODUCTION

Let me compliment Simon Jenkins for his thorough, interesting and informative review of the history of hypnosis. As a practicing psychoanalyst in the field of sport psychology, I have been asked to respond to parts or the whole of his work. I will focus on the underlying issue of patient expectation regarding hypnosis and how this expectation demonstrates an underlying belief on the part of the hypnotist and patient that growth and improvement will be facile and fast.

Most adults and athletes are familiar with the process of hypnosis. As Simon Jenkins has shown, it conjures up images of stage craft, mesmerism and spiritual trance states. Hypnosis has been used for thousands of years and engages man's belief system to induce positive behavioral changes. Medical hypnosis is used for smoking cessation, diet control and behavioral changes of various kinds. Sport psychologists have used hypnosis to help athletes with anxiety, pain tolerance, focus, and anger control.

STRESS

Let us first review the predominant reasons athletes come a calling. As a psychoanalyst treating stressed professional athletes for my entire career, I have come to see that there are essentially four problem areas that will drive an athlete into treatment: i) anxiety (playing in front of huge crowds produces incredible amounts of anxiety); ii) anger (the amount of pressure and physical trauma they face induces anger that the athlete typically deals with through either drug or alcohol abuse); iii) pain (all athletes get injured and this physical damage produces both pain and fear which must be treated); and iv) loss (disappointment in the career will often lead them into depression which needs treatment). We have terms for all these conditions which include anxiety disorder, drug or alcohol dependence, post-traumatic stress and dysthymia. Make no mistake; these are very real and very serious disorders which take skill, effort and patience to cure. A sport psychologist's greatest mistake is to trivialize these conditions and assume the neurotic or the psychotic athlete can be cured by a few fast and easy sessions. They cannot.

HYPNOSIS AND COGNITIVE-BEHAVIORAL TECHNIQUES

I consider hypnosis to be similar to a host of other cognitive-behavioral methods that have been developed over the last fifty years. Simon Jenkins' discussion of neurolinguistic programming and inner mental training reveals how these techniques can be packaged as a series of cognitive-behavioral techniques under the umbrella of hypnosis. They use relaxation training, goal setting, anxiety control, positive self talk, visualization and similar methods in an effort to suppress and modify affect, cognition or behavior. It all sounds so good in principle. But the reality is they do not hold up under intense competitive pressure as any athlete or experienced sport psychologist will tell you.

It took Frank Gardner and Zella Moore's impressive text *Clinical Sport Psychology* [1] to prove this point. They demonstrated through review and meta-analysis how surprisingly limited and ineffective short-term behavioral interventions were. The techniques are all an intellectual exercise which leaves the athlete's sense of identity, self image or unconscious conflicts untouched. Hypnotists insist that they are 'entering the client's unconscious' when in fact they are not even close. And so armed with these rather superficial techniques, the athlete returns to battle to fail again and then to drop out of therapy. This is the predominant pattern of sport psychology.

The underlying self and the unresolved traumas are quite powerful and have been in place for a very long time. Giving behavioral or hypnotic messages to the athlete is like putting jet fuel into an old car. The car will take off real fast, but the frame and shocks are so worn that the car will fall apart when it reaches 60 mph.

When the athlete arrives in my office, I see my job is to dispel the fantasy that the cure will be quick and easy. I establish a working relationship and begin the laborious work of getting to understand the athlete's debilitating anxiety, anger, fear or despair. One must assess the triggers, the history; and one must work hard to develop a trusting relationship. Only after all this does the real work begin of working through the cure, week after week. They will need to learn how to be more forgiving, how to repair a destroyed self-image, how to manage fear of injury, how to solace the self, and how to lower anxiety in the heat of battle.

I see hypnosis like all short-term behavior therapy where the therapist joins with the patient's resistance as they both pretend that the work will be cheap, easy and fast. It never is. The pressures are too great and the damage done is too profound. To assume the work will be fast trivializes the problems to a laughable degree.

TRANCE AND DISSOCIATION

I do think hypnosis has made a substantial contribution by introducing the concept of trance. To me, they are referencing the state of dissociation. What I have come to realize is that many high-level international athletes have had at least ten years of very painful training they have endured. What this does to them is to promote a dissociated state that they all seem to enter into in order to withstand the enormous pain of training and competition. This state is alluded to when one reads about 'the zone,' which has been mythologized as an easy-to-enter state that one should have access to without strain or pain. In fact, dissociative states and dissociative identity are developed through years of painful suffering. Most elite athletes do this and never tell anyone about it for fear they will be called crazy. But most tell me that, in fact, they do hear internal voices in this state that prompt them to withstand pain, ignore pain and minimize pressure in order to crush the competition. These are the tiger personalities that they all seem to have inside and rarely talk about to others. These fugue states are actually very common in elite athletes. It is remarkable to me that, to my knowledge, almost nothing had been written about dissociative states in champions yet the ones I treat all seem to have this defensive system in place. And so I think hypnosis is the only field that is keeping this concept alive. More research is needed.

CONCLUSION

There is no easy way to teach athletes to develop methods to cope with the intensity of the competitive sport experience. It takes energy, time, insight and patience. There is no short cut to this and I believe that hypnosis promises this kind of short cut. Using hypnosis to treat a troubled athlete is like planting flowers in a toxic waste dump. The flowers look good alright, but they will be dead within 24 hours. Hypnosis is also a lot like Valium. It works for a little while, but has a half life of 12 hours. Then it's back to who you really are.

REFERENCE

1.   Gardner, F.L. and Moore, Z.E., *Clinical Sport Psychology*, Human Kinetics, Champaign, IL, 2005.

Editor's Note: Tom Ferraro, Ph.D., is a sport psychologist and psychoanalytic psychotherapist. (Http://www.drtomferraro.com)

Sport Psychology, Hypnosis and Golf:

A Commentary

Simon Robinson

School of Applied Global Ethics, Leeds Metropolitan University,
The Grange, Beckett Park Campus, Headingley, LS6 3QS, UK
E-mail: S.J. Robinson@leedsmet.ac.uk

INTRODUCTION

Simon Jenkins' article is very useful. It helpfully focuses on key theories of hypnosis while also attending to some of the major issues arising from different views. If I were a professional golfer, it would leave me thinking twice before I made use of hypnosis.

PERSONAL AUTONOMY

I suppose the main question I would want to raise would be how hypnosis might affect my autonomy. The use of hypnosis stage shows sharply focuses this issue. Paul Mckenna and others insist that nobody would get involved in hypnosis unless they wanted to, and only do things in that situation that they wanted to. Theorists about hypnosis might also suggest that this is not some mystical state, but is rather a simple acting out of a role. However, it is clear for other theorists that such an acting out is more complex than passive acceptance of the hypnotist's words. There are cognitive strategies involved as well, at least enabling an interpretation of the hypnotist's words. In turn, this would seem to suggest that the social context of the relationship has a major effect on the response. Some would connect a form of crude hypnosis to cults (New Religious Movements). The key point about cults, however, is precisely the social context. The dynamic of cults involves setting up a dependency relationship where the member feels valued. This unconditional acceptance, so called 'love-bombing', seems in stark contrast for many to previous relationships, not least in the family, in which acceptance has seemed highly conditional. The problem then with cults is that acceptance becomes, over time, conditional on reciprocal commitment, and the acceptance of polarized ways of thinking that reinforce the power of the leader. This both reinforces McKenna's point and at the same time raises more questions. If hypnosis is used in cults, then it is not the hypnosis that causes the dependency. The prior need for acceptance and the response of the cult is what builds up the dependency relationship, something reinforced in some cults by 'discipling', where new members are given mentors who build up a close and disciplined relationship [1]. This relationship in turn makes the cult member want to serve the group, to accept the views of the leader, and to proselytize. If there is any use of hypnotic techniques, they are simply reinforcing what the person already wants to do.

They want to be compliant, because that makes them feel good, and precisely avoids having to take responsibility for dealing with previous relationships that were causing problems. Being part of the cult even gives the person courage to stand out against old relationships, but only at the price of accepting the cult's way of thinking, something reinforced by affective ritual.

But here lies the problem, this may be what the person wants, but it certainly isn't autonomy, at least not in the sense of a moral maturity that can handle ambiguity, diversity, and critical thinking. Much the same dynamic was seen in the rise of the Third Reich [2], with well-being associated with polarized thought and dependency, reinforced by ritual, myth, mystery and by fear. Hence, even if a form of hypnosis were used in politics, it would still come down to the voters wanting this approach. Faced by uncertainty, this made them feel good and thus they gave the regime their allegiance.

Transfer to the stage and we have most of these things in place: ritual, mystification (accepted by McKenna himself) and an audience there for fun and wanting to believe. All it lacks is the imposition of polarized thinking, and in its place is short-term entertainment.

COACHING, HYPNOSIS AND MEDITATION

So how does all this relate to serious golfing? The good news is that self-hypnosis or hypnosis used by the coach will not lead to dependency and the like. Where hypnosis is based in contract and used for clear utility, in this case improving focus for playing, then that is what the player wants. It becomes simply a technique to achieve that end. The question then is how hypnosis differs from the techniques of spirituality. There is some evidence that such techniques help in centring the athlete and that this improves performance. Indeed, such evidence also indicates improvement in creativity in general [3].

Meditation is an obvious technique around the development of mindfulness, and it is suggested that this includes effects like hypnosis while also developing a deeper sense of consciousness [4]. At one level, this enables centredness, a better capacity to focus on the necessary action, and thus to exclude attention to other areas of experience that connect to an uncontrolled affective response, be they immediate or recalled, and that might put off the golfer. At another level, deeper awareness involves an increased awareness of the self and of the social and physical environment, in such a way that creative connections can be made. It is precisely this level of awareness that might be critical for a rugby player and not for a golfer.

CONCLUSION

Of course, this leaves many further questions, not least around whether effective centredness involves focusing on the task to the exclusion of the surrounding environment, or whether it actually involves an embracing of that environment, such that it does not affect performance. In all that, is hypnosis only able to achieve the first of these (as some of Jenkins' article suggests) or could it enable deeper engagement?

And what about autonomy? That comes back to the golfer and what he or she wants out of this. Self-governance requires critical conversation around purpose, objective and social context, and focus that connects intention to practice. Provided hypnosis is used in this critical context, which I take good coaching to provide, there is every reason to believe hypnosis can assist focus for effective practice, without negatively affecting autonomy.

REFERENCES

1. Robinson, S., *Ministry to Students*, SPCK, London, 2004.

2. Burleigh, M., *The Third Reich*, Pan, London, 2000.

3. Bachner-Melman, R., Dina, C., Zohar et al., A.H. et al., *AVPR1a* and *SLC6A4* Gene Polymorphisms Are Associated with Creative Dance Performance, *PLOS Genetics*, 2005, September.

4. Ding-E Young, J.D-E. and Taylor, E., Meditation as a Voluntary Hypometabolic State of Biological Estivation, *News in Physiological Sciences*, 1998, 13(3), 149-153.

Editor's Note: The Reverend Simon Robinson, Ph.D., is Professor of Applied and Professional Ethics at Leeds Metropolitan University.

Using Mental Skills to Improve Golfing Performance: A Theory-Based Case Study for Golf Coaches

Jon Finn

Carnegie Faculty of Sport and Education
Leeds Metropolitan University, Leeds, LS6 3QS, UK
E-mail: J.Finn@Leedsmet.ac.uk

ABSTRACT

The manner in which golfers think on the golf course significantly influences their performance. In 2008, the author provided an overview of golf-specific mental skills with the intention of raising golf coaches' awareness of psychological techniques they could use to help their golfers think more effectively. The aim of this paper is to follow up the author's overview by providing an introduction to mental skills interventions, specifically focusing on how they can be tailored to individual golfer's needs, and how they can be applied, analysed, and evaluated to facilitate the performance of competitive golfers. This five-part paper will: 1) outline the current state of formal mental skills education among golf coaches; 2) introduce selected theories that underpin mental skills interventions; 3) address the role of golf coaches in delivering these interventions; 4) suggest some frameworks which might help to increase the effectiveness of these interventions; and 5) illustrate the practical application of these theories and frameworks by describing a mental skills intervention that was used with a tour-level golfer to improve playing performance.

Key words: Coaching Education, Cognitive Behavioural Modification, Mental Skills Intervention, Sport Psychology

INTRODUCTION

The relationship between psychology and successful golf performance seems perpetual. This special connection has been recognised by both successful golf professionals [1-3] and academics who research golf performance [4-6]. More

---

Reviewers: Patti McGowan (Lake Nona Golf Club, USA)
            John Stevenson (Grand Valley State University, USA)

recently golf coach education programmes [7, 8] have also supported the role of psychology within golf. However, given the contemporary nature of these programmes, many golf professionals have not received a formal education in golf psychology and therefore their application of psychological principles within golf coaching may be haphazard and unstructured [9]. The primary aim of this paper is to aid golf coaches in their application of psychological techniques by illustrating their use within a case study based on the author's work with a tour-level golfer.

In 2008 Finn [10] offered golf coaches an overview of golf specific mental skills. A useful way to consider Finn's overview is to frame it within the taxonomy of cognitive learning. Anderson and Krathwohl's [11] taxonomy of cognitive learning classifies how we learn new information in the following six stages: 1) *Remembering* and the ability to recall information, such as recalling the different mental skills that golf coaches might use; 2) *Understanding* and explaining how different mental skills might help golf performance; 3) *Applying* and being able to discuss mental skills with clients and suggesting where mental skills might be able to help an individual's golf performance; 4) *Analysing* and breaking down the specific components of individual mental skills to see how they function in a golfing context; 5) *Evaluating* and critiquing the impact mental skills have made on a client's performance; and 6) *Creating* and being able to modify the application of mental skills as needed, tailoring unique mental skills interventions to individual clients.

This hierarchal model suggests that we learn in stages, conquering one stage before we can move onto the next. For example, in order to master the analysing stage we must also have first comprehended the remembering, understanding and applying stages. Although this is an over-simplified description of Anderson and Krathwohl's model, it aims to highlight that, as a coach, you learn in stages, thus becoming proficient in an area such as mental skills training will take time and practice.

Finn's overview aimed to fulfil stages 1 and 2 of Anderson and Krathwohl's taxonomy; providing coaches with a knowledge of what mental skills consist of, and with an understanding of where and when different mental skills might be used within their coaching. A rational progression from Finn's overview would be to help golf coaches progress their knowledge of mental skills up the taxonomy by providing further information on mental skills in golf.

The aim of the current article is to raise golf coaches' awareness of how to use mental skills interventions to improve the performance of their clients, specifically detailing how to apply, analyse, evaluate and create these types of interventions. A case study, based on work with a tour-level player, will be used to highlight these dimensions of a golf-specific mental skills intervention.

HOW CAN I USE MENTAL SKILLS TO IMPROVE THE PERFORMANCE OF MY CLIENTS? A CASE STUDY OF A TOUR-CALIBRE PLAYER

The following case study is based on a sport psychologist's work with a professional tour golfer, where a mental skills intervention was utilized to improve performance. After providing a brief overview of the case study, the paper will consider: i) selected psychological theories which underpin mental skills interventions, explaining why mental skills might help golfers to think more effectively; ii) the role of the golf coach in delivering mental skills; iii) selected frameworks that might help to maximise the impact of mental skills interventions, and iv) a detailed account of a golf-specific case study, moving from initial contact with the golfer, through the intervention process, and finally to the outcomes of the intervention.

WHO IS THE GOLFER?

The identity of the golfer has been kept anonymous, so we'll call him Bill. Bill was a 37-year-old PGA Professional playing full time on a professional tour. Bill felt his game lacked consistency and that he did not always perform as well as he knew he could. One bad shot was all it seemed to take for Bill's good performances to quickly turn into bad performances. Bill felt that he could improve the mental aspect of his game and decided to approach a sport psychology consultant to investigate further.

The next three sections aim to answer questions which the author has often been asked by golf coaches when they have been considering the use of mental techniques with their own clients who were suffering from similar problems to Bill.

HOW WOULD A MENTAL SKILLS INTERVENTION HELP BILL OR MY CLIENT TO THINK MORE EFFECTIVELY ON THE GOLF COURSE?

How Bill thinks, as how any golfer thinks, will largely determine how he feels and behaves [12]. For example, if Bill thinks that he cannot successfully hole short putts under pressure he most likely won't be able to. A fear of not being able to hole short putts is generally not innate, but something that has been learned through our own experiences, including watching or listening to others [12]. Psychologists have suggested that if we can learn maladaptive thoughts (e.g., 'I always miss these important short putts) and behaviours (e.g., standing over the ball longer than you normally would do because you are anxious) which negatively impact on performance, we can also learn to modify these thoughts to enhance performance. A popular way to modify these thoughts has been termed Cognitive Behavioural Modification (CBM) [12, 13]. Mental skills such as imagery, self-talk, arousal regulation techniques and goal setting can be used to help modify our thoughts and behaviours. For example, imagine that you have to hole a short putt to win an important competition. You are feeling extremely anxious because the last time you were in this position you missed the hole, knocking the ball six feet past, and you subsequently missed your next putt. Consequently, your thoughts are driven by those images with your self-talk reminding you of what happened last time. Physically, your shoulders are tense and your arms become very stiff. In this situation, you could make use of specific mental skills to modify your maladaptive thoughts and behaviours. For example, you could change thoughts such as the negative images and self-talk that you might be experiencing into positive images and self-talk. Further, arousal regulation-based mental skills (e.g., relaxation techniques) could help to reduce maladaptive behaviours such as developing tension in your shoulders and arms. So when golfers are prone to experiencing maladaptive thoughts and behaviours in relation to their golf, CBM interventions, which are largely mental-skills based, can be used to modify and regulate more facilitative thoughts and behaviours.

CAN I DELIVER MENTAL SKILLS TO PLAYERS LIKE BILL IF I AM NOT A QUALIFIED PSYCHOLOGIST?

As CBM techniques are rooted within psychology, you would assume that in a sport setting sport psychologists would deliver these types of interventions. However, it is often the case that sport psychologists are not well placed to do this. Increasingly, coaches are developing and facilitating CBM interventions as it is felt that they are better placed to do so, although many will be supported by sport psychologists from a distance [14]. To facilitate this growing trend, many governing bodies now actively train their coaches to use mental skills within their coaching.

The use of the CBM approach and mental skills interventions has proven to be very popular and largely successful within sport [15, 16]. However some criticism has been levelled at the effectiveness of these types of interventions within sport psychology. It has been suggested that this style of intervention often only act as sticking plasters (or band aids) to athlete's problems, sometimes only managing symptoms when deeper issues need to be considered [17]. For example, if your golfer is in a state of clinical depression due to problems in their personal life, it is highly unlikely that performance psychology-based interventions such as CBM will effectively resolve the bouts of concentration loss that may be resulting on the golf course. As the criticisms of CBM within sport psychology seem valid, it is important that these types of interventions are applied appropriately, and that if deeper psychological issues do need to be considered, coaches call in the appropriate professionals. An overriding aim of this article is to encourage coaches to use mental skills with their clients. However, it is not advocating that coaches act as psychologists, as this would jeopardizes ethical boundaries and some cases athlete's mental well-being [18].

IF I WAS WORKING WITH BILL OR ONE OF MY OWN CLIENTS HOW COULD I MAXIMISE THE IMPACT OF THE CBM APPROACH AND MENTAL SKILLS INTERVENTIONS?

If a CBM approach to enhancing your golfer's performance is deemed appropriate, there are several frameworks which can be employed to maximise intervention effectiveness. This article will provide an overview of the following three established frameworks, and then utilize these frameworks with the present case study of Bill: 1) Thomas's [19] model of a seven-phase performance enhancement process; 2) Bull and Shambrook's [20] considerations for adherence in psychological skills training; and 3) Deci and Ryan's [21] social cognitive motivational theory of self-determination.

Thomas's [19] model describes the seven general phases a practitioner (sport psychologist or a coach) might employ during a psychological intervention when working with an athlete or team of athletes, or in this case a golfer.

- *Phase 1 (Orientation)* concentrates on getting a feel for the type of help a client is looking for and how committed they are to improving their performance. For example, whether a golfer has a specific problem with their game or whether they just want you to help them raise their general awareness of mental skills training.

- *Phase 2 (Sport Analysis)* focuses on gaining a deeper understanding of what it takes to compete in the sport you are working in. If you put yourself in the shoes of a sport psychologist, this phase is very applicable as many practitioners will work in sports that they have never competed in, or had any involvement in before. If this is the case, practitioners will need to develop an understanding of what athletes need to do to achieve and compete in this particular sport. A golfing equivalent might be that if you are a golf coach working with tour players, but you have never played or experienced tour golf before. Therefore, developing a deeper understanding of what it takes to compete on tour will be very important for this coach.

- *Phase 3 (Individual/Team Assessment)* is the initial assessment stage where information such as questionnaires, interviews and performance data is gathered regarding an athlete's current performance and where strengths and weaknesses might be. A practitioner's approach to this phase is often very individual, with different practitioners using their own unique combination of measures.

- *Phase 4 (Conceptualization)* combines what has been learned from phase 3 and therefore what needs to be done in phase 5. This phase will often entail going to the literature to develop a deeper understanding of your client's problems.

- *Phase 5 (Psychological Skills Training)* considers and introduces the skills and techniques which might help to improve your client's performance. For example, if your client is suffering from anxiety on the first tee, arousal regulation techniques might be introduced.

- *Phase 6 (Implementation)* considers the integration of the skills and techniques introduced in phase 5 into your client's everyday training, and their performances.

- *Phase 7 (Evaluation)* aims to evaluate your client's adherence to the interventions which have been implemented, measure any performance impact the interventions have had, and understand any problems or difficulties your client might have faced.

- Finally the model has a closed-loop function moving the practitioner from phase 7 back to phase 1 where they reassess the initially stated aims and objectives.

In summary, Thomas [19] proposes that the practitioner should consider the following phases: i) what does your client want from you? ii) what does your client need to perform in their chosen sport? iii) what does your client's current performance look like? iv) which areas of your client's current performance can be improved? v) which psychological skills might help your client to improve? vi) how can you implement these skills into their performance? vii) how can you evaluate the impact of the intervention? and viii) does your client need to revisit these phases for further interventions?

Thomas's [19] model provides a good general overview of how a practitioner might implement a CBM-based intervention. Although this model oversimplifies the process of an intervention and does have some limitations, it is recognised as a framework which is reflective of contemporary practice [22].

Thomas's [19] model provides a good framework to work around, but used alone it will not maximise the effectiveness of your intervention. Two of the biggest barriers a practitioner will face when developing a successful intervention will be keeping the client motivated and ensuring intervention adherence.

When considering motivation, Deci and Ryan's [21] social cognitive motivational theory of self-determination has recently been popular in sport psychology. To be self-determined is to be able to do what you chose to do, and free to make the choices you want to make. Self-determination theory suggests that you provide autonomy, competence and relatedness in order to maximise a self-determined mindset within your clients. To enable these three core components of self-determination you should consider the following behaviours suggested by Mageau and Vallerand [23]: don't tell your client what to do; provide them with options and choices when developing interventions; value their thoughts and options; give them good positive feedback; if you are asking them to do things they don't necessarily agree with, rationalise why you are asking them to do it; encourage them to focus on the improvements they are making on the small areas of their game that you are working on, and not how their overall game might currently compare with their peers.

In order to maximise adherence to mental skills interventions, Bull and Shambrook [20] suggested that practitioners should consider the following four strategies: i) working in partnership with the athlete to develop the intervention; ii) developing the intervention within a sound goal-setting framework in order to ensure a specific outcome target; iii) putting in place clear processes of measurement, achievement and evaluation; and iv) encouraging the athlete to use a diary to longitudinally reflect, record and evaluate the intervention.

Utilizing these three frameworks in combination within your intervention will help you to maximise intervention efficacy. Furthermore, these frameworks may also be useful in maximising the impact of other parts of your coaching practice.

IF I WAS WORKING WITH BILL HOW COULD I IMPLEMENT AN EFFECTIVE MENTAL SKILLS INTERVENTION USING THE PREVIOUS THREE FRAMEWORKS?

PHASE 1 (ORIENTATION)
Bill was a 37-year-old PGA Professional playing fulltime on a professional tour. Bill approached a sport psychology consultant as he was interested in improving the mental-skills aspect of his game. Bill indicated that he would like to pursue a one-to-one psychology-based intervention with the sport psychologist.

PHASE 2 (SPORT ANALYSIS)
The psychology consultant was comfortable with the sport of golf as he had played

the game for a considerable period of time. He had also worked closely with the Professional Golf Association of Great Britain and Ireland and clearly understood the key psychological principles which underpinned elite golf performance. In deciding whether developing the psychological elements of Bill's game would be beneficial, the consultant considered two influential points: a) Bill was making a living playing on tour as a professional golfer, and b) several of Bill's peers reported that he was a very talented golfer, but they felt he had never fulfilled his potential of playing golf at a higher level; i.e., the PGA European Tour. Based on this evidence, the consultant concluded that enhancing Bill's psychological performance skills might be beneficial to his overall game, helping him to get closer to fulfilling his potential.

PHASE 3 (INDIVIDUAL/TEAM ASSESSMENT)

The assessment process took place over a three-week period. Several sources of data were collected allowing a triangulation effect, where the same variables are considered from three or more perspectives, reducing the potential bias that may occur when only limited data sources are referenced [24]. The data collected were as follows; self-report data from Bill in the form of a performance profile [25] (see appendix 1 for an example of a performance profile) and several semi-structured interviews; self-report data from Bill's friends, playing partners and coach in the form of semi-structured interviews; the practitioner's observations of Bill practicing and playing competitive golf; objective data in the form of Bill's competitive golf statistics which he had collected over a period of time. Periodic reports combining subjective data, objective data, assessment of the problem(s), and plans for intervention (SOAP) were constructed throughout the data collection process [26]. This allowed the consultant to reflect on his interactions with the client and consolidate the multiple sources of data that were collected, thus bringing to the fore any important issues that emerged. Further measures that might be appropriate within the assessment phase, but were not used in the current intervention, are personality profiles and learning style inventories. Some of these types of assessment tools would facilitate the development of interventions that consider the underpinning motivations and behaviours of your client, and also their optimal learning style, helping you to build more effective interventions.

PHASE 4 (CONCEPTUALIZATION)

Several themes emerged once the data had been evaluated. It seemed that the weakest areas of Bill's game were his fairway play and his putting. It was apparent that Bill changed the way he played these areas of his golf game on a regular basis. For example, he often changed the type and style of his golf equipment, his pre-shot routines (PSR) as he approached each shot, and the way he swung the golf club. This inconsistency in Bill's game led to him being given the nickname, 'The Tinker Man' by other players and coaches, a nickname which Bill seemed to be fond of and wanted to live up to.

By contrast, the strongest area of Bill's golf was his driving off the tee. In this area of his game, Bill used a consistent PSR prior to every shot and was confident in his swing. Self report, observational and performance data suggested he consistently hit fairways and greens from the tee. Bill did not tinker with this area of his game.

After hitting a shot that he perceived to be of unacceptable quality, Bill would engage in high levels of negative self-talk and physical gestures of dissatisfaction. A side effect of his negative mindset would often manifest in his next similar shot. Here Bill believed that he would become overly conscious of his golf swing technique, describing his 'swing thoughts', which seemed to be similar to the concept of swing keys [27], as being focused on the movements he needed to make to perform his swing. For example, Bill reported that he would consciously think about the mechanics of his golf swing as he hit the ball.

To summarize, it seemed that the major psychological problem with Bill's game was that he did not display consistent behaviours on the golf course and was intolerant of any shot he believed to be inferior of his best. This did not necessarily reflect the finishing position of the shot, but the way the shot looked and felt. This frustration led to negative self-talk and body language. When Bill was unhappy with a particular shot, he would become upset which would result in him tweaking his PSR and consciously monitoring the mechanics of his swing on the next similar shot. When he was unhappy with a round, or sequential rounds, he would change a club. Bill seemed to justify his title as 'The Tinker Man'.

It seemed Bill was in a vicious cycle which once entered was difficult to escape. He would hit what he perceived to be a bad shot because it didn't look or feel as good as it could, getting angry at himself, and subsequently trying to change his swing which would lead to him to hitting an even worse shot. Bill was unable to accept bad shots, consciously thinking about his swing on the next shot in order to try and improve his performance. He was in a negative downward spiral and he could not seem to get out of it.

Once the areas that were believed to be detrimental to Bill's game had been identified, it was important to gain a clear understanding from the research literature of why these factors might be having a negative impact. Once these factors were clearly understood, a much more effective intervention could be developed.

DO GOLFERS ALWAYS NEED TO HIT PERFECT SHOTS?

Anecdotal reports from Ian Woosnam stated that he became a world-class player when he began to accept that he would hit four to five bad shots per round [28]. Qualitative research [29] found that during peak performance a sample of touring and club professional golfers were unconcerned by the negative consequences of poor shots. Furthermore data collected by Thomas and Over [6] suggested that the lower handicap golfers in their sample were less inclined to dwell on missed opportunities, past mistakes and other negative thoughts whilst performing in competitions.

Golfers may be frustrated by unsatisfactory shots as they are susceptible to cognitive biases during shot selection [30]. Human information processing is thought to be affected by a wide variety of cognitive biases [31]. Cognitive biases, which have also been termed positive illusions, have been suggested to manifest themselves in well-adjusted children and adults [31]. Individuals who indulge in positive illusions tend to overestimate their success in tasks which are important to them [32]. Bill may have therefore been overestimating his ability to hit every shot optimally and therefore suffering from the effects of positive illusions.

CAN NEGATIVE SELF-TALK BE DETRIMENTAL TO GOLF PERFORMANCE?

Negative self-talk is largely thought to be counter-productive during sporting performance due to the internal distractions it causes [33]. Specifically, negative self-talk can potentially have an adverse impact on anxiety, concentration, confidence and motivation [33, 34]. Research also suggests that negative-self talk and associated behaviours may have a positive impact on your opponent's performance [35, 36].

CAN INSTRUCTIONAL SELF-TALK BE DETRIMENTAL TO GOLF PERFORMANCE?

Bill's dissatisfaction with poor shots led him to engage in instructional self-talk [37], where his internal dialogue focused on the mechanics of his swing. It has been suggested that for someone of Bill's high skill level the use of instructional self-talk, while swinging the club, would be detrimental to his swing mechanics, and therefore the quality of his shot [38]. This is based on the conscious processing hypothesis, which suggests that when a skill has become automatic, too much conscious thought about the mechanics of that skill will result in the skill breaking down. For example, many highly skilled golfers report that they have very few thoughts when swinging the golf club. This suggests their golf skills are automatic and, therefore, if they begin to think too much about making movements by using instructional self-talk, their golf skills will begin to breakdown.

CAN A CONSISTENT PSR HELP TO ENHANCE GOLF PERFORMANCE?

Within golf, a PSR can be thought of as the routine pattern of thoughts and behaviours used before and as a golfer hits the golf ball (for example see Table 1). Well-practiced and consistent PSRs are thought to have several advantages. Shaw [39] suggested that they facilitate good mental preparation, helping the golfer turn on concentration, focus in on the present shot, and displace previous negative shots. Further, the

Table 1. Example of a Golf-Specific Pre-Shot Routine (PSR)

Behaviours	Thoughts
1. Put your glove on	1. Self-talk – 'turn concentration on'
2. Pace out to nearest yardage marker	2. Imagery – 'start to see the types of shots you could play'
3. Select club and pick it out of your bag	3. Self-talk 'stay in the present'
4. Stand behind the ball using your club to line up the target	4. Imagery – 'see, feel and hear the shot you want to play and how you want the shot to behave when it lands'
5. Stand over the ball and set up	5. Self-talk – 'take a nice slow deep breath feeling the air slowly fill up your belly as you breathe in through your nostrils, and feeling your shoulders sink as the tension is released. Then once your belly is full slowly release the air back out through your mouth'
6. The swing	6. Self-talk – 'smooth' or '1, 2, 3' (striking the ball on 3). Imagery – 'see the ball flight you want to achieve'

automatic subconscious process of the swing is thought to be enhanced by a consistent PSR [40, 41].

WILL MECHANICAL THOUGHTS DURING MY SWING FACILITATE GOOD PERFORMANCE?

Consciously being aware of movements during a well-learned skill may lead to unravelling the automaticity of that skill [42, 43]. Within golf, there has been much indirect discussion of automaticity in the form of 'trusting your swing'. The term trust, in this case, refers to the performance skill of releasing any conscious control over motor program execution; for golf, this means the ability to give up trying to control the swing mechanics during execution of the golf swing [44, 45]. Rotella [46] has discussed the role of players trusting their swings when they were performing exceptionally well, and were on what he termed a 'hot streak'. Rotella reported that players did not think about the mechanics of their swings while hitting the ball when on hot streaks. Jenkins' [27] research supported the idea that thinking about swing mechanics might be detrimental to competitive performance, suggesting that swing keys are used to fill the void between the continuum of thinking about swing mechanics and the seemingly impossible 'thinking about nothing'. Most recently the work of Stevenson and colleagues on tee shots, pitch shots and putting highlighted the superior performance advantages for golfers who trusted their swing mechanics [44, 47].

WHAT DOES THE ANECDOTAL AND RESEARCH EVIDENCE SUGGEST ABOUT BILL'S PERFORMANCE?

After considering the literature, it seemed that the cognitions and behaviours which were debilitative to Bill's performance were as follows: 1) the belief that he should always hit perfect shots; 2) becoming angry at himself when he hit bad shots; 3) not having consistent PSRs in his fairway and putting game; 4) consciously thinking about the mechanics of his swing while swinging. As illustrated in Figure 1, these four areas are interconnected: 1) as Bill believes that every shot must be perfect, he becomes frustrated when every shot is not perfect; 1-2) this frustration results in negative self-talk; 2-3) Bill's negative self-talk and general dissatisfaction with his previous shot leads him to change his thoughts and behaviours during his PSR, making it inconsistent; 3-4) due the inconsistent nature and lack of automaticity in

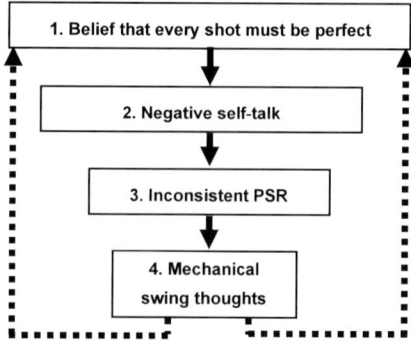

Figure 1. Cognitions and Behaviours that Appeared to be Detrimental to Bill's Golf Game

Bill's PSR, and his lack of trust in his swing, he allows mechanical swing thoughts to occur; 4-1) these mechanical swing thoughts could result in dissatisfactory shots that are not perfect.

PHASE 5 (PSYCHOLOGICAL SKILLS TRAINING)

In phase 5, it is important that you reach a consensus with your client about the cognitions and behaviours which are deemed to be detrimental to their performance. This can be facilitated through raising the awareness of your client by educating them and using the information from phase 4. When an understanding between your client and yourself has been achieved, you can begin to consider which types of mental skills and interventions might facilitate positive change in their debilitative thoughts and actions.

In this case, both Bill and the practitioner agreed that they would aim to modify the following cognitions and behaviours (Figure 2): 1) belief that every shot must be perfect, to belief that not every shot will be perfect; 2) negative self-talk after a bad shot, to positive self-talk after a bad shot; 3) inconsistent PSRs in fairway and putting play, to consistent PSRs in fairway and putting play; 4) mechanical swing thoughts during swing, to no mechanical swing thoughts during the swing.

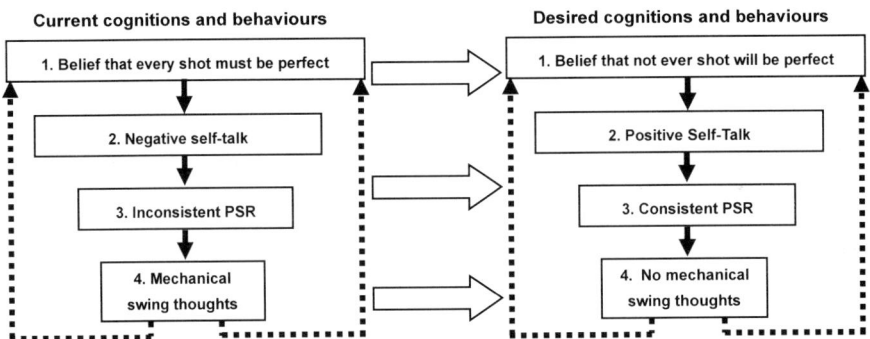

Figure 2. Bill's Current Cognitions and Behaviours Modified Through Interventions to Desired Cognitions and Behaviours

SOME STEPS TO PROMOTE ADHERENCE AND SELF-DETERMINATION IN YOUR CLIENT

As you begin to work together with your client to select appropriate interventions, it is important that you consider the suggestions made to increase self-determination and adherence in the first part of the paper. For example, work in partnership with your client and also encourage them to keep a reflective diary of the intervention process [20]. Provide your client with choices regarding the interventions they may wish to pursue [23].

A further consideration might be that not all clients will be familiar with sport psychology techniques. If this is the case, it may be beneficial to introduce them to the potential benefits of using these techniques [48]. For example, emphasise the growth in the number of athletes using psychological skills to enhance performance and the success these athletes are experiencing [49, 50]. Localise the use of psychological skills in golf and give world-class examples of their use. For example, discuss peer-reviewed published articles [16, 51] and anecdotal reports from Tiger Woods and Ernie Els, two prominent golfers who publicise their use of psychology. It will also be important to explain that their proficiency in psychological skills will be reflected through the amount of time and practice which they afford to developing and learning those skills [33].

DEVELOPING THE FOUNDATIONS OF THE INTERVENTIONS
It was agreed by both Bill and the practitioner that the intervention would be comprised of two components. As illustrated in Figure 3, the first part of the intervention, Part A, would target Bill's thoughts that every shot he hit needed to look and feel perfect. The second part of the intervention, Part B, would be directed at Bill's negative self-talk, inconsistent PSRs and mechanical swing thoughts.

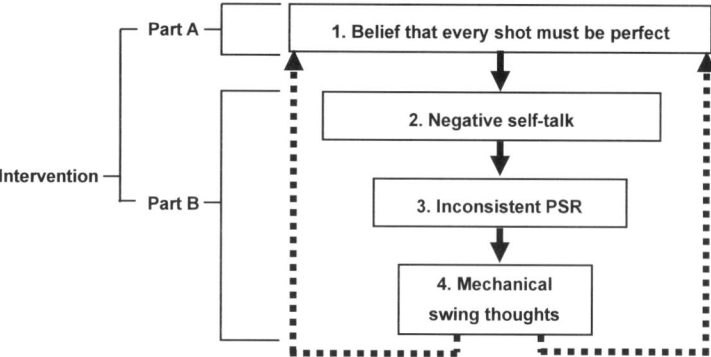

Figure 3. Target Cognitions (Part A) and Behaviours (Part B) of the Interventions

PART A
Both the practitioner and Bill felt that the education session, based on the material in phase 4 regarding not having to consistently hit perfect shots, had made a significant impact in modifying Bill's thinking on this area. However, to further reinforce the educational sessions, the practitioner asked Bill to complete two further tasks. First, Bill was to attend a major tournament, which was being held close to Bill's home in the near future, and monitor the number of imperfect shots that world-ranked players were hitting [52]. Secondly, Bill was asked to recall from his memory occasions when he and playing partners had hit bad shots, but still recorded good scores [52].

Bill and the practitioner also agreed that a golf-course coping strategy to manage Bill's expectations of hitting perfect shots would be used. It was decided that a coping strategy called positive focusing [51] might be beneficial for Bill. Positive focusing combines both motivational general mastery imagery and motivational mastery self-talk [10]. The aim of positive focusing is to direct attention towards good and better shots and away from problematic and negative shots. Focusing on positive performance in sport has been suggested to facilitate better performance [53, 54].

PART B

As Bill's cognitive and behavioural problems seemed to stem from hitting what he believed to be substandard shots, both Bill and the practitioner agreed that the PSR would be a good place to develop the second part of the intervention. Further, as PSRs generally only consider thoughts and behaviours prior to skill execution; i.e., the golf swing, it was also deemed important to consider the post-shot routine (Post-SR) where Bill's self-talk was sometimes very negative.

In targeting Bill's pre-shot and post-shot fairway and putting routines, it was hoped that consistency could be developed, mechanical swing thoughts could be reduced, and negative self-talk could be changed into positive self-talk. Based on the evidence presented in phase 4, it was agreed that this was the best way to proceed.

PSR DEVELOPMENT

The construction of PSRs is a very individual process. The practitioner provided Bill with some golf-specific PSR literature and supported him in the development of his fairway and putting routines. The practitioner asked Bill to strike a balance between both behavioural and cognitive PSR components (for example see Table 1). Bill was also encouraged to direct his attention to relevant stimuli during the routines and not focus on previous mistakes or his golf swing [39, 41]. Bill was advised on the roles imagery, self-talk, arousal regulation and goal-setting might play in his PSRs [10]. The consultant and Bill also used a video recorder to help Bill develop and learn the behavioural components of his PSRs. Primarily this technique was used to allow Bill to see his new routines from several different external perspectives, both immediately after recordings were made, and also at home in Bill's own time. In addition to helping Bill to learn his new PSRs, it was also hoped that this technique would increase Bill's confidence in using his new PSRs.

POST-SHOT ROUTINE DEVELOPMENT

As the Post-SR was specifically targeting negative self-talk, both the practitioner and Bill agreed that the use of a coping strategy to combat this would be beneficial. Bill agreed to introduce the four rules of React [51] into his Post-SR. React is based on motivational general mastery imagery and motivational mastery self-talk (see Finn [10]) and aims to reduce negative self-talk. The four rules of React are: i) use only positive verbal comments about your game and yourself; ii) defend yourself against negative comments from others; iii) keep your attributes adaptive (e.g., focus on external factors such as an unlucky bounce); and iv) use the 4-F technique to stay optimistic (see below).

The 4-F technique [51] would be used as another tool to help Bill react positively after hitting a bad shot: i) Fudge (an exclamation of dissatisfaction after hitting a bad shot); ii) Fix (redo the swing using a practice swing to correct the problem); iii) Forget (forget about the problematic shot, remembering nobody plays perfect golf); and iv) Focus (focus your attention on the next the shot in a positive manner).

It was agreed that Bill would use the four rules of React after every shot he hit during both practice and competition in order to make it a consistent part of his Post-SR.

PHASE 6 (IMPLEMENTATION)

Once the client has begun to learn the skills presented in phase 5, these skills can start to be integrated into the client's practices and performances. When considering Bull and Shambrook's [20] thoughts on adherence, it is important that a sound goal-setting framework is used as well as clear processes of measurement, achievement and evaluation. Further, during this important implementation process, it has been suggested that the practitioner contacts the client on a daily basis with a view to increasing adherence [55].

INTERVENTION A

Organisation. Positive Focusing was initially integrated into Bill's game over a two-week period.

   Expected Outcomes. Bill and the consultant set moderately difficult goals for him to attain [56]. The short-term goal for Positive Focusing was to record at least one good shot after each hole that Bill played in both game-specific practice and competition. The long-term goal for Positive Focusing was to be able to disregard all negative thoughts regarding his game while on the course and only concentrate on the positives.

   Measurements. To enable positive focusing, Bill would ask himself after a shot "Did I hit that shot basically where I wanted it to go?" If the answer was "Yes," then Bill agreed that he should consider it at least a 'good shot'. Bill would make a note of at least one good shot after every hole. For example, if Bill had hit a good drive on the second hole, it was suggested that he mark down a D (drive) on his adapted scorecard (Figure 4) next to the second hole in the Pos Foc row. If he hit a good long putt on the first hole it was suggested that he mark down LP (long putt) next to the first hole on his adapted scorecard. The number of good shots he recorded should be equal to or greater than the number of holes he played. Percentages could also be calculated. Bill was then to imagine these good shots in between holes to replace any negative thought he may be having. A self-report diary was also used to record Bill's positive thinking patterns and strategies [21].

INTERVENTION B

The organisation, expected outcomes, measures and evaluation processes of the React intervention in Bill's Post-SR were almost identical to those used for the Positive Focus intervention. The only difference was that Bill used the Post-SR (React) column in the adapted scorecard to record his use of this strategy. This process for the implementation of the PSR is explained below:

   Organisation. Once Bill had consolidated the behavioural and cognitive components of the fairway and putting PSRs that he wanted to use, we began to monitor their use.

   Expected Outcomes. It was agreed that Bill's short-term goal would be to implement and begin to use consistent and systematic PSRs in his fairway play and putting. Bill's long term goal would be to use consistent PSRs before every shot he played, both during a round of golf and in the practice area when working on game-specific play.

   Measurements. Bill would record every time he used a PSR on the adapted score

Hole	1	2	3	4	5	6	7	8	9	Out
White Tees	190	334	502	168	423	452	394	362	161	2986
Yellow Tees	180	305	494	159	375	431	383	348	149	2824
Par	3	4	5	3	4	4	4	4	3	34
Stroke Index	10	9	14	15	2	3	6	13	11	
Score										
Pos Foc										
Post-SR (React)										
PPRs										
Stroke Index	18	10	4	14	12	2	8	6	16	
Par	4	4	5	3	4	4	4	4	3	35
Red Tees	217	305	476	156	303	365	326	338	149	2635

(Positive Score Card)

Hole	10	11	12	13	14	15	16	17	18	In	Tot	Hc	Nt
W. Tees	369	319	430	196	363	356	411	493	302	3239	6225		
Y. Tees	357	298	416	191	357	326	406	475	290	3116	5940		
Par	4	4	4	3	4	4	4	5	4	36	70		
Stroke Index	8	18	1	7	17	4	5	16	12				
Score													
Pos Foc													
Post-SR (React)													
PPRs													
Stroke Index	7	17	3	11	13	1	5	9	15		Pos Foc + React		
Par	4	4	5	3	4	4	4	5	4	37	72	=	/36
R. Tees	322	243	422	148	356	268	363	454	240	2816	5451	=	%

No of FW/greens hit from tee

Total No Putts

No of greens hit from FW

Figure 4. Adapted Score Card Used to Measure the Cognitive and Behavioural Interventions Used by Bill (based on [51])

card in the PSR column. The number of PSRs versus shots made per round could then be calculated to give a gross value and percentage of how often Bill was using the routines. A self-report diary of pre-shot routines would also be kept to record Bill's thoughts on this area [21].

PHASE 7 (EVALUATION)

It was agreed between Bill and the practitioner that he should aim to achieve his short-term goals within a two-week period of the intervention being implemented, and his long-term goal within two months. The actual number and percentage of times Bill successfully used the Positive Focus, Post-SR and PSR strategies would be recorded on the adapted score card (Figure 4) every time he played a round of golf. These data would provide one measure of Bill's progress.

A further evaluation measure would be Bill's golf performance. Bill would use the adapted score card to record the number of putts, and the number of greens hit from the fairway per round. Bill's diary and own thoughts on the intervention would also be an important component of the evaluation process.

CLOSED-LOOP FUNCTION

Once the intervention had been thoroughly evaluated, it would be clear if it had been successful or if further work needed to be done on these specific areas of Bill's game. In the first instance – the intervention had been successful – Bill might decide to target another area of his game which he felt needed to be improved, beginning again at phase 1 of the model. In the second instance – the intervention had not been successful – Bill and the practitioner would have to re-evaluate why and move back into phase 1 of the model.

CONCLUSION

The way golfers think ultimately impacts their ability to perform on the golf course; therefore, the capability to improve the way that golfers think might be an important commodity for a golf coach. This paper used the case study of Bill as a genuine example of a mental-skills intervention to raise the awareness of golf coaches wishing to develop these types of interventions with their own clients.

If coaches want to use these types of interventions successfully, it is important that they: i) theoretically understand why and how mental skills help golfers to improve their performance; ii) have a repertoire of mental skills that they can successfully use with their client; iii) approach interventions systematically; and iv) consider their client's motivational needs and levels of adherence when implementing interventions. In combination, these four attributes should help to develop mental skills interventions which have a positive impact on the way clients think and perform on the golf course.

It is important to recognize that mental skills interventions can be extremely complex. If you do wish to start applying, analysing, evaluating and creating mental skills interventions, you should begin by working in partnership with an experienced sport psychologist. This will not only further your understanding of these performance-enhancing techniques, but also maximise your abilities to make mental skills work in your coaching, ultimately helping your clients to think more effectively on the golf course. Finally, it is hoped that the combined examples of the current article and Finn [10] will bring golf coaches a step closer to understanding and successfully implementing mental skills interventions with their own clients.

REFERENCES

1. Nicklaus, J., *Play Better Golf*, King Features, New York, 1976.

2. Faldo, N., *Life Swings*, Headline, St Ives, 2004.

3. Tiger Woods, "How I play the game II". *Golf Digest*, http://findarticles.com/p/articles/mi_m0HFI/is_11_52/ai_79352566/ (Web page accessed on 28/03/2009).

4. Crews, D.J. and Boutcher, S.H., The Effects of a Pre-Shot Attentional Routine on a Well Learned Skill, *International Journal of Sport Psychology*, 1986, 18, 30-39.

5. McCaffrey, N. and Orlick, T., Mental Factors Related to Excellence Among Top Professional Golfers, *International Journal of Sport Psychology*, 1989, 20, 256-278.

6. Thomas, P.R. and Over, R., Psychological and Psychomotor Skills Associated with Performance in Golf, *The Sport Psychologist*, 1994, 8, 73-86.

7. PGA.info, Http://www.pga.info/PGANationalTrainingAcademy/34791421.htm (Web page accessed on 01/03/2008).

8. University of Birmingham, http://www.education.bham.ac.uk/programmes/applied_golf_management_studies.shtml (Web page accessed on 12/04/2009).

9. Kingston, K. Thomas, O. and Mitchell, I., Psychology for Coaches, in: Jones, R., Hughes, M. and Kingston, K., ed., *An Introduction to Sports Coaching: From Science and Theory to Practice*, Routledge, Abingdon, UK, 2008, 28-40.

10. Finn, J., An Introduction to Using Mental Skills to Enhance Performance in Golf: Beyond the Bounds of Positive and Negative Thinking, *Annual Review of Golf Coaching*, 2008, 2, 255-269.

11. Anderson, L. and Krathwohl, D., *A Taxonomy for Learning, Teaching and Assessing: A Revision of Bloom's Taxonomy of Educational Objectives,* Longman, New York, 2001.

12. Hill, K., *Frameworks for Sport Psychologists: Enhancing Sport Performance*, Human Kinetics, Champaign, IL, 2001.

13. Mace, R., Cognitive Behavioural Interventions in Sport, in: Jones, G. and Hardy, L., eds., *Stress and Performance in Sport,* John Wiley & Sons, Chichester, UK, 1995, 203-230.

14. Smith, R.E. and Johnson, J., An Organizational Empowerment Approach to Consultation in Professional Baseball, *The Sport Psychologist*, 1990, 4, 347-357.

15. Weinberg, R.S. and Williams, J.M., Integrating and Implementing a Psychological Skills Training Program in: Williams, J. M., ed., *Applied Sport Psychology: Personal Growth to Peak Performance,* 6th edn., McGraw-Hill, New York, 2006, 425-457.

16. Thomas, P. and Fogarty, G., Psychological Skills Training in Golf: The Role of Individual Differences in Cognitive Preferences, *The Sport Psychologist*, 1997, 11, 86-106.

17. Nesti, M., *Existential Psychology and Sport: Theory and Application*, Routledge, Abingdon, 2004.

18. Brewer, B., Doing Sport Psychology in the Coaching Role in: Andersen, M. B., ed., *Doing Sport Psychology*, Human Kinetics, Champaign, IL, 2000, 237-248.

19. Morris, T. and Thomas, P. R., Approaches to Applied Sport Psychology in: Morris, T. and Summers, J., eds., *Sport Psychology: Theory, Applications and Current Issues*, John Wiley & Sons, Chichester, UK, 1995, 215-252.

20. Shambrook, C.J. and Bull, S.J., Adherence to Psychological Preparation in Sport in: Bull, S.J., ed., *Adherence Issues in Sport and Exercise,* John Wiley & Sons, London, 1999, 169-197.

21.   Ryan, R.M. and Deci, E.L., Self-Determination Theory and the Facilitation of Intrinsic Motivation, Social Development, and Well-Being, *American Psychologist*, 2000, 55, 68-78.

22.   Hardy, L., Jones, G. and Gould, D., *Understanding Psychological Preparation for Sport*, John Wiley & Sons, Chichcester, UK, 1996.

23.   Mageau, G.A. and Vallerand, R.J., The Coach-Athlete Relationship: A Motivational Model, *Journal of Sports Sciences*, 2003, 21, 883-904.

24.   Miles, M.B. and Huberman, A.M., *An Expanded Sourcebook: Qualitative Data Analysis*, Sage, London, 1994.

25.   Butler, R.J. and Hardy, L., The Performance Profile: Theory and Application in Sport, *The Sport Psychologist*, 1992, 6, 27-46.

26.   Andersen, M.B., Beginnings: Intakes and the Initiation Relationships, in: Andersen, M.B., ed., *Doing Sport Psychology*, Human Kinetics, Champaign, IL, 2000, 3-17.

27.   Jenkins, S., The Use of Swing Keys by Elite Tournament Professionals, *Annual Review of Golf Coaching*, 2007, 1, 199-217.

28.   BBC Five Live, http://www.bbc.co.uk/fivelive/programmes/des_meets.shtml (Web page accessed 22.06.05).

29.   Cohn, P.J., An Exploratory Study on Peak Performance in Golf, *The Sport Psychologist*, 1991, 5, 1-14.

30.   Kirschenbaum, D.S. and O'Connor, E., Positive Illusions in Golf: Empirical and Conceptual Analyses, *Journal of Applied Sport Psychology*, 1999, 11, 1-27.

31.   Tversky, A. and Kahneman, D., Judgement Under Uncertainty: Heuristics and Biases, *Science*, 1974, 183, 1124-1131.

32.   Taylor, S.E. and Brown, J.D., Illusion and Well-Being: A Social-Psychological Perspective on Mental Health, *Psychological Bulletin*, 1988, 103, 193-210.

33.   Weinberg, R. S. and Gould, D., *Foundations of Sport and Exercise Psychology*, 4th edn., Human Kinetics, Champaign, IL, 2007.

34.   Van Raalte, J. L., Brewer, B. W., Rivera, P. M. and Petitpas, A. J., The Relationship Between Observable Self-Talk and Competitive Junior Tennis Players' Match Performance, *Journal of Sport and Exercise Psychology*, 1994, 16, 400-415.

35.   Greenlees, I., Bradley, A., Holder, T. and Thelwell, R., The Impact of Opponents' Non-Verbal Behaviour on the First Impressions and Outcome Expectations of Table-Tennis Players, *Psychology of Sport & Exercise*, 2005, 6, 103-115.

36.   Greenlees, I., Buscombe, R., Thelwell, R., Holder, T. and Rimmer, M., Impact of Opponents' Clothing and Body Language on Impression Formation and Outcome Expectations, *Journal of Sport & Exercise Psychology*, 2005, 27, 39-52.

37.   Hardy, J., Hall, C.R. and Hardy, L., Quantifying Athlete Self-Talk, *Journal of Sports Sciences*, 2005, 23, 905-917.

38.   Masters, R. S., Knowledge, Knerves and Know-How: The Role of Explicit Versus Knowledge in the Breakdown of Complex Motor Skill Under Pressure, *British Journal of Psychology*, 1992, 83, 343-358.

39.   Shaw, D., Confidence and the Pre-Shot Routine in Golf: A Case Study, in: Cockerill, I., ed., *Solutions in Sport Psychology*, Thomson, London, 2002, 108-119.

40.   Baumeister, R.F., Choking Under Pressure: Self-Consciousness and Paradoxical Effects of Incentives on Skilful Performance, *Journal of Personality and Social Psychology*, 1984, 46, 610-620.

41.   Boutcher, S.H., The Role of Pre-Performance Routines in Sport in: Jones, G. and Hardy, L., eds., *Stress and Performance in Sport*, John Wiley & Sons, Chichester, UK, 1990, 231-247.

42. Magill, R., *Motor Learning and Control: Concepts and Applications,* McGraw-Hill, New York, 2007.

43. Beilock, S. and Carr, T.H., On the Fragility of Skilled Performance: What Governs Choking Under Pressure?, *Journal of Experimental Psychology*, 2001, 4, 701-725.

44. Moore, W.E. and Stevenson, J.R., Understanding Trust in the Performance of Complex Automatic Sport Skills, *The Sport Psychologist*, 1991, 5, 281-289.

45. Stevenson, J., Moore, B., Pinter, M., Stephenson, P., Liley, M., Elliot, D. and Brossman, M., Effects of Trust Training on Tee and Pitch Shots in Golf, *Annual Review of Golf Coaching*, 2007, 1, 47-66.

46. Rotella, R. and Cullen, R., *Golf is Not a Game of Perfect*, Simon & Schuster, New York, 1995.

47. Stevenson, J., Stephenson, P. Hoffman, M., Jager, T., VanEngen, E. and Pinter, M., Effects of Trust Training on Putting Performance of Skilled Golfers: A Randomized Control Trial, *Annual Review of Golf Coaching*, 2007, 1, 67-86.

48. Maniar, S.D., Curry, L.A., Sommers, F.J. and Walsh, J.A., Student Athlete Preference in Seeking Help When Confronted with Sports Performance Problems, *The Sport Psychologist*, 2001, 15, 205-223.

49. Greenleaf, C., Gould, D. and Dieffenbach, K., Factors Influencing Olympic Performance: Interviews with Atlanta and Nagano US Olympians, *Journal of Applied Sport Psychology,* 2001, 13, 154-184.

50. Vernacchia, R.A., McGuire, R. T., Reardon, J.P. and Templin, D. P., Psychological Characteristics of Olympic Track and Field Athletes, *International Journal of Sport Psychology*, 2000, 3, 5-23.

51. Kirschenbaum, D.S., Owens, D. and O'Connor, E., Smart Golf: Preliminary Evaluation of a Simple, Yet Comprehensive, Approach to Improving and Scoring the Mental Game, *The Sport Psychologist*, 1998, 12, 271-282.

52. Duda, J. and Treasure, D., Motivational Processes and the Facilitation of Performance, Persistency, and Well-Being in Sport in: Williams, J. M., ed., *Applied Sport Psychology: Personal Growth to Peak Performance, 6th edn.,* McGraw-Hill, New York, 2006, 57-81.

53. Kirschenbaum, D.S., *Mind Matters: Seven Steps to Smarter Sport Performance*, Cooper, Carmel, 1997.

54. Kirschenbaum, D.S. and Tomarken, A.J., On Facing the Generalization Problem: The Study of Self-Regulatory Failure in: Kendall, P., ed., *Advances of Cognitive Behavioral Research and Therapy,* Academic Press, New York, 1982, 121-200.

55. Bull, S.J., Personal and Situational Influences on the Adherence to Mental Skills Training, *Journal of Sport and Exercise Psychology*, 1991, 13, 121-132.

56. Kyllo, L.B. and Landers, D.M., Goal Setting in Sport and Exercise: A Research Synthesis to Resolve the Controversy, *Journal of Sport and Exercise Psychology*, 1995, 17, 117-137.

APPENDIX 1: EXAMPLE PERFORMANCE PROFILE

Name: Joe Bloggs *Handicap:* +3 *Date:* 01/07/09

Quality	Sub-Quality	Meaning	Current Rating	Short Term Goal
Technical	Driving off the tee	I am confident that I will hit the area of fairway I want 90% of the time.	8	10
	Mid-fairway irons	The green generally looks pretty big from about 150-180yds in. I'm nearly always on.	7	10
	Chipping	My chipping has let me down in the past sixth months. On one or two occasions I have ended up off the other side of the green.	6	8
	Short Putting	I just don't seem to be able to hole out when it matters. It used to be a strength, but now I find anything from 8ft to 4ft really difficult.	4	7
Mental	Concentration	My focus during short putts and chips is often on my technique because I feel so tense.	5	8
	Confidence	My belief in my ability to hold short putts has almost gone.	4	7
	Motivation	I like getting out there and getting my practice in at least 4 times a week. However, I think I can sometimes improve on the quality .	8	10
	Anxiety	I get really anxious when it come to short putts and chipping	5	8
Physical	Tension	I feel lots of tension in the top of my back shoulders and arms when I get anxious.	5	7
	Suppleness	I am aware I have really tight hamstrings, but I often forget or can't be bothered to stretch them. However, I do realise this might cause me problems in the future.	6	8
	Stamina	I find it easy to get around 18 holes and even if I have to do 36 in the day, I don't feel tired.	9	10

Using Mental Skills to Improve Golfing Performance: A Theory-based Case Study for Golf Coaches

A Commentary

Nigel Edwards
Director of Player Development & Coaching
Golf Union of Wales Ltd
Catsash, Newport, South Wales, NP18 1JQ, UK
E-mail: nigel.edwards@golfunionwales.org

INTRODUCTION

Having read Jon Finn's article on the mental skills for performance golf, it is quite interesting how it has now become vogue, cool or chic to thank your psychologist or performance coach or at least refer to this aspect of your golf. Jon's article confirms all my previous experience as a player and an interested party in how competitors in any environment perform at the highest of standards. I agree with Jon's conclusion that professional advice on this subject is vital and from my personal experience I confirm that the way we think affects performance.

Over the years, the Welsh Golfing Union and now the Golf Union of Wales have been proactive in getting players to help themselves more in a very simplistic way. As has been proven many times the simplest methods are usually the best and from experience players/performers want the quickest route to success, but in a simple form.

FEEDBACK AND SELF-MONITORING OF PERFORMANCE

The better players feedback their knowledge in a simple way, but also providing great details, whereas the not so successful will use phrases, words or terms such as 'I drove it well', 'I putted well' or 'I putted badly', rather than getting to the bottom of how they perform each part of the game successfully for themselves. We are getting the players to understand how they play well, rather than *us* telling *them* how they should play well. We are constantly 'drip-feeding' them information and reminding them of their *keys* they have previously mentioned that enhance their performances. Some players have really taken on board the feedback and are precise in what makes them tick, but even the most conscientious 'forget' what makes it all for into place.

We have an extremely varied group of individuals ranging through the Mens, Ladies, Boys and Girls National squads with differing levels of commitment, desire, dedication and intelligence. While not all players grasp the reasoning behind the system, it is perhaps best described using the example of an examination in school: your *keys* are your crib notes, whether they be in the form of key phrases such as commit, focus, enjoy or just simple reminders in the yardage booklet. I would suggest that the very elite performers from Major golf champions to Olympic gold medalists have *keys* that enable them to succeed, so why shouldn't an amateur golfer? From our experiences, the players who perform best have *keys*, understand their feedback, and also know when to use the information and to what extent so that it doesn't 'overcrowd' them. Performance still has to be fun and enjoyable – the moment a player becomes over-concerned with the exact science of success then performance dips. Successful performance is a fine blend of art and science. We have other players who show little interest for this constant monitoring of performance, but we have evidence they have little consistency especially when it comes to performing at the higher levels.

SOME OF MY KEYS TO PLAYING AND THINKING WELL

As a current elite amateur player myself, here are my recent keys:

PUTTING

Using the chalk line in practice gives me confidence for holing out. Plenty of pace putting to the edges of greens, but also competitive practice like lag and drag. In terms of my technique/feelings/thoughts, I have putted better recently by making a fluid stroke (not hitting at the ball) and committing to the line of a putt, trusting and letting go.

CHIPPING

Making it very simple, several practice swings/strokes to try and get the feel, visualising the shot, committing to the shot and accepting the outcome. I also feel that I chip better when I stand taller to the ball at address and not "slouch".

PITCHING

Good yardages give me confidence and then during the practice round hitting pitches from different distances not too much but several times during a round. At the moment, I am visualising the shot very clearly.

BUNKER PLAY

Being positive about the selection of the shot, committing to that choice of shot and then executing. I try not to have many technical thoughts as I become too focused on making sure I do the technique right.

TEE SHOTS / IRONS

Not jumping away from the ball, taking the club what feels to me outside the line and then feeling as if I'm releasing like Geoff Ogilvy. I pick a very clear target and commit to the shot.

MENTAL SKILLS

I have to have clear goals for the day and the week. I play my best golf when I'm relaxed, having fun (despite not playing my best) and enjoying the golf. They are big keys for me.

PREPARATION
Ideally I'd like to play half a practice round hitting shots, chipping, putting, etc., but then play competitively on the back 9. If the other players don't want to, then I need to simulate a competitive environment. Good course planner is essential.

CONCLUSION
While many players expect performance to change overnight, the reality is that performance change usually comes as a result of a player having tried, tested, and re-tested different methods until they have found their formula; i.e., *keys* that work. Some players have listened intently to lots of different advice trying to find the missing ingredient, but they have also had the presence of mind to know when to disregard information while still having the option of going back to that information in the future.

Editor's Note: Nigel Edwards has represented Great Britain and Ireland in the Walker Cup on four occasions, including the victories of 2001 and 2003; and has been a member of three Great Britain and Ireland winning teams in the St. Andrews Trophy.

Selective Attention in Golf: Managing the Keys to the Door

Ronald G. Marteniuk[1] and Christopher P. Bertram[2]
[1]Human Performance Consultant, 110 Seymour View,
Anmore, BC, V3H 4X9, Canada
E-mail: ron_marteniuk@sfu.ca
[2]University College of the Fraser Valley,
Human Performance Laboratory,
Department of Kinesiology and Physical Education,
33844 King Road, Abbotsford, BC, Canada, V2S 7M8

ABSTRACT

An information processing approach is taken to explain the concept of selective attention as it occurs in planning and executing the golf swing. Selective attention is likened to a door that has access to the central planning and execution centres. Principles of controlling the door to allow only relevant information to enter the movement planning and execution processes are discussed. Practical implications of this information processing model are given.

Key words: Information Processing, Pre-Shot Routine, Swing Thoughts

INTRODUCTION

Almost every highly skilled athlete reports that at some time or other during their performances they become totally focused on their game or skill so much so that their performance is automatic and they are completely unaware of distracting or irrelevant information such as cheering crowds or other distracting events. As a result, their performances are very good and feel effortless and automatic. This state of awareness and performance is called "the zone" and it is something that all athletes try to reach.

One golf example describes how a professional woman golfer was preparing a putt which, if successful, would win the tournament. During these preparations and while she was actually putting, a nearby noisy train passed the golf course. She was successful in making the putt and when interviewed later, a reporter asked how she dealt with all the noise from the train while she was attempting to make her final putt.

Reviewers: Kim Kincer (Eastern Kentucky University, USA)
               Matt Pinter (Ferris State University, USA)

She replied: "What train?"

This ability to block out information irrelevant to the planning and execution of movement is called selective attention. The phenomenon of attention is a brain process that allows one to focus on information that comes from the environment, ideas or thoughts originating in the brain, preparation and execution of movement, or on sensory feedback from one's movements in regard to the success or failure of these movements [1]. However, as will be discussed below, an individual has a limited ability to attend to this information so controlling where attention will be focused is crucial for successful performance.

Of course, attention can at times be scattered and one becomes unable to attend to any one specific source of information for any given amount of time. The ability to focus on relevant information in regard to intended actions is called selective attention and this ability is the focus of the current article.

One can think of selective attention as a doorway in the brain that leads to the movement planning and execution centers. Passing through this door are all sources of information that come from our senses (vision, kinesthesis, touch, sound) and our thoughts (e.g., past successes and failures in this situation, fears, doubts). When one is attempting to prepare a golf swing, sensory information concerning the conditions under which the swing will be made must be analyzed (e.g., the ball is in the middle of the fairway with a downhill lie, there is a strong wind coming straight toward you, and the hole in the green you are trying to reach is 60 yards away). In addition, we have past thoughts or memories of how we have handled this kind of shot in the past that might pass through the door and influence our planning and execution processes. However, part of these past experiences have been failures and so there are doubts and fears that also have access to the selective attention door.

SELECTIVE ATTENTION AND PLANNING OF THE GOLF SWING

The importance of selective attention for golf is that our ability to prepare and execute a golf swing is directly correlated to the quality of the information that we let through the selective attention door. Any doubts, incorrect or irrelevant information, or memories of past failures will produce "noise" within our central nervous system [2] that will hinder or prevent the development and execution of a high-quality swing.

This "noise" can take one of several forms. For example, anxiety about an upcoming shot may overly activate muscles involved in the swing and cause muscular tension to interfere with the 'automatic' execution of the swing [3]. Another source of noise is the activation of inappropriate muscles that then cause a poor swing or putting stroke [4]. Recent scientific studies have shown that if one thinks about an upcoming movement, areas in the brain responsible for planning and executing the movement become activated [5]. This process can be thought of as a priming action that prepares our nervous system for the upcoming swing. If one has the image or idea of the correct swing and selectively attends to this information, then useful priming occurs. However, if one is in a situation and thinks about what not to do, and this information enters through the selective attention door, the muscles responsible for the incorrect swing become primed and may actually be activated instead of the correct muscles.

Thus the role of selective attention, or in this analogy, the door, is to allow only relevant information to enter and contribute to planning and execution of the golf swing.

SELECTIVE ATTENTION CAN BE INTENTIONAL

What this means is that the door can be operated such that only information we want to let in will be let in. Hence, the highly skilled athlete lets in information that is correct and relevant to successful performance. This is a learned ability and comes from intelligent practice and playing [6]. Note, however, a performer can also intentionally let in irrelevant or incorrect information. In golf, such errors or misjudgments are made due to the very nature of the game which requires the player to make 'educated guesses' at factors such as wind influence, the lie of the ball, the break of a putt, and so on.

SELECTIVE ATTENTION CAN BE UNINTENTIONAL

Perhaps the best example of this is when golfers let past failures or fears of the present situation affect the planning and execution of the swing. How many times have we been in a situation where we must drive over a body of water to a fairway on the other side? We know we must ignore that irrelevant information and make a normal swing, but more times than we like, a swing emerges that puts the ball into the water. In essence, by letting through the door the memories of our past failures, we allow this information to influence the plan for our swing and hence its execution.

SELECTIVE ATTENTION HAS A LIMITED CAPACITY

Put another way, and in terms of our door analogy, a golfer can only effectively attend to a limited number of inputs [7] at the door and once this capacity is reached, no other information can enter through the door. Thus, if one is totally attending to hitting the ball to a target, one will likely not be able to pay attention to other events in the environment or thoughts coming from memory (like our putting example at the beginning of this article). This is the positive side of the limited ability to selectively attend to events relevant to a good golf swing. The negative side is if one pays attention to incorrect or irrelevant information (e.g., fear of failure or the sound of a passing train) then chances are the relevant information will not be fully attended to or will be completely blocked by the door.

One can appreciate that the above three characteristics of selective attention are not unrelated. For example, if an experienced golfer intentionally attends to a correct source of information about the swing, because of the limited capacity of selective attention, all other distracting and non-relevant information will be blocked out. Similarly, unintentional information can totally occupy the doorway to our swing planning process, and in so doing, preventing or hindering the processing of relevant information.

SELECTIVE ATTENTION AND GETTING INTO THE ZONE

The ability to control the flow of information coming from your senses as well as your thoughts, including memories of past experiences, is difficult to say the least. Highly proficient athletes continuously work at developing and using this ability with very few becoming consistently successful. This is one of the reasons that the use of sport psychologists has become so common over the past several years. Sport psychologists help athletes become familiar with how to control selective attention so that only relevant information is processed during the athletes' performances.

SELECTIVE ATTENTION IS AFFECTED BY EXPERIENCE AND KNOWLEDGE.

There is no doubt that the professional golfer has a much easier time at attending to relevant information about the type of shot necessary given current conditions and past experiences than the novice golfer. The professional golfer has a huge store of past experiences that can be brought to bear on the current shot. For example, lies in the rough require different address positions and steepness of backswing depending on how much of the ball is buried in the rough. Through countless encounters with these kinds of shots the professional can quickly decide on the best swing and thus attend to only relevant information in planning and executing the swing.

What about the novice or intermediate player? These players are bombarded with a vast array of information from the environment (e.g., what's the difference in the swing for a ball half covered by the rough versus a ball fully covered and how will the ball react once it is out of the rough?). Additionally, the higher handicap player is simultaneously coping with past, oftentimes negative, experiences of shots from the rough. Such experiences can conjure negative memories and fears that must be dealt with, and create uncertainty in the task at hand.

To deal with this uncertainty, the novice or intermediate person must substitute experience on the golf course with knowledge gained from reading and watching others perform. The principle to be followed is that in any situation on the golf course it is important to have a clear and simple plan for your swing – one that avoids ambiguity, uncertainty and fear. Even if the plan is not entirely correct, it is better to have a positive idea about your swing than a nagging doubt about whether it is the correct swing and whether you should be swinging in a different way [8]. A practical example of this would be finding a specific target prior to swinging the club, and then wholly committing to hitting that target. By doing so, the player's attention will be focused on important and relevant information and as a result, they will reduce, and possibly eliminate, the unwanted influences of doubt and uncertainty.

To help you have a positive approach to planning a swing in adverse conditions like sand bunkers and rough, you should have a rudimentary understanding on how to adjust your stance and address position in these circumstances and any deviation from a normal swing that is necessary. It does not have to be tremendously complicated and detailed. Have two and, at the most, three thoughts about what you have to do differently in each of these situations. Then, when you are faced with a shot from the sand or rough take a practice swing while attending to these two or three thoughts. Once the practice swing is completed, follow your normal routine in preparing for the swing and only have the target in mind when you take the swing. The practice swing should allow the real swing to be prepared and executed with the appropriate changes incorporated into the swing.

As you gain more experience through practice and playing, you will find that your ability to attend to the relevant information in these adverse settings will increase and this knowledge will pass through the selective attention door and help develop the swing plan and its execution in a more automatic way. But remember, at first keep your plan simple and think only positive thoughts about this plan as well as its execution.

ATTENDING TO RELEVANT INFORMATION: WHAT SHOULD YOU FOCUS ON?

Focusing your attention during the planning and execution of a swing is the equivalent of attempting to let only relevant information through the selective attention door. The question is, where should you focus your attention? There are two broad areas that a golfer can concentrate on during the planning and execution of a swing. The first area is the swing itself – attending to something about the upcoming swing like the club take away, the rotation of the trunk, the start of the downswing, or the tempo of the swing. We'll call these kinds of thoughts *swing thoughts.*

The second broad area for focusing your attention on is the cues or landmarks that are outside the body of the golfer and that occur in the environment. We'll call these *external cues* and chief among these are the golf club, the ball and the target a golfer is aiming at.

The golf research literature on focus of attention has mostly been done on putting [9] and pitch shots [10, 11] and this research indicates there may be an advantage for golfers to concentrate on external cues. Thinking about the path of the ball on the green, or the target one is aiming at, or on the club head as it contacts the ball has been shown to be superior to concentrating on movements of the body – grip pressure, shoulder movement, arm movement, etc. As well, most golf books written by professional coaches and sport psychologists suggest that for shots using metals or irons, one should focus attention on the target one is attempting to hit the ball to. While this seems to be widely accepted, there is very little evidence to base this strong advice on.

So, while there is a paucity of research on focus of attention in the golf swing, it is fairly certain, however, that once the plan for a swing has been made, one should have a definite strategy for focusing one's attention during movement execution. This controls the selective attention door and helps prevent irrelevant and harmful information from entering the planning and execution process.

To find out what is best for your swing, during practice, try out different ways of focusing your attention on both swing thoughts and external cues. Find out what is most comfortable and successful for you. Then take this method of focusing to the next game and try it out. To be successful, however, remember that you should have very few thoughts during preparation and execution of the swing; in fact, the fewer the better. Try limiting yourself to one swing thought or external cue to begin with. Stick with it to see what happens. If it does not work, try another one. Over time, you may find that one that is comfortable for you and that is successful in focusing your attention. If you do not like experimenting with your attention like this, then focus on what most golf professionals recommend: the target.

DEVELOPING A ROUTINE TO HELP CONTROL YOUR SELECTIVE ATTENTION

We have all seen or read about professional golfers who are almost ritualistic in preparing for a swing. The process starts with the club selection (some golfers insist on taking the club out of the bag instead of having it handed to them by the caddy) and ending with a waggle before initiating the swing. This routine includes taking one or more practice swings, usually behind the ball facing the target, and then a series of moves involving addressing the ball which ends with the correct stance and posture.

While there are many reasons for this routine, one surely involves the control of selective attention. By having a routine, the golfer's thoughts are systematically directed to the task at hand. The door is occupied by these thoughts leaving little or no room for negative thoughts or noise from the environment. The practice swings taken during this routine are also helpful for the same reason. Facing the target during the practice swings, the golfer can visualize the kind of shot needed to be successful and then physically rehearse it by doing a practice swing. This activates the appropriate brain movement planning and execution centers which then prime the appropriate muscles involved in the swing. In this way, the *whole* capacity of the selective attention process is occupied with very relevant information leaving little room for irrelevant or harmful information to be processed.

The pre-shot routine starts with having a clearly defined goal for the upcoming swing. It then involves taking in information from the environment that is relevant to this goal. These two sources of information are then used to generate an idea or image of the required swing. All this is done before approaching the ball. If a practice swing is required, we suggest this be done three or four feet behind the ball and while looking at the target. This procedure aids the central nervous system in selecting the right swing from our 'golf swing schema' (i.e., our general knowledge about how to swing a golf club). Once we have the image or idea of the movement, we then move to take up our stance at the ball, perhaps attend to a swing thought, and then initiate the swing.

If we engage our selective attention process in the above routine, we will not have any capacity to think about negative thoughts or let irrelevant information through the door of selective attention. We also stand a chance of establishing a zone of thinking that is entirely concerned with swing preparation and execution. It is this state of mind that is free from distractions and where movements seem to be executed without thought. In essence, it is just the result of a thorough planning process. Thus, to improve your ability to control your selective attention, work during practice and the game on developing a consistent routine for all your swings, including putting.

CONCLUSION

The goal of the present article was to explain the concept of selective attention as it relates to planning and executing the golf swing. We explained that attention is a process that allows our brains to focus on potential sources information from within the body, the mind, and the world around us. All of this information is clamoring at the door of selective attention and vying to be included in the planning and execution of your golf swing. By putting forth an explanation of the basic sources of information, and providing strategies as to where, how and when to focus your attention, we hope that both high- and low-handicap players will increase their probability of success on the course.

REFERENCES

1. Neumann, O., Theories of Attention, in: Neumann, O. and Sanders, A.F., eds., *Handbook of Perception and Action: Vol. 3: Attention*, Academic Press, San Diego, CA, 1996, 389-446.

2. Schröger, E., Giard, M.H. and Woff, C., Auditory Distraction: Event-Related Potential and Behavioral Indices, *Clinical Neurophysiology*, 2000, 111(8), 1450-1460.

3. Adler, C.H., Crews, D., Hentz, J.A., Smith, A.M. and Caviness, J.N., Abnormal Co-Contraction in Yips-Affected But Not Unaffected Golfers: Evidence for Focal Dystonia, *Neurology*, 2005, 64(10), 1813-1814.

4. Smith, A.M., Adler, C.H., Crews, D., Wharen, R.E., Laskowski, R., Barnes, K., Valone Bell, C., Pelz, D., Brennan, R.D., Smith, J., Sorenson, M.C. and Kaufman, K.R., The 'Yips' in Golf: A Continuum Between a Focal Dystonia and Choking, *Sports Medicine*, 2003, 33(1), 13-31.

5. Roland, P.E., Larsen, B., Lassen, N.A. and Skinhof, E., Supplementary Motor Area and Other Cortical Areas in Organization of Voluntary Movement in Man, *Journal of Neurophysiology*, 1980, 43, 118-136.

6. Holmes, P. and Calmels, C., A Neuroscientific Review of Imagery and Observation Use in Sport, *Journal of Motor Behavior*, 2008, 40, 433-445.

7. Miller, G.A., The Magical Number Seven, Plus or Minus Two: Some Limits on Our Capacity for Processing Information, *Psychological Review*, 1956, 63, 81-97.

8. Bell, R.J., Skinner, C.H. and Fisher, L.A., Decreasing Putting Yips in Accomplished Golfers via Solution-Focused Guided Imagery: A Single-Subject Research Design, *Journal of Applied Sport Psychology*, 2009, 21(1), 1-14.

9. Poolton, J.M., Maxwell, J.P., Masters, R.S.W. and Raab, M., Benefits of an External Focus of Attention: Common Coding or Conscious Processing?, *Journal of Sports Sciences*, 2006, 24(1), 89-99.

10. Wulf, G. and Jiang, S., An External Focus of Attention Enhances Golf Shot Accuracy in Beginners and Experts, *Research Quarterly for Exercise and Sport*, 2007, 78(4), 384-389.

11. Wulf, G., Lauterbach, B. and Toole, T., The Learning Advantages of an External Focus of Attention in Golf, *Research Quarterly for Exercise and Sport*, 1999, 70, 120-126.

Book Reviews

by Simon Jenkins

Homer Kelley's Golfing Machine: The Curious Quest that Solved Golf

Scott Gummer
Gotham Books, New York, NY, 2009
ISBN: 978-1-592-40452-0

Scott Gummer is a book and magazine author who lives and coaches high-school girls' golf in the California wine country. In writing this book, Gummer had exclusive access to Homer Kelley's archives.

Homer Kelley intended *The Golfing Machine* "to serve as the Duffer's Bible, the Golf Nut's Catalog, the Circuit Player's handbook, and the Instructor's Textbook" (p. 114). However, Gary Wiren, who served as director of education, learning and research at the PGA of America, denied Kelley's request that *The Golfing Machine* be adopted as the PGA's golf instruction manual:

> "I've always felt that the reason Gary Wiren did not espouse The Golfing Machine was because he felt that if he asked the membership to take such a step they would rise up in a righteous wrath and dispense with him," Kelley said. The reality, says Wiren, was that while the PGA was open to the concept of adopting and promoting a universal golf instruction vocabulary, it was never going to be Kelley's physics babble. "When you write it in English," Wiren half-joked with Kelley, "it's going to be a big seller." (p. 133)

The above account is in need of some clarification:

> I never used the word "babble" in referring to Homer's writing. I did joke with Homer about the English part. That simply was saying that most golfers don't relate to an engineer's writing style as it is too complex to assimilate without making it a study. Studied thoroughly, it presented a logical approach to the varieties of ways a golf club be swung. Homer was a kind man with a mission. I recognized that and was able to get him on two PGA programs so that people could hear his message. *The Golfing Machine* is a textbook of cause and effect in swinging a golf club. To me, it is not a method but a guide.
> (Gary Wiren, Personal Communication with the Reviewer, July 2009)

Kelley's story, as told by Gummer, is an extraordinary one. In addition to Kelley himself, the key characters are Ben Doyle, a golf teacher who was also ranked as the leading dealer of Ben Hogan golf equipment in 1963; and Bobby Clampett, who became famous for leading the field by seven shots through five holes of his third round in The Open at Troon in 1982. Gummer describes Kelley, Doyle, and Clampett as "the oracle, the disciple, and the chosen one," which "may have been God's will, though it may also have been just pure luck:"

> Kelley needed a teacher who could grasp his concepts and translate them for golfers of all stripes; Doyle needed a deeper understanding of how to explain golf and not just describe it. Clampett needed a coach/father figure/friend; Doyle needed a student who was ready, willing, and able. Kelley needed a champion to take forth and validate his message; Clampett needed a system he could trust unconditionally. (p. 160-161)

Kelley was a Christian Science practitioner, which teaches that 'from right thinking right actions must follow' (p. 107), but it was his eight years of working with Boeing that appeared to really shape *The Golfing Machine*:

> In addition to discovering a golf instruction book [Alex Morrison's *A New Way to Better Golf*, published in 1932] that approached the game from a scientific standpoint, Kelley also finally found a job that utilized his analytical and mechanical aptitude... . In 1941, Kelley wrangled a job with the Boeing Airplane Company in Seattle as an electrician developing wiring for the B-17F bomber. Kelly was in his element assembling books for circuit diagrams for functional test crews...
> ...
> While he was not an engineer, in his eight years with Boeing Kelley not only effectively functioned as one but also trained scores of engineers in the art of methodical problem solving; identifying the issue, gather information, define alternatives, anticipate conflicts, evaluate options, select and implement the solution. Kelley applied these same principles to his increasingly consuming quest to discern the science behind the golf swing. (p. 23-24)

In 1954, Kelley had his "dandelion ephiphany" (p. 43):

> It hit him while swinging at a dandelion.
> As Kelley's club met the flower he noticed that his left hand was aligned with the clubshaft. However, whenever he swung at a golf ball his hand was curved, with the back of his palm getting ahead of his wrist. With the dandelion he allowed the club to follow its natural path, but he tried to steer the golf ball. The resulting scooping motion allowed the clubhead to pass ahead of the hands before impacting the ball. The cause was a subconscious effort to help get the ball airborne, but the effect was a deceleration of centrifugal force. (p. 31)

Years later, in 1983, Kelley was struggling with questions about the flat left wrist at a clinic for twenty golf professionals, when Tom Tomasello, who was hosting the event, interjected:

> "Mr. Kelley, let me boil that down into one simple thing that I think everybody can understand. If you were going to smash something with the back of your left hand – smash it! In what position would your hand be? Would you have your thumb on top? Would you have your left wrist bent? Or would your hand look a lot like a fist? Wouldn't it? If you were going to smash something?" (p. 207)

Scott Gummer has produced an enthralling account of Homer Kelley's life and how he developed *The Golfing Machine* and a network of Authorized Instructors. The final chapter is about Morgan Pressel, who became the youngest player in the modern era (male or female) to win a major golf championship:

> "Everything I have taught Morgan came right from Homer Kelley," says Martin Hall. "She is a *Golfing Machine* baby." (p. 262)

Hank Haney's Essentials of the Swing: A 7-Point Plan for Building a Better Swing and Shaping Your Shots

Hank Haney
John Wiley & Sons, Inc., Hoboken, New Jersey, 2009
ISBN: 978-0-470-40748-6 (Cloth)

While Hank Haney's first two books were based on fixing swing problems (p. ix), this book explains his "vision of what every aspect of the swing should look like" (p. ix). He explains how he moved from emphasizing short-term to long-term change in his students with respect to John Jacobs, the teacher he influenced him most and whom he considers to be "the greatest teacher the game of golf has ever known" (p. 2):

> John was a genius when it came to quickly and accurately diagnosing swing problems, so his emphasis was on getting students to make quick corrections to whatever ball flight they were struggling with. ... Every golf swing has good aspects to it, but equally, within every swing there are mistakes. If you have an even number of mistakes – each canceling out another – you can hit good shots and play good golf. But the closer your number of mistakes is to zero, the more consistent you are likely to be.
> There's a danger in that line of thinking, though. It can easily lead to a swing that is full of compensations. In other words, if your shots are tending to finish, say, to the right of where you want them, one way of fixing that might be to turn your hands to the right on the club, thereby strengthening your grip.

...

But what happens is that, over time, you end up doing exactly what you are trying not to do in your swing. You are building a method on mistakes, one piled on top of the other.

Still, if I'm honest, that system of "quick fixes" worked well for me as a teacher. I had a lot of success helping students, although it was a transitory success. It was never long before most of them were back with their new and latest problem. (p. 3-4)

Haney believes that three factors work against the process of long-term change: boredom, fatigue and patience (p. 4-5). In this book, Haney's vision of the perfect swing – "perfectly neutral and devoid of compensations or mistakes" (p. 6) is described in careful detail and is copiously illustrated with photographs of Haney himself. The book is a must-buy for all players and coaches, especially with the insights it provides on Tiger Woods' warm-up and practice routines. A highlight of Haney's technical work with Tiger concerns his 'stinger':

In 1998, I went to the Dunhill Cup at St. Andrews with my student Mark O'Meara. He had won the Masters and the British Open that year, so he made the U.S. team along with Tiger and John Daly.

It was a very windy week and the course played hard. One day we were on the range and Tiger appeared (this, of course, was long before we started working together). Mark and I were working on hitting low shots into the wind, especially one that he would need at the short 11th hole. As we did so, Tiger mentioned that he didn't really have that shot. The only low one he had was the result of putting the ball back in his stance and "leaning" on the ball through impact. That produced a left-to-right flight that was less than ideal when the wind was into him and off the left.

The ideal shot, of course, was a low draw that would hold the ball up into the wind. But that wasn't something Tiger felt he could do at the time. So Mark and I showed Tiger the proper release to that shot. The feeling is that the back of the left hand squares and bows down at impact to take loft off the clubface and then there is a relaxing of the elbows through impact. That softening of the elbows breaks the momentum of the release and produces a lower shot. In other words, the club finishes low and the ball follows suit.

Tiger was curious, but after we showed him the shot and how Mark was playing it, his reaction was that he wasn't strong enough to do it. Of course that wasn't the case, but his perception was that to "hold off" the finish in that manner took an incredible amount of strength. Even after we explained that the key wasn't strength but technique, he still didn't believe he could do it.

Years later, early in our working relationship, I was showing Tiger that same shot in preparation for a trip to the British Open. He got it. He knows now that the more you relax your arms and the less you use your strength, the more able you are to get that proper release for a low shot. (p. 137-138)

Zen Putting

Joe Parent
Gotham Books, New York, NY, 2007
ISBN-13: 978-1-592-40267-0 (Hardcover)

Dr. Joe Parent has coached the mental game in golf, business, and life for over thirty years and was named by *Golf Digest* magazine as one of the "Top Ten Mental Game Experts" in the world. He holds a Ph.D. in psychology from the University of Colorado. His aims with this book are "to help golfers get out of their own way and excel at putting" and "to help people get out of their own way and better enjoy their lives (p. xix). He provides "a unique perspective that applies modern psychology and the ancient wisdom of the Buddhist and martial arts traditions to the mystery of putting" (p. xix).

"Zen, and Buddhism in general," writes Parent, "is known as the Middle Way: free from extremes in body, speech, and mind, such as the extremes of a life of pure self-indulgence versus one of continuous self-denial" (p. 41). In his coaching, he often refers to a theme from the fairy tale of Goldilocks and the Three Bears:

> When she entered the bears' house, Goldilocks encountered three versions of everthing: two extremes and one balance between the two. Papa Bear's porridge was too hot, Mama Bear's porridge was too cold, but Baby Bear's porridge was *just right*. Papa Bear's char was too hard, Mama Bear's chair was too soft, but Baby Bear's chair was *just right*. For every shot they choose, for every target they aim toward, for every putt they plan, I encourage golfers to find the middle way between the extremes of risk and reward. Like Goldilocks, I prefer that they choose the path that is not too risky, not too conservative, but *just right*. (p. 41-42)

While there are numerous golf books that apply Zen and other systems of Eastern thought to golf, it is the clarity and accessibility of Parent's thinking about psychology that will make this book particularly valuable to golf coaches. This can be shown by the way he distinguishes between 'mindful action' and 'self-consciousness':

> It is not helpful to self-consciously watch what you're doing with a critical eye, directing yourself while you're doing it, and bringing to it a sense of judgment and worry about how well you're doing it. In mindful awareness, you're being an objective observer, simply noticing how you're moving through any action, without any judgment about the quality or results. Mindful awareness in action is an opportunity for discovery and exploration, uncovering subtleties that you didn't know about. Self-consciousness is trying to do things in a particular way, trying to make them come out right, and worrying about whether or not you're succeeding.
>
> Ideally, we want to be mindful of the process of making a putt or any golf swing. We want to be present, aware of what we're doing while we're doing

it, without self-consciously looking over our shoulder. When we apply mindful awareness to our golf game, we can recognize our patterns, reinforce the successful ones, and learn from our mistakes. We can train our mind to be a great vehicle as we travel the path of continual improvement. (p. 59)

Inevitably in a book on putting, there is coverage of the yips. Parent argues that the key to overcoming the yips is to accept them and to have a sense of humour, as taking ourselves too seriously and feeling embarrassed by them is part of the "self-punishment" cycle that characterises the yips. The favourite slogan of Parent's teacher, Chögyam Trungpa, is "Not Afraid to be a Fool"; the opposite of taking oneself too seriously, it represents total freedom from self-consciousness:

Taking oneself too seriously is an expression of attachment to one's self image. It betrays an underlying lack of confidence in one's inherent worth as a person. Behind it is usually a need to be seen a particular way by others in order to feel valid.

I was working with a young pro who had qualified for and was playing in a higher-level tournament than those on his regular tour. After a mediocre first round, he said, "Well, at least I didn't embarrass myself out there."
…
If you are afraid to look like a fool, you'll rarely make a free swing on a long putt, and you'll be terrified of short ones. … The very fear of looking like a fool by missing a two-foot putt becomes a self-fulfilling prophecy.

Maintaining a sense of humor about one's foibles is not only healthy but also appreciated by others. … If you're not afraid to be a fool, making a mistake won't embarrass you.
…
Great players look for opportunities. … They are not afraid to take the risk of being a fool if they can have the chance to be the hero. (p. 189-190)

The Putting Prescription: The Putt Doctor's Proven Method for a Better Stroke

Craig L. Farnsworth
John Wiley & Sons, Inc., Hoboken, NJ, 2009
ISBN: 978-0-470-37101-5 (Cloth)

This book follows the author's *See It and Sink It* (1997), which was published in the wake of his "innovative putting system" helping Nick Faldo to win the 1996 US Masters:

Obviously, I was pleased to share the detailed insight that helped one of my favourite and most talented Tour professionals win a major championship. Nonetheless, since that book's printing, I have acquired a broader focus to every aspect of putting, from both technical and physiological standpoints. (p. 2)

As a sports vision expert turned golf instructor, it is not surprising the emphasis the author places on the importance of the dominant eye dictating the stance (p. 17), finding a posture that facilitates perception of the correct target line (p. 19), and also shoulder alignment and front-arm dominance:

> If you are a same-sided dominant player, you no doubt fight a tendency toward open shoulders, caused by your body being pulled around by your back eye so it can better appreciate the target line. This brings us to another important part of the setup: the need for you to get both your shoulders and your forearms parallel to each other and parallel to the target line. (p. 21)

The book includes numerous prescriptions and diagnostic tests, including a prescription for "the Putt Doctor's Stroke", which (among other things) is based on a curved (i.e., in-to-square-to-in) putting path.

The author provides many insights from his work with Tour players and his involvement in the elite golfing community, for example:

> A little-known fact concerning Tiger Woods' historic win at the 1996 U.S. Amateur – his third in a row – was a putting tip he picked up during practice rounds at Pumpkin Ridge from a student of mine, who was in the field. He had been a friend of Tiger's through junior and collegiate golf. Tiger noticed him putting well and wondered what he was doing.
>
> …
>
> Tiger watched my student closely during the practice rounds and then commented, "I see what you are doing. You're using a line you drew on your ball to aim at your target!"
>
> …
>
> I would approximate the number of players on the PGA Tour that used the logo to align to the target as being barely a handful before my first book was published in 1997. A recent survey by a major golf publication showed that 91 per cent of the Tour players now use the logo for aiming. Most of them use an "enhanced" (longer, bolder) logo line.
>
> My research has shown that drawing at least a 2-inch long bold line will improve your aiming accuracy compared to using the manufacturer's lettering already on the ball.
>
> …
>
> A number of players, including Tiger Woods, draw a line freehand. (p. 85-87)

The Art of the Short Game:
Tour-Tested Secrets for Getting Up and Down

Stan Utley with Matthew Rudy
Gotham Books, New York, NY, 2007
ISBN 978-1-592-40292-2 (Hardcover)

As a Tour player, Stan Utley was a short-hitter off the tee and had to chip and putt above average to compete. (p. xi) He played more than ten years on Tour and set a PGA Tour record for the fewest putts for nine holes – six at the 2002 Air Canada Championships ("I missed a bunch of greens, but holed out two bunker shots, made a putt from the fringe and left myself tap-ins on all my other chips") (p. xvi). He is now short-game coach to numerous Tour players and goes to twelve of fifteen events a year to work with players who are specifically looking for his help (p. 110).

In this book, the distinction between a chip and a pitch is important:

> I define a chip shot as a shot that is played with a de-lofted clubface position. I'm hitting the ball first and making contact with the ground with the leading edge of the clubface out in front of the ball. A pitch shot uses more wrist action, and I'm making contact with the ground with the bounce on the bottom of the club. (p. 142)

When playing himself, Utley carries a 48-degree pitching wedge, 52-degree gap wedge and a 58-degree sand wedge. On chipping, he only uses his 58-degree sand wedge:

> You might be wondering why I use my 58-degree club instead of something with less loft. I've never been a proponent of using lots of different clubs around the green – say, using a 7-iron for a long, running chip and a sand wedge for something closer that requires a high-lofted shot. I think it's easier to develop confidence and touch with one club and adapt your trajectory with your swing, versus learning the feel of half your set to play shots around the green. I also think the 58-degree club is more versatile than a regular iron. Its sole is designed to perform a variety of functions – dig into the grass if you play with the leading edge forward, skid across if you play the sole more flat, or bounce if you play it more open. (p. 48-49)

This book explains Utley's philosophy and describes his techniques in detail, with insights from his work with Tour players, and should be useful to all golf coaches and serious players. Utley does recognise individual differences in technique; for example, while he likes to see a neutral grip he asks:

> Does that mean you can't hit great shots with a strong grip? Of course not. Paul Azinger is one of the greatest short-game artists of all time, and he's been phenomenal with a strong grip. But Paul uses a different technique than I do. He's awesome at hitting his short-game shots without rolling his arms.

To hit a chip shot, he takes loft off his wedge by bowing his wrists rather than rotating his forearms, like I teach. Paul plays to his strengths. He has always played more low shots. If you have a strong grip like Paul, you have to recognize that you'll close the clubface on the backswing. This reduces loft and eliminates the club's bounce. Starting from a more fundamental grip will speed your ability to learn different shots around the green. (p. 20)

This Round's On Me: Lorne Rubenstein on Golf

Lorne Rubenstein
McClelland & Stewart, Ltd., Toronto, Canada, 2009
ISBN: 978-0-7710-7857-6 (hard back)

Lorne Rubenstein writes for Canadian newspaper *The Globe and Mail* and many magazines. In the foreword, Curtis Gillespie, states that "to call Lorne a traditionalist is really to say that he values a kind of authenticity that he promotes with every story he writes" (p. ix). This is a collection of his best and favourite articles from 1993 to 2008, divided into eight chapters. There is a chapter devoted to Canadian player Mike Weir, whom Rubenstein wrote about in his best-selling book, *Mike Weir: The Road to the Masters*; and, inevitably, a chapter on Tiger Woods: "certain subjects and events demand consideration. This was the case when Mike Weir defeated Tiger Woods in their singles match at the 2007 Presidents Cup, and when Woods' father, Earl, died" (p. 2).

The opening chapter, "Reflections", focuses on "the pleasures of being with friends on the course, and the ways in which golf captures the imagination of so many, transporting us to places where cultures, ideas, languages, and people intersect" (p. 3).

"The Swing and the Psychology" is a chapter and Rubenstein admits to "a sometimes unhealthy fascination with the swing and the mental side of the game – unhealthy because I've probably thought so much about related subjects that my game has suffered" (p. 2). In this chapter is an article entitled, "Letter from Ben Hogan", which was published in *The Globe and Mail* on 22 May 1993. In the 1950s ten disciples visited Hogan and each paid $500 to spend the week with him. Hogan later wrote to one of these disciples. It is written differently from his classic *The Modern Fundamentals of Golf*, which was shaped by Rubenstein's idol, Herbert Warren Wind. In the letter, Hogan emphasized "correct leg work and body position": "Why, look how Babe Ruth leaned into the ball when he it. Pictures of the Babe verify the fact that he did use his legs with tremendous effect and his head remained in one place throughout his murderous assault of the baseball and golf ball" (p. 63). As Rubenstein remarks in his article, 'keeping one's head still' is "a tenet of golf much challenged today" (p. 63).

A Son of the Game: A Story of Golf, Going Home, and Sharing Life's Lessons

James Dodson
Algonquin Books of Chapel Hill, NC, 2009
ISBN-13: 978-1-56512-506-3

James Dodson is author of seven books, including *Final Rounds* and *Ben Hogan: An American Life*. This book is billed as being about Dodson's "chance to pass along his love of the game to his own son, Jack, just as his father had done for him". Dodson is a good friend of Arnold Palmer, whose wife, Winnie, died in 1999:

> My book about my dad and his father had brought Arnold and me together. *Final Rounds* had been Winnie's favorite book – the primary reason Arnold invited me to help him write his long-awaited memoirs. His relationship with his dad, Deacon Palmer, was the key to understanding Arnold Palmer, Winnie pointed out. (p. 238-239)

A central character in this book is Edward Harvie Ward, who beat out his longtime college rival Arnold Palmer to win the U.S. Amateur Championship in both 1955 and 1956 before disaster struck:

> Following a wave of scandals that emerged from IRS [Internal Revenue Service] investigations into huge illegal payouts given to amateur players at amateur golf tournaments held at several prominent private clubs, Ward became the scapegoat of the darkest episode in USGA history, alleged to have been financially subsidized – essentially paid to play golf as an amateur. In a sweeping sanction that shook golf to its core, the governing body of golf in America suspended Ward's amateur status and prevented him from going after an unprecedented third consecutive National Amateur Championship, a fall from grace that effectively ended the age of the golden amateur.
>
> Harvie Ward disappeared quietly into a whiskey bottle and effectively stayed there for the next thirty years, bitterly drinking away the most promising game, many felt, since Bobby Jones. (p. 6)

Years later, in 1985, Ward became coach to Payne Stewart, "then almost thirty years old and searching for a replacement for the only teacher he'd ever had, his own father, William Lewis Stewart, who had died that year from bone cancer:"

> "Payne was in grief, and I'd been in grief for decades – so we were a team made for each other," Harvie quipped.
>
> "Payne and I had a productive but volatile relationship from the start. He was a spoiled rotten kid with a Rolls-Royce swing but as good as anybody I ever saw from one hundred yards in. He just needed to get his head on straight and learn how to win again. That's a father's role in life – and he's

lost his. So I sort of filled in. I think I helped Payne begin to realize something about patience and dedication – but also about getting your heart and head to work in the same direction. (p. 212-213)

Payne Stewart's career flourished while working with Ward:

> He jumped into the top ten on the money list and won several big tournaments. When Stewart came to Pinehurst in 1989 and informed his teacher that he wanted to learn how to work the ball like Seve Ballesteros, the darling of pro golf at that moment, famous for his daring recovery shots from anyplace on the golf course, Ward advised him not to tamper with his swing. A short time later, Ward found out that Stewart had acquired a new teacher. That same year, Payne won his first major, the 1989 PGA Championship. (p. 213)

Dodson provides a lucid, reflective, account of his relationship with his son Jack. Like his own father, he viewed golf as "a splendid way of staying connected to my son through the ups and downs of life":

> On a more personal level, Jack was decidedly reserved in expressing his golf passion, a young man who observed everything but often kept his feelings close to the vest. He reminded me of myself at this age – quiet, maybe a little too much inside his own head. In time, however, playing golf with my dad and eventually a larger group of buddies helped draw me outside my anxious teenage head. It taught me to respect traditions, to honor the rules of fair play, and most of all to have a hell of a good time using little more than a pitching wedge and my imagination to solve problems and overcome obstacles – serving, at the end of the day, as a reminder that everything is a game if you choose to make it so.
> That's what I thought – and hoped – golf could do for Jack.
> Silly dad.

Shooting for Tiger: How Golf's Obsessed New Generation is Transforming a Country-Club Sport

William Echikson
PublicAffairs, New York, 2009, Xiii + 272 pages
ISBN: 978-1-58648-578-8 (hardcover)

A former staff correspondent for periodicals such as the *Wall Street Journal*, the author is now director of European Communications for Google. This book is about the American Junior Golf Association (AJGA), which was founded in 1979. It originally catered for 16-18 year olds, but this was eventually reduced to 12 year olds (executive director Stephen Hamblin would not allow 11 year-old Michelle Wie to play in 2000) (p. 3). As it can cost in excess of $100,000 per annum to play on the

AJGA circuit, the AJGA has a scholarship program that grants more than $200,000 each year to less-privileged golfers (p. 9). About two-thirds of the National Collegiate Athletic Association (NCAA) Division 1 men's golfers and about one-half of the Division 1 women's golfers come from the AJGA.

The author presents an insider's view of the AJGA and especially some of the prominent players such as Marika and Isabelle Lendl, daughters of former tennis star Ivan; and Peter Uihlein, son of Titleist CEO Wally, whose company sponsors the AJGA; and Vicky Hurst, "whose family is reminiscent of Tiger Woods'":

> Earl Woods was a Great Beret and lieutenant colonel. Hurst's father, Joe Hurst, was an Air Force colonel, who retired from service after twenty-six years. Woods's mother, Kutilda, is Thai. Hurst's mother, Koko, is Korean. Earl Woods met Kutilda when he was stationed in Southeast Asia, Joe Hurst met Koko when he was stationed in Korea. Both Hurst and Woods know what it's like to lose their biggest fan. Earl Woods died of cancer in June 2006 when his son was an established superstar and an expectant father. In April 2006 Hurst's father died after a stroke. His daughter was only fifteen. When her mother called her with the news, she was waiting out a thunderstorm during a qualifying event for an adult Ladies Professional Golf Association (LPGA) tournament in Orlando. It was the only time she withdrew from a golf event.
>
> For both Tiger and Vicky, mothers have played crucial disciplinary roles in their lives... Insiders like Tiger's junior golf rival Ted Purdy say Kutilda was a driving, determined mother who rivalled her husband's involvement in her son's golf career. ...
>
> Behind her calm appearance, Koko Hurst displays the same side of Asian parenting, an uncompromising demand for strong work ethic and unfailing obedience. (p. 35-36)

As for his own son, Samuel, who is 15; he played a full tournament season in Europe, winning a tournament in France. By the end of 2008, he was ranked twentieth among all male golfers in Belgium with a handicap of 1.3. The plan for 2009 was to play in "the most prestigious European and American junior tournaments" (p. 248). One of the strengths of *Shooting for Tiger* is that the author provides a balanced account of the pros and cons of young golfers joining the David Leadbetter Academy or other academies such as the International Junior Golf Academy. He concludes his book with the following reflection:

> I often wonder whether I have found the correct balance between pushing my son and encouraging him. My intentions are benevolent: I want to see Samuel realize his potential, and above all, be happy. But I also know that his success gives me pleasure and pride. Many times I wonder what the best path for both of us is. Should I send Samuel to sunny Florida and the Leadbetter Academy? Samuel reassures me that he doesn't want to go, and we both agree that such dogged concentration on golf runs the risk of hurting his academic progress and turning a passion into an onerous obligation. Like

all parents, I fear the moment Samuel leaves the parental cocoon and steps out on his own, and at the same time recognize his need for independence. My son may have the talent to become a golf professional. He may end up choosing that path. More likely, after college he will move in another direction. For as Samuel often reminds me, there's only one Tiger. (p. 249)

An Old Caddie Looks Back: Reflections from a Town that Loves Golf...and Tiger

Tom Warren
iUniverse, Inc., New York, 2009
ISBN: 978-0-595-47583-4 (pbk)

This is the story about Rockford, Illinois, "a community that has been one of America's most supportive golf towns for generations" and serves as "a case study in how to keep the game healthy and strong" (p. xi). Tom Warren, Emeritus Professor of Education at Beloit College, tells the Rockford story from the late 1940s to the early 1960s, and then from 1989 when he met Earl Woods and his 13 year-old son. A friend of Warren, Bill Stark, had become regular playing partner of Tiger and Earl. Stark introduced Warren to the Woodses and they hatched a plan to bring Tiger to Rockford; a plan which materialised on July 1, 2001 when the Tiger Woods Foundation Junior Golf Clinic came to town.

When Warren played a round of golf with Stark and the Woodses in February 1989; he made the following observation:

> That day Earl Woods impressed me as a parent-teacher who respected his son. He urged Tiger to bear down as they worked together on fundamentals. The pupil was motivated, but like all young learners, Tiger needed guidance and an occasional wake-up call. At one point Earl said, "Remember what the video showed us about hitting out of a downhill lie from a greenside bunker?" Followed by, "Look at your position NOW" (Earl almost shouted). (p. 141-142)

The author draws attention to Charles "Chick" Evans from Chicago, who won both the US Amateur and US Open in 1916 before establishing the Charles Evans Jr. Trust in 1928 to provide scholarships and other educational opportunities for caddies. The Western Golf Association became its sponsor 1930 and by 2008, more than 8,000 caddies had graduated as Evans Scholars. Warren himself was a young caddie in the 1950s and he laments the decline of caddying:

> Caddying at one time was a step up on the ladder toward upward social and economic mobility for countless youngsters in Rockford and beyond. Caddies see the empowerment of golf close up. ... The disappearance of caddies from all but a few elite private clubs has diminished the opportunities of contemporary young aspiring golfers. (p. xi – xii)

Gypsy Joe: Bare-Knuckle Fighter, Professional Golfer

Joe Smith
London Books, London, UK, 2009
ISBN: 978-0-9551851

In this book, "doing battle" is the metaphor used to understand being both a golf professional and a bare-knuckle fighter. Joe Smith's grandfather, Rymer Smith, was "a legend among Romany folk" as a bare-knuckle fighter at fairground booths before becoming a professional boxer. When he was 6 years-old, Rymer encouraged Joe to reject the family tradition of fighting and take up the sport of golf. When Rymer suffered a heart attack and died on the golf course Joe promised his grandfather that he would one day become a professional golfer. At the age of 15, Joe won the London Junior Open, but was soon forced to resign from his golf club as a result of his father refusing to pay a sandwich bill (believing that the sandwiches were complimentary for Joe's group) at another golf club where Joe was playing in a tournament:

> For a short while I was incensed with my dad… Why didn't he just pay for the fucking sandwich bill? He could have done. Why did he make a stand? I was short and snappy with my parents and I regret that, but I was mixed up. Soon though I could see clearly again and could see it was prejudice and nothing else why I was kicked out. Those club officials may not have known it (and probably would not have cared), but their decision set me on a road that partially closed and soured my open mind and which would end up nearly killing me and hurting many others along the way. (p. 61)

Not only did Joe return to bare-knuckle fighting, but he also found that his muscle was in demand for hire as a gang enforcer. However, he eventually returned to golf and made it to the final qualifying of The Open on three occasions. He also decided to fight legitimately and won the London Heavyweight title.

At the Final Qualifying for The Open in 1991, Joe was on the practice ground at Birkdale, which was also being used for adjacent Hillside, whose practice ground was being used as a car-park. He was facing into a fierce wind:

> Myself and Constantino Rocca were having our fun on the practice ground, seeing who could keep their drives lowest and not even the Italian Ryder Cup star could match me in that department. As I stood over one shot and prepared to hit it, my brother whispered, 'You better make this a good 'un bruv, yer man's here!'
> I knew exactly what he meant. Shaking a bit, I made a good swing and struck the ball nicely then turned round and sure enough my hero Bernhard Langer put his practice balls down on the ground right beside me.
> 'Hello Bernhard,' I mumbled.
> 'Hello, Joe,' he replied.
> I was flattered he remembered me and knew my name. Golf-wise Bernhard was my hero and had been almost since I first picked up a golf club and I

first met him and spoke to him at the RAC club. I suppose an eight-year-old gypsy kid quizzing you up on golf technique might stick in your mind… (p. 137-138)

Billed as a story of redemption and "an unlifting account of a young man determined to realise his dream", this book will not only help to promote diversity and inclusion in golf, but it will also be valuable in terms of reflection on issues of values, personal identity and self-esteem.

The Art of Getting Out of Your Own Way: Why Can't I Do That All the Time?

Fred Brattain
CreateSpace, 2009
ISBN: 978-1441481115

This simple and passionately written book could be considered to represent the Zeitgeist in golf coaching in that it echoes the mantras of sport psychology such as "be process oriented rather than results oriented" and those of golf psychologies inspired by Eastern thought such as "getting out of your own way". With regard to the latter, the author emphasizes that "self interference", "getting in your own way", "listening to the voices in your head", and "a lack of faith" all mean the same thing.

The author is a fan of the book by Pia Nilsson and Lynn Marriott:

In this book they suggest the following routine, which I fully support and recommend to all my students. It is called "Decision Box / Play Box".

When you are preparing to hit a golf shot…imagine a line drawn on the ground about 3 feet behind the ball, at right angles to the target line. This is the Decision line. Behind the line is the Decision Box, in front of the line, next to the ball is the Play Box. The object is to do all of your thinking, planning and practice swings in the Decision Box, not in the Play Box. In the Decision Box you determine what shot you want to hit, what club to use, how you want to hit the shot, your complete visualization of the shot, the SINGLE swing thought you will employ when playing the shot. Only after you have made all the decisions and performed all of your practice swings do you step across the line into the Play Box.

The Mental Side of Golf

Charles Bonasera
CreateSpace, 2009
ISBN: 978-1442139879

The author is a psychotherapist who began working with athletes in many sports in the mid-1980s a result of his daughter's figure-skating coach asking him to work with a group of her students (p. 15). His slogan is "Enjoy your Game. Have Fun. Enjoy Your Life, Stay Well and PRESS ON!

He provides a number of interesting perspectives; for example, he emphasizes that perfection is unachievable: "The need for perfection doesn't come from being human; it comes from unwillingness to accept our humanity" (p. 80). A highlight is a short chapter on a woman who came to him to cure a putting problem after a golf instructor had indicated her grip was the cause of the problem. The author asked her to give him a lesson, during which he intentionally gripped the putter with a 'death grip':

> She asked me top loosen my grip but I loosened only a little bit each time and missed most of my putts. She chastised me and said that I apparently was not receptive to a necessary change. Clearly, she was very frustrated with me. I said that I was frustrated as well and asked that she show me how to do it. I set up five golf balls at different locations and distances from the cup and told her that I would watch while she stroked each of them into the cup.
> She began by gripping her club tightly as she usually did, but knowing that I was watching her intently, she consciously relaxed her grip. By the time she struck the fifth ball her grip and stroke were more relaxed. She gave me a big grin when she finished and begrudgingly said, "OK, I get the message." (p. 88-89)

EFT and Golf: The New Mental Game Manual

Jack Eason Rowe
Booklocker.com, Inc., 2009
ISBN: 978-1-60145-776-9

Energy psychology is the application of the principles of acupuncture (without needles) to psychological issues. Emotional Freedom Techniques™ (EFT™) is a version of energy psychology developed by Gary Craig. It involves tapping on or near the end point of acupuncture energy meridians.

The biggest chapter in this book is on the yips, which the author believes is "simply a social phobia:"

> Social phobias involve anxiety about performing a task in the presence of others. ... Our subconscious mind is trying to protect

us from the pain of embarrassment and our conscious mind just wants us to make the putt and move on. (p. 214-216)

The author recommends applying EFT to cure the yips; a summary of the EFT basics from an earlier chapter in the book is as follows:

Step 1...you tuned in, focused, or thought about the specific problem and you assigned a label to it. ... You can realign your body's energy meridians regarding anything that happened in the past by tuning in to that situation and stimulating the energy meridians using EFT.

Step 2...you rated the intensity of the distress on the 0 to 10 SUDS scale [Subjective Units of Distress Scale].

Step 3...you corrected for psychological reversal ["self-sabotage"; intending to do one thing but doing the opposite] if it was present, by tapping the side of the hand and saying you accepted yourself even though you had this problem.

Step 4...you balanced your chi ["a fundamental energy that is the foundation of all of the other systems in the body"] by tapping the endpoints of your energy meridians.

Step 5...you reassessed to see what progress you've made and repeated the process with some modifications. You continued that process until your distress level went down to zero.

Step 6...if you got stuck, you tried different solutions. (p. 69-70)

The Golf Guru:
Answers to Golf's Most Perplexing Questions

John Barton
Quirk Productions, Inc., 2009
ISBN: 978-1-59474-322-1

John Barton, editor-in-chief of Golf Digest International, is the "Golf Guru", which is also a monthly column that reaches millions of readers via *Golf Digest* and its 25 international editions. This book is six-years worth of "Golf Guru" columns in *Golf Digest*, from September 2002, divided into chapters on: Rules, Instruction, Equipment, Fashion, History, and Etiquette. The foreword is written by Arnold Palmer, who states:

My first golf guru was my father. Pap worked as the golf professional and greenskeeper at the Country Club in Latrobe, Pennsylvania, where he first put my hands around a cut-down golf club when I was just three years old. He taught me about the game – not only how to play it but also about its rules, culture, and traditions. He taught me manners, how to greet other people, how to behave, how to live. (p. 7)

Each "Golf Guru" features a question from a Golf Digest reader, followed by an answer. For example:

> [Q:] Hey, Guru, I use the logo on my ball to help with alignment on the tee and the green. I line up the logo, then set up and swing accordingly. Is this legal?
>
> Ed Cochard, Battle Creek, Michigan

> [A:] Yes, it's legal. The professionals all do it, too. Alignment is so important – it shouldn't require any great skill to get right, yet it's the source of most bad shots. It's easy to lose your way in this funny old game. Step back from time to time and check that you're heading in the right direction. A friend can help. If you don't have a target or a goal or a dream, then you aren't aiming at anything, in which case the game has no point at all. (p. 39)

What's a Golfer to Do?

Ron Kasprikse & the Editors of *Golf Digest*
Artisan, New York, 2009
ISBN-13: 978-1-57965-373-6

This book features "343 techniques, tips, and tricks from the best pros" divided into chapters on full swing, short game, putting, speciality/trouble shots, playing strategy, rules and etiquette, helpful skills, and equipment.

An example of one of the 343 entries is entitled "How to watch Tiger play a round" and is written by Ron Kaspriske himself:

> Getting up close to the world's greatest golfer is a lot like getting close to Oscar nominees on the red carpet. A little planning and good timing, and you'll catch more than a glimpse. Here are a few suggestions:
> • If it's a practice round, Tiger almost always plays at first light, so get to the course before the sunrise.
> • If it's a regular round, use the three-holes-ahead method and you should get to see him five or six times. After you watch him play through, jump ahead three holes to another viewing spot. Note: Standing behind him when he tees off with a driver is something every golf fan should do at least once.
> • Late in the day, go to the driving range. There's a decent chance he'll be one of the guys out there practicing – especially at the majors. (p. 188)

Golfology: Daily Inspiration from the Fairway and the Rough

Loretta Marra

Sunbelt Publications, El Cajon, CA, 2008
ISBN: 978-0-9729663-0-2

The author is an avid golfer and an impressionistic/portrait painter. Her aim in writing the book is "to inspire us to take each day and make it an opportunity for growth whether in the fairway or rough" (p. 7). Each page has a quotation, an anecdote or story and a "Golfology", which is "a thought to take with us to the tee" (p. 7). The subject matter ranges from golf instruction and rules/etiquette to cooking recipes. The 365 quotations range from the Bible to the philosopher Ludwig Wittgenstein, and from P.G. Wodehouse to Kultida Woods.

This book may inspire the reader to start their own daily, reflective journal; using the Internet to search for quotations that are helpful for their golf and meaningful to their life.

How to Master the Inner Game of Golf

Maxine Van Evera Lupo

Taylor Trade Publishing, Lanham, MD, 2009
ISBN-13: 978-1-58979-416-0 (pbk)

Formerly a teaching professional at the Rancho Santa Fe Golf Club and a faculty member at the San Diego Golf Academy, the author contends that being "in the zone" is "attributable to a crystallization of knowledge and technique" and "a positive attitude toward the sport's challenges" (Back Cover). The premise is that "when players learn to recognize and deal with factors such as their own attitude, personality, emotions, and even character and integrity, suddenly their concentration, confidence, and ability improve significantly" (Back Cover).